Dad,

Wishing you a very Merry Christmas.
Happy reading! - another bit of Polish
history.

Much Love,

Richard, Jenny, Hannah, Bethany
& Tom xxxxx

THE
FORGOTTEN
FEW

THE
FORGOTTEN
FEW

The Polish Air Force
in the Second World War

ADAM ZAMOYSKI

HIPPOCRENE BOOKS
New York

First published in 1995 by John Murray (Publishers) Ltd.,
50 Albermarle Street, London W1X 4BD

Hippocrene edition, 1996.

Second Hippocrene printing, 2001.

For information, address:
HIPPOCRENE BOOKS, INC.
171 Madison Avenue
New York, NY 10016

ISBN 0-7818-0421-3

Printed in the United States of America.

TO

THE MEN AND WOMEN OF THE POLISH AIR FORCE

WHO FOUGHT

SO LONG AND SO HARD FOR SO LITTLE

Contents

Illustrations

(between pages 112 and 113)

The author and publishers wish to thank the following for permission to reproduce illustrations: Plate 1, J. B. Cynk Polish Aircraft Archives; Plates 2–30, Polish Institute and Sikorski Museum, London.

MAPS

Preface

MOST PEOPLE IN this country know that there were Poles fighting alongside the RAF during the Second World War, and colourful stories of their doings have become part of British folklore. But very few have any idea of the extent of their involvement, or how they came to be here.

Some 17,000 men and women passed through the ranks of the Polish Air Force while it was stationed on British soil. They not only played a crucial part in the Battle of Britain, they also contributed significantly to the Allied war effort in the air. They shot down 745 enemy aircraft, with another 175 unconfirmed, destroyed a further 25 on the ground and damaged 259. They shot down 190 flying bombs aimed at London. They dropped 13,206 tons of bombs, and laid 1,502 mines. They sank three ships, eight miniature submarines and two U-boats, damaging another thirty. They destroyed 1,171 tanks, armoured cars and other vehicles, 84 rail engines and 606 railway coaches. They flew a total of 102,486 sorties, notching up 290,895 operational flying hours, and took part in virtually every type of RAF operation. They achieved this at a cost of 1,973 killed and 1,388 wounded. They won 342 British gallantry awards, including 9 DSOs and 191 DFCs, as well as 15 American ones.

This book is not intended as a history of the Polish Air Force, and it does not set out to be comprehensive or definitive in any sense. I have taken scores and figures from printed sources considered to be authoritative. Nor does it pretend to assess the exact contribution of these men and women to the Allied cause in the Second World War. The intention is merely to give some idea of who they were, where they came from, how they got here, and what they did; and also to take a look at their sometimes strained but ultimately successful collaboration with the RAF, and their sometimes difficult, often notorious, but ultimately happy relationship with the British people.

It is the story of a large number of men and women. Some of them, and some of those who knew them well, will inevitably feel that justice has not been done to individuals and units. Others will disagree with some of the generalizations or assessments they will find here. But it is not possible to do justice to heroism and suffering on such a scale, and no generalization can hope to characterize so many people in so many differing situations. The more I listened and the more I read, the more I came to realize that each one of those 17,000 could be the subject of a fascinating book. All I could hope to do was to give some idea of the collective experience.

I am very grateful to all those who agreed to talk to me about their experiences, and to the staffs of libraries and archives I used, including the Polish Library, London, the Polish Army Museum, Warsaw, and the Imperial War Museum and Public Record Office in London. I am also grateful to Group Captain J.R.D. Morley, station commander of RAF Northolt, and Flight Lieutenant Steve Partridge for their enthusiastic co-operation. The staff of the Polish Institute and Sikorski Museum in London, earned my deepest gratitude, particularly Captain Wacław Milewski, whose untiring courtesy could serve as a model to any curator, Andrzej Suchcitz and Krzysztof Barbarski. I should like to thank Mr Jerzy Cynk, the ultimate authority on all things Polish and aeronautical, for his assistance, and above all Elżbieta Rogerson, who traced many an old warrior for me and used her charm to unlock his memory.

I was encouraged to write this book by the Polish Air Force Association, and it was the support of its President, Air Vice-Marshal Aleksander Maisner, and of other members, such as Tadeusz Kwiatkowski, Stanisław Wandzilak, Andrzej Jeziorski and Ludwik Martel – all delightful companions as well as brave men – that made my task not only much easier, but vastly more agreeable.

Preface to the 60th Anniversary Edition

The idea of writing this book was originally put to me by a group of veteran Polish airmen, and I embarked on the task largely out of a sense of respect for their heroism, almost out of a sense of duty, as an elegiac tribute to their extraordinary though ultimately fruitless achievements.

The story is so magnificent, so full of drama, of humour and of tragedy, that I knew this would be a pleasure to research and write. I was also confident that it would make a great book. I knew it would be well received in the United Kingdom, where memories of the Battle of Britain are sacred to many generations, and where the image of the brave Poles who flew alongside the 'Few' at that defining moment in British history hovers at the back of peoples' consciousness.

But I was somewhat taken aback at the success of the book in other quarters. In a free Poland, it has been greeted with enthusiasm by a younger generation which had no idea of the extent of the Polish airmen's contribution to Allied victory. They not only lapped up the spectacular heroics, they also warmed to the examples of courage and integrity set by the airmen, virtues that have not been much in evidence in Poland itself in recent times.

The book's phenomenal success in the United States has similar, but deeper causes. From reading the letters that have poured in and the references that come up in discussion groups on the internet, it is obvious that the book has played a major part in awakening the pride of Polish Americans.

Reading up the history of Poland can help to give a young Polish American a sense of identity and a sense of worth, but it requires a certain amount of study and reflection. The story told on these pages is so poignant, so universally accessible and understandable to anyone, that it strikes an immediate chord. It is not just about the facts and figures of history, it is about people. And what people! Reading of their exploits, one can only feel pride at the thought of belonging to the same nation.

I am happy that the book has stood the test of time, and as this new revised edition goes to print, on the 60th anniversary of the Battle of Britain, I hope that it will continue to inspire not only Polish Americans, but everyone young and old who chances upon it.

Adam Zamoyski
London, September 2000

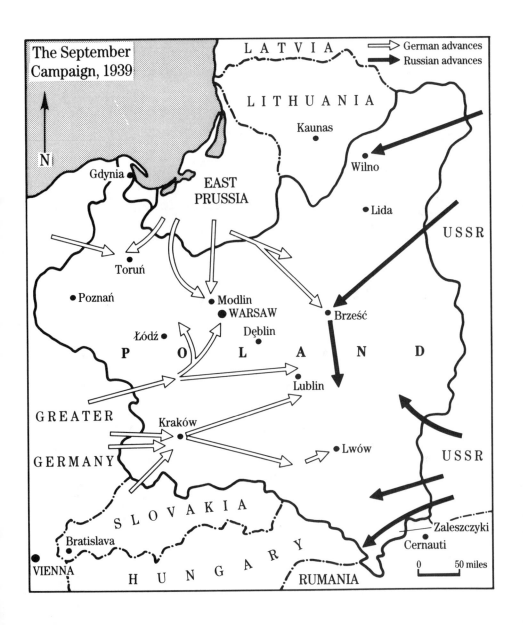

The September Campaign, 1939

N

German advances
Russian advances

LATVIA

LITHUANIA

Kaunas

Wilno

Lida

USSR

Gdynia

EAST
PRUSSIA

Toruń

Poznań

Modlin

WARSAW

Brześć

Łódź

Dęblin

P   O   L   A   N   D

Lublin

Kraków

Lwów

USSR

GREATER

GERMANY

SLOVAKIA

Bratislava

Zaleszczyki

Cernauti

VIENNA

H U N G A R Y

RUMANIA

0   50 miles

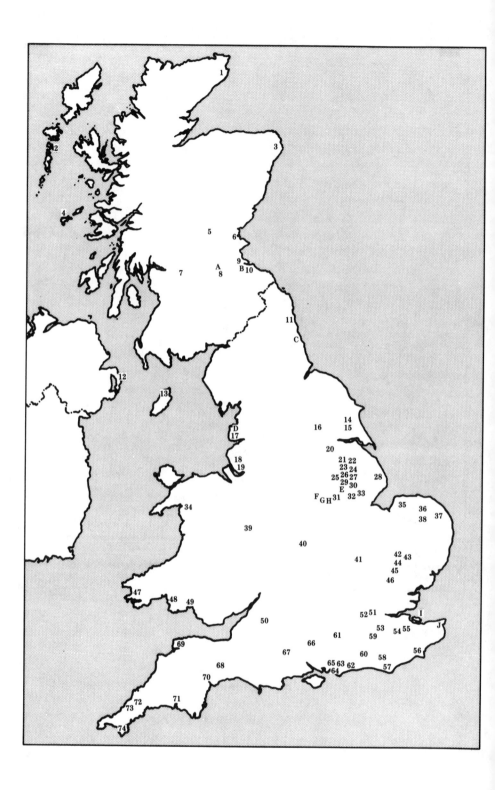

Principal Airfields on which Polish Units Were Stationed, 1939–1945

AIRFIELDS

1. Wick
2. Benbecula
3. Peterhead
4. Tiree
5. Findo Gask
6. Dunino
7. Renfrew
8. Kirknewton
9. Turnhouse
10. Drem
11. Acklington
12. Balleyhalbert
13. Jurby
14. Hutton Cranswick
15. Leconfield
16. Church Fenton
17. Squires Gate
18. Woodvale
19. Speke
20. Lindholme
21. Blyton
22. Kirton-in-Lindsey
23. Hemswell
24. Faldingworth
25. Ingham
26. Cammeringham
27. Dunholme Lodge
28. Winthorpe
29. Swinderby
30. Coleby Grange
31. Syerston
32. Wellingore
33. Digby
34. Llanber
35. Docking
36. Hethel
37. Coltishall
38. Swanton Morley
39. Kenley
40. Bagington
41. Tempsford
42. Snailwell
43. Chedburgh
44. Castle Camps
45. Debden
46. Andrews Field
47. Dale
48. Pembrey
49. Fairwood Common
50. Colerne
51. Northolt
52. Heston
53. Croydon
54. West Malling
55. Detling
56. Brenzett
57. Friston
58. Chailey
59. Horne
60. Coolham
61. Lasham
62. Ford
63. Tangmere
64. Westhampnett
65. Apuldram
66. Chilbolton
67. Deanland
68. Church Stanton
69. Chivenor
70. Exeter
71. Harrowbeer
72. St Eval
73. Perranporth
74. Predannack

TRAINING SCHOOLS

A. Grangemouth
B. East Fortune
C. Usworth
D. Blackpool
E. Newark
F. Hucknall
G. Bramcote
H. Newton
I. Eastchurch
J. Manston

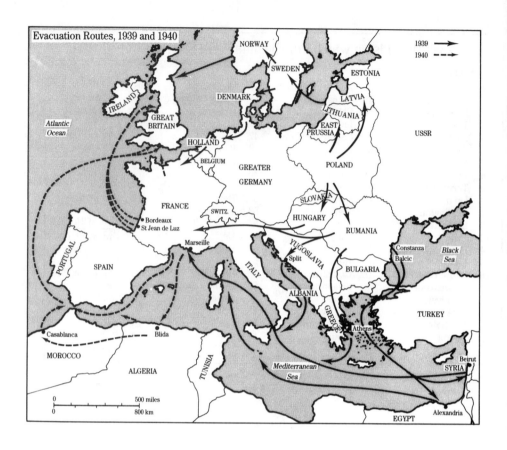

1

Knights Errant

ON THE MORNING of 10 July 1967 a Second-World-War
Douglas B-26 bomber with a shark's eyes and gaping jaw
painted garishly over its nose swooped low over the tree-tops on
the approach to the Nigerian airfield of Makurdi. It had been
purchased for $25,000 at a scrapyard outside Paris a couple of
months earlier, and it represented the entire air force of the
breakaway state of Biafra. As it had not been used for military
operations for twenty years, its plexiglass nose had been replaced
with an aluminium cowl. Through a hole drilled in this poked
the barrel of an infantry machine-gun clutched nervously by an
Ibo tribesman staring at a wall of aluminium, his only 'eyes' a
cord tied round his arm and held at the other end by the pilot.
Pulled once, it signified 'open fire!', pulled twice it told him to
stop. The bomb-bay, manned by two more Ibo tribesmen, held
tall thin cauldrons furnished by Colonel Ojukwu's personal arti-
ficer, Mister Willy, with the assurance that they were 'terrific
bombs'. The order to release the bombs would be the buzzer
originally meant as a signal for the crew to bale out. Since
none of the crew had a parachute, there was unlikely to be any
confusion.

As the Makurdi airstrip came into view, the pilot saw three
Nigerian Air Force DC–3s, a fuel tanker beside them, and a helicopter standing by the control tower. As the planes came into his
improvised gunsight, he pulled the cord attached to the front
gunner. The sightless Ibo gave a furious burst from his machine-
gun, which promptly jammed. The pilot then activated the

buzzer. The 'bombardiers' detached the cooking-pots from their fastenings, primed them and tipped them out of the bomb-bay. The tail-gunner, who *could* see what he was doing, as he was perched over a hole in the fuselage, also opened fire. The bombs were indeed 'terrific': loud detonations were followed by sheets of flame and clouds of smoke.

The bomber banked and overflew the airfield once more. The pilot noted with satisfaction that the three planes, which represented the only reliable supply-line for the Nigerian forces moving against Biafra, were ablaze. The helicopter, which had been trying to take off, crashed to the ground and exploded in a ball of fire. As the Biafran Air Force headed for its home base of Enugu, they heard over their radio the Makurdi control tower calling HQ in Lagos to inform them that the chief-of-staff of the Nigerian army had been killed in the helicopter. An unexpectedly successful operation, reflected 'Mr Brown', the pilot.

That night, after a celebratory dinner, Colonel Ojukwu held him back as the other Biafran commanders were leaving. 'By the way, Mr Brown,' he said, pouring him a large whisky, 'who are you? I know nothing of your background.' It was a good question. 'Mr Brown' was in fact Wing-Commander 'Johnny' Zumbach, DFC and Bar, a regular officer of the pre-war Polish Air Force. He had shot down eight German planes during the Battle of Britain in 1940 and gone on to command 131 RAF Fighter Wing during the Allied invasion of Germany.

In Warsaw, a few months after the Makurdi raid, Colonel Stanisław Skalski was discharged from the Polish Air Force. He too had been a regular officer before the war, and had fought in a fighter squadron when the Germans invaded Poland. On the morning of 1 September 1939 he had shot down a German bomber, one of the first Allied air kills of the Second World War. He too had distinguished himself during the Battle of Britain, destroying 17 German planes. In 1946 he had turned down offers of jobs in the RAF and the USAAF, preferring to go back to his Soviet-dominated country to help build an air force for it. In 1948 he was accused of being a British spy. He was interrogated, tortured and condemned to death. In 1950 his sentence was commuted to life imprisonment. After the end of the Stalin era, in 1956, he was released but forced to go back into uniform.

Both these men were fairly standard Polish casualties of war. They were neither the bravest nor the most enterprising of the men and women of the Polish Air Force, and they were certainly among the lucky ones. Many of those imprisoned with Skalski did face the Communist firing squads. Many more had been killed in action during the war. Others had been shot by the Germans on capture or after attempted escapes. Yet others perished in Auschwitz and other concentration camps. Some had survived, but had bought their survival at a barely believable cost.

Władysław Cehak lives quietly in small-town America, but he still has nightmares. He was a navigator in a Polish bomber when he was shot down by the Germans, on 14 September 1939. The pilot managed to crash-land the blazing plane, and Cehak leapt clear. 'I had been shot in the face, my right arm was almost shot off, I had four bullets in my right leg, and my uniform was on fire,' he recalls. The field-hospital he was transferred to was in eastern Poland, which was invaded by the Soviets three days later, and he fell into the nursing care of the NKVD. After a couple of months without medicine, his wounds wrapped in packing-paper as bandages, and with little food, he lapsed into despair. 'I made a noose with a towel, and kicked myself off the bed,' he writes. 'But I was untied and revived. I was too weak even to accomplish that simple act. But for the NKVD I was still a threat.' The inmates of the hospital were being evacuated to camps at Kozielsk and Starobielsk, staging posts on the road to the mass graves in the forest of Katyn.

A Polish doctor drafted in to work at the hospital gave Cehak an injection and wrote out a death certificate, and his apparently lifeless body was taken to the morgue, whence it was spirited away by the Polish underground. After a few months in hiding, he felt strong enough to attempt an escape to join the Polish forces in the West, and he set off across the snow-covered Carpathian mountains. He was caught and fed into the merciless machine of the gulags. In the far north of Siberia, where he ended up, the prisoners lived in sub-zero temperatures, without adequate food or clothing. They were driven to hard labour with blows and kicks, and died in their thousands. The other prisoners, many of them criminals, were always trying to steal what little food or clothing he had, and he killed four times to survive. In the short Siberian summer he supplemented his diet as best he could. 'I devoured grass, poisonous mushrooms, the bark of aspen trees, the liver of a dead Lithuanian prisoner.' He should have been freed in 1941 when the Soviet Union joined the Allies, but they did not let him go: he had been sentenced for life. It was not until ten years later that he was released.

Even the luckiest members of the Polish Air Force could not escape what was perhaps the heaviest, and certainly the bitterest blow of all. It fell on Konrad Stembrowicz, a pilot flying Mustangs in one of the Polish fighter squadrons, in the mess of RAF Andrews Field in Essex on a drizzly 13 February 1945. 'The war was slowly drawing to a close,' he writes. 'Nobody had the slightest doubt that the Allies would win, and that the Polish squadrons would soon be landing on their own native soil, freed at last from the Nazi invader. In the officers' mess, a huge Nissen hut, British and Polish officers were sitting around in large green armchairs reading newspapers or magazines. Others stood by the long bar, behind which a British corporal in a spotless white tunic served small tankards of beer.' At one o'clock the wireless was turned on for the news. 'The next few minutes seemed to me the very worst of my life. I felt as though I had been hit by a thunderbolt – only this image can describe how I and all other Poles must have felt when they heard on that momentous day of the agreement reached at Yalta.' Roosevelt and Churchill had conceded all Stalin's territorial demands at the expense of Poland and effectively left him in control of the country. 'The British officers were thunderstruck. They lowered their heads and avoided looking at the Poles. Incredulity, horror and shame were painted on their faces. I looked round the room – only one pair of British eyes met mine. It was Tony; there were tears running down his cheeks . . .'

At the Victory Parade held in London in June 1946, detachments of every Allied force marched past proudly between the jubilant crowds lining the pavements. But there was one ally missing from the parade – Polish units were not allowed to take part, so as not to offend Stalin, who had declared them to be 'Fascists'. Flight Lieutenant Jan Preihs, a native of Pomerania who had flown a Spitfire in defence of Britain, turned and walked away from the parade. An old lady came up to him and asked: 'Why are you crying, young man?'

The end of any war makes a nonsense of the fine words and illusions conjured up to help win it and fills those who fought in it with mixed feelings. From being indispensable they suddenly find themselves redundant. The risks they took and the sacrifices they made are never fully understood, let alone appreciated. Ordinary people wishing to return to peacetime normality do not like to be reminded of the war. Those who did not fight even slightly resent the implied reproach embodied in those who have returned from battle. Very rarely is the home-coming hero treated like one. And the more he has put into the fight, the greater the feelings of bitterness he experiences.

The Polish airmen had given more than is usual of themselves in defence of their homeland. Many of them were born when it was still torn into three parts, each a colony of one of its three powerful neighbours, Russia, Germany and Austro-Hungary. At their mothers' knees they were fed on a rich diet of Polish patriotism. They were taught self-sacrifice and endurance, and to hope against all hope for a free future. Suddenly, when they were still small children, the unbelievable happened: first Russia in 1917, then Austria and Germany in 1918, disintegrated into chaos, and the Poles were handed their chance. In the last days of the First World War, Polish underground units began to disarm the German and Austrian soldiers occupying the country, and on 11 November 1918 Poland declared her independence.

The children who watched these events, and their younger siblings, were so conscious of the great miracle that had occurred, and so imbued with the happiness and pride of having their own country to build up and live in, that they were committed to its defence as a matter of almost natural instinct. A twenty year old Polish pilot was deeply shocked by a conversation with a French airman in 1940. 'It transpired that as far as he was concerned, his family came first, then himself, and only then his country – that is really extraordinary and incomprehensible,' he wrote. Johnny Zumbach's colleague Witold Urbanowicz, another Battle of Britain ace, agreed. 'My generation was brought up on books that told only of those who had sacrificed their lives in the good cause,' he wrote. As he was saying goodbye to his girlfriend in Warsaw on 5 September 1939, she stuffed a scrap of paper into his pocket without him noticing. He found it later, in the chaos of the general retreat. On it was written one sentence: 'You will have no other aim in life until your country is free once more.' It was more than patriotism – for that generation it was an article of personal faith.

2

Growing Wings

T HE FIRST POLISH operational flight took off on 5 November
1918 from Lewandówka airfield against Ukrainian national-
ist forces attacking the city of Lwów. It was carried out by Janusz
de Beaurain, the son of a doctor from Zakopane, and Stefan
Bastyr, an officer in the Austro-Hungarian air service. They were
piloting a contraption composed of salvaged parts of at least
three different aircraft, and assembled under fire by mechanics
who had to interrupt work frequently in order to repel attacks on
the airfield. The flying machine, proudly painted in the Polish
colours of white and red, bumped along the grass runway and
rose unsteadily into the air. It puttered over the Ukrainian lines
and dropped two bombs, causing more astonishment than
damage, and then returned safely to Lwów. The Polish Air Force
was born.

Everything that attended this birth – the uncertain political
situation, the lack of resources, the improvisation, and the
diverse human element – was to characterize the Air Force's
further development and account for its strengths and failings
over the next decades.

By the middle of November 1918 all the German and Austrian
airfields on Polish territory had been taken over and, with them,
a veritable museum of some 250 machines, in various states of
decrepitude. Men quickly came forward to repair and fly the
planes. They were from the most varied backgrounds and represented a mine of skill and experience, for the Poles were not new
to flying. Countless engineers, amateurs and country gentlemen

swept up by the romance of flight had flopped and crunched their way onto the rubbish-heap of aeronautical history at the turn of the century. But there had also been solid achievements. It was a Pole who built the first helicopter in Russia, in 1903. Prince Stanisław Lubomirski had established a small aircraft works and flying school at Mokotów just outside Warsaw, where the first Polish-designed plane was built in 1910. In the same year, Grzegorz Piotrowski had flown from St Petersburg to Kronstadt, a record of 23 miles over water. In 1914 Jan Nagórski had been the first to fly over the Arctic.

During the First World War Poles had to fight in the armies of one of the three powers occupying their country, and dozens joined the Russian, German or Austro-Hungarian air forces. They fought with distinction on many fronts against various enemies, and when the armies in which they were forced to serve disintegrated, they made their way back to Poland. It was the personal badge of one of them, an ace in the Austro-Hungarian flying service who landed his plane at Warsaw in December 1918, that was adopted as the insignia of the new Polish Air Force – a chequer pattern in the Polish colours.

Earlier still, during the Russian Revolution, a large number of the Poles serving in the Tsarist army had split off and set up a Polish army on Russian territory. By March 1918 it had a squadron of twelve fighters and one bomber. This army was surrounded and disarmed by the Bolsheviks, but another such Polish force arose in Odessa in 1918, and this too had an air arm – consisting of a single, somewhat patched, Breguet bomber.

This bomber flew into Poland in June 1919, piloted by Captain Ludomił Rayski. Rayski, whose father had been exiled after taking part in the 1863 rising against Russia and taken refuge in Turkey, had served in the Turkish Air Force in the First World War. But he was by no means the most exotic figure in the new Polish Air Force. On 14 July 1919 two American pilots, Major Cedric E. Fauntleroy and Captain Merian C. Cooper, were moved at the sight of Polish units that had fought with the Allies on the Western Front parading up the Champs-Elysées. Hearing that Poland was threatened by invasion from Russia, they assembled another fifteen American pilots and set off for Warsaw. They were seconded to the 3rd Fighter Squadron, which was renamed the Kościuszko Squadron (in memory of the Polish patriot who took part in the American War of Independence), and they fought with distinction in the Polish–Bolshevik war of 1919–21.

By the end of that war there were twenty Polish air squadrons, consisting of some 200 pilots flying a bizarre collection of planes kept airborne by the skills of a small army of mechanics. They were organized into three air regiments, stationed at Warsaw, Kraków and Poznań. In 1926 this number was swelled to six. Each regiment had fighter, bomber and reconnaissance squadrons, and its own support groups. Armaments came low on the list of priorities as the devastated country started to rebuild after a century of foreign occupation and seven years of war; the immediate one was to mobilize the human resources.

Three flying schools were set up. They were manned by French instructors, and it was hoped that they would bring a degree of uniformity to the force. The different military backgrounds – Russian, German, Austrian, Turkish and American – did not sit easily together. Each of these armies had its own style and its own way of doing things. Those brought up in German military service with its Prussian stiffness found it difficult to work with those who had been schooled in Russian formations, whose attitude was more casual, and who in turn resented the overbearing and bureaucratically-minded products of the Austrian army. The imposition of French military norms over these three traditions was only a partial success.

Creating armed forces for the new Polish state was no easy matter, and the officer corps as a whole did not present an edifying picture. According to 1928 statistics, only 14 per cent of all officers had a degree from an institution of higher education. This was partly the result of studies having been interrupted by the Great War, partly because the new republic had to take its cadres wherever it could find them. The officer corps nevertheless considered itself a social élite, and was ensnared in a web of codes and practices that reflected this. Regiments vetted newcomers and froze them out if they were considered socially unsuitable. Officers' schools taught subalterns the elaborate manners of another age. Duelling, theoretically illegal and strictly banned by the military code, was tacitly approved as the only honourable way of settling disputes, and hundreds of duels were fought between officers in the 1920s. In 1928, when two officers of the 4 Toruń Air Regiment had a minor disagreement, the regimental commander himself sent a plane to Warsaw to pick up a pair of duelling pistols so they could resolve it. In 40 per cent of cases the duels ended without a scratch, honour having been satisfied by the mere discharge of pistols, but a staggering 25 per cent ended fatally.

Many of the duels were triggered by drunken provocation or disagreements over card games. Poker and szminka (*chemin de fer*) were preferred to the more respectable bridge, and stakes tended to be ruinous in relation to the low pay of the officers. Women were another frequent cause of duels. Officers' messes were more like social clubs than their counterparts in other countries. They included sitting-rooms, libraries and ballrooms, and there was no bar on bringing in women.

Officers were not allowed to marry before the age of twenty-four or before attaining the rank and pay of captain, whichever came sooner. In the air force, marriage was discouraged among pilots on the grounds that 'the bravery of fighter pilots should be enhanced through celibacy', in the words of one report. Even senior officers were often refused permission to marry on account of the young lady's alleged social unsuitability. One major who had commanded a squadron in the 1920 war and would do so again in Britain in 1940 had to leave the air force in the late 1920s on account of such an 'unsuitable' marriage.

Many of these problems were amplified in the air force. It drew the enterprising and the restless to its ranks, many of them former cavalry officers. These imagined the air force to be the cavalry of the future and assumed that once a pilot was airborne he could do whatever he liked, like some kind of medieval knight-errant. Only 2.8 per cent of air force officers had a degree, the lowest ratio of any service in the armed forces. Their attitude to discipline was hardly more promising. 'Leaving aside the technical question of flying, [the air force] is indolent, capricious and undisciplined in every other function,' a general wrote in his report after carrying out inspections of three air regiments. 'It is characterized by staggering lack of punctuality in the carrying out of orders, glaring evidence of poor discipline, which is occasionally made up for by good will, whimsy, sympathy for superiors or good humour.' Granted that they were equipped for the most part with ancient machines (the French Caudrons had a nasty habit of losing their wings in the air), and that they liked to show off in them, it is astonishing that the air force only lost 14 per cent of its pilots in accidents between 1919 and 1929.

The problem of drunkenness was also magnified in the air force. As there were not enough planes for them to fly and a shortage of fuel, the airmen were often idle. Most of the airfields were some way from larger towns, so there were few distractions. The 5 Air Regiment stationed at Lida was a case in point. The mess was a long wooden bungalow, the library's shelves lined not with books but with bottles. An officer posted there from Warsaw was horrified when, invited to lunch by the colonel, he found that this consisted of one pickled herring and a litre of vodka. In the early 1920s the whole air force suffered from what Major Rayski described as 'a plague of alcoholism', and he went on to say that 'although there still wasn't anything you could properly call an air force, it was already in appalling shape'.

Matters improved radically after the appointment, in 1926, of Rayski, now a colonel, to overall command. He was an energetic, sensible man, and he was a real airman. He did his best to create an infrastructure for the air force and to improve the quality of the cadres. In 1928 he moved the main pilots' school to Dęblin, where it had four runways, custom-built workshops, modern installations, comfortable accommodation, and a magnificent officers' mess in the eighteenth-century country residence of a princely family. He supplemented this with another officers' training school at Radom, a junior training school at Warsaw, and a ground-crew training centre at Krosno. He changed the uniform of the air force from standard military khaki to steel blue, with its own insignia and eagle cap-badge. With their black leather flying outfits, their walking-out uniforms and their evening kit, including dark blue trousers with a black stripe and airman's dagger, the air force officers now had eight different kinds of uniform, and were only outdone in terms of sartorial elegance by naval officers. Rayski also obtained a separate flag for the air force, incorporating the chequer pattern. These measures went a long way towards creating a sense of cohesion among the next generation of airmen and turning them into a professional élite. This was reinforced by the reforms of 1933, which gave them extra pay for flying and raised them financially above the norm in the armed forces. But there was still a long way to go before the Polish Air Force could become an effective military machine.

One of the reasons for this lay in the very motivation of the men who joined it in the late 1920s and early 1930s. While the slaughter of the First World War had plunged the populations of Great Britain and France into gloomy reflection on the horrors of modernity, it had made only a slight impression on the Poles, who had endured over a hundred years of sometimes bloody repression. And if the war had shaken most Englishmen's and Frenchmen's faith in the future, it had given the Poles an ardently longed-for independence. The average Briton had come to believe that progress bore the fruits of destruction, but the average Pole saw endless promise in it.

This promise was intensified by the fact that the national liberation of 1918 had also been a social liberation. Having been hemmed in by the rigid social systems of the three empires that ruled over them, Polish peasants and workers had suddenly become full citizens of a new and largely classless Poland. To be sure, there was still an enormous discrepancy between land-owning aristocrats and the deprived sections of the population, but the political culture and the ethos of the new state favoured the latter rather than the former. This gave rise to an astonishing degree of social mobility, as the sons and daughters of peasants and workers pursued their aspirations with vigour. And it was pre-cisely the areas of applied science that offered them the greatest scope for satisfying these aspirations. Technological progress and modernity beckoned towards a brave new world, with none of the irony that the phrase came to hold in Britain, and young people of all backgrounds embraced this faith with exuberance. To many, the most striking symbol of this new world was the aero-plane.

'When I was at school,' recalls a later ace, 'virtually every schoolboy in Poland was enthused by the exploits of our leading pilots.' This was hardly surprising. Polish Air Force officers devoted an inordinate amount of time to sporting events and competitions, and achieved some notable successes. Major Bolesław Orliński's flight from Warsaw to Tokyo in 1925 was one such feat, another was Captain Stanisław Skarżyński's solo cross-ing of the Atlantic from Dakar to Brazil in 1933. They and others went on to win aerobatic competitions and long-range races on both sides of the Atlantic. Their feats were widely publicized, generating interest and enthusiasm among young people.

Wojciech Kołaczkowski was barely a teenager when a plane made a forced landing on his father's estate in 1918, and from the moment he saw the machine, he made up his mind to become an airman. He took flying instruction while still at school, but then his father died and he had to manage the estate. He could not long resist the lure of the air, and he soon left the estate to an agent and joined the air force. Bolesław Drobiński too, while still at primary school, became fascinated by the sight of planes in the sky, and determined to become a flier. 'Every young man dreamt of being a pilot,' recalls another. It was certainly true of Anna Lęska, who was taken to an air show at the age of eleven, and determined to be a pilot. Her parents tried to knock this notion out of her head by giving her a pony, but it did not distract her for long. She joined a gliding club, learnt ballooning, and finally obtained her pilot's licence.

It was the romance of flying and the challenge of conquering the ether that drew people to the air force, not the prospect of fighting. Many of the least militaristically-minded young men, when faced with the obligation of national service, opted for the air force. Others saw it as a cheap way of learning to fly. When civil aeroclubs began to proliferate in the early 1930s, the number of applicants to the air force went down dramatically. Colonel Rayski attempted to bring the aeroclubs under air force control, but the connection only served to underline the sporting mentality of the air force. It was thus a very different kind of force from the great war-machine that was the *Luftwaffe*, the large professional *Armée de l'Air*, or even the small and similarly amateurish RAF, with its upper-middle-class and public school ethos.

The Polish Air Force attracted people from all levels of society. There were noble landowners such as Kołaczkowski and there were sons of peasants, such as Wacław Król, whose father could not read or even sign his name and farmed a smallholding of six hectares. There were sons of tram-drivers, miners and artists. Competition for a place at the Dęblin officers' school was stiff – 6,000 applicants for the 100 places in 1935 – and neither background nor connections played a part in securing one. The accent was laid heavily on good eyesight, speed of reaction and physical fitness. 'It was enough to have a spot on your nose to be rejected,' a successful candidate noted.

Every entrant had to spend his first three months attached to an infantry unit. Conditions were gruelling. The cadet was subjected to spartan conditions, route marches and obstacle courses in order to test his endurance and toughen him up. Only after completing this stint did the officer-cadet go to Dęblin. Discipline there was strict, with reveille at 4 a.m. Flying instruction was nothing if not thorough, beginning with theory, mechanics and navigation, and moving on to gliding and ballooning. The cadet only climbed into the cockpit of an aeroplane once he had a profound knowledge of the principles of aerodynamics. He then had to master a variety of planes. Many were fairly primitive and poorly designed. All were old and liable to malfunction. The radio hardly existed and airfields were equipped with none of the facilities that pilots came to expect only a decade later. All this encouraged constant alertness, improvisation and initiative, if only in the interests of self-preservation.

It was probably the best flying school in the world. 'Our level of training compared to that of the RAF, even after the war, was very high indeed,' claims Stanisław Wandzilak, one of its last pupils. He should know. He crowned his career in the 1960s as a Group Captain, with overall responsibility for flying instruction in the RAF.

Graduates of the Dęblin school either became officers in the reserve, in which case they had to put in a certain amount of flying every year, or they remained in the air force as regular officers. These continued to train in the course of service. Fighter pilots would do stints on bombers and vice versa, and they took courses in night-flying and navigation. The aim was to give them as complete a grasp as possible of every aspect of aerial warfare. All this, and the introduction of parachutes in 1928, dramatically reduced the number of lives lost in accidents, which had been depleting the cadres.

The training of ground crews was equally thorough. 'Looking back with all the wisdom of hindsight and the experience of the war at the technical aspects of air force training in Poland, I have to say that it was carried out with remarkable vision and prescience, for the knowledge and skills that we acquired then turned out to be virtually one hundred per cent useful in the war years, and they gave us the conviction that we knew what to do in every situation and how to do it,' claims Jerzy Kaliniecki, who became a senior technical officer in the RAF after the war. The connection between the air force's servicing units and the aeronautical industry was close, and ground crews underwent part of their training in the factories, which gave them a grasp of the theory and design aspects of the aircraft they were called upon to service. And they too were constantly faced with the necessity to improvise and get by with the poor resources at their disposal.

Their high degree of training, their similarly varied social origins, and the fact that there were far fewer of them in relation to flying personnel than in any other air force, meant that the ground crews were not regarded, as they usually were in other air forces, as inferior creatures. Unlike other services, the Polish Air Force did not expect ground staff to act as orderlies or batmen to officers. At the same time, they were paid extremely badly. Yet many demanded and received the full respect due to them from the flying officers. The chief mechanic at Dęblin was in his sixties, but refused to take retirement. He had spent four years in Siberia under the Tsars, two years in a German gaol during the war, and had fought as an infantryman in the Polish–Bolshevik war of 1920, during which he had been wounded three times. The officer cadets called him 'Papa', but they trod warily, as he could tell from the state of their engines whether they had been flying correctly, and voiced his judgements forcefully.

Despite Rayski's efforts, the air force remained stubbornly unmilitaristic in many respects. It was regularly lambasted in reports for its lack of punctiliousness, and the military inspectorate was in a permanent state of irritation at the airmen's attitude to dress. They wore their favourite bits of every type of uniform as and how they pleased, in incorrect combinations. One officer of the Warsaw Regiment went further, on a bet. He streaked, wearing nothing but his cap and boots, from a well-known brothel to the regimental air base, right through the centre of Warsaw, pursued by a growing crowd of policemen.

The tendency to show off was characteristic. A favourite pastime was to fly planes under bridges or down streets. A smart cavalry officer could be humiliated by flying so low over him that his horse bolted; a girl-friend could be surprised at her *toilette* by flying past her window. Airmen would take girls up in their planes, an excellent opportunity for breaking the ice in an era of formal courtship. They would take off for a routine flight and develop 'engine trouble' over a nice looking country house, where they might then spend a few days of stylish living. One airman actually used his plane to steal a girl from a strictly enclosed convent.

The equivocal position of the air force within the military machine was mirrored by the airmen's position within society as a whole. The officers of 2 Air Regiment stationed in Kraków gave splendid balls and were always outdoing one another by flying between the spires of St Mary's Church or under the bridges over the Vistula, but while this delighted the girl-friends for whose benefit it was done, cavalry uniforms dominated in Kraków's salons. The Rakowice airfield just outside Kraków, the home of the regiment, was separated only by a flimsy fence from the barracks of the smart 8th Lancers, the darlings of Kraków society. But the officers of the two regiments ignored one another. A young aristocrat doing his national service in the 8th Lancers slipped through a gap in the fence one evening and appeared in the airmen's mess in what he considered a perfectly natural gesture of camaraderie. 'They all stared at me as though I had landed from the moon,' he recalls; 'it was clear they had never seen one of our uniforms in their mess before.' It was not a question of class or snobbery, though these undoubtedly played a part. The cadets of the pilots' school at Grudziądz fraternized quite happily with the officer-cadets of the cavalry training centre in the same town.

The main air force officers' training school at Dęblin was the centre of a vibrant social life. The balls given by the airmen in their palatial mess were as glittering as any. Girls came down by train from Warsaw, from a nearby women's agricultural college and from surrounding manor-houses. Every summer students from the Warsaw Academy of Fine Arts came to a nearby beauty spot for a summer course which had more to do with picnics, bathing in the Vistula and dancing in the Dęblin mess's underground 'Hades' than with painting.

So the air force in Poland was certainly not a poor cousin in the social sense. It was just that the airmen lived in their own world, a forward-looking world centred upon things aeronautical. They had their own admirers, largely among the sporting enthusiasts. They spent their leave skiing in Zakopane or sailing on the Baltic coast. Kołaczkowski took part in the Monte Carlo Rally. Although it lacked the ethos of a modern military formation, its men were as well trained as those of any air force in the world, if not better, and their patriotism and morale were not in doubt. What *was* in doubt was the role they were supposed to play in the event of war, and how they were to fulfil it with the equipment at their disposal.

The air forces of Europe and the United States all started as part of the army and remained under its control for varying lengths of time. The army could see no use for planes beside tactical support, liaison and reconnaissance. Airmen naturally resented such limitations and their enforced subservience to army imperatives. But there was little they could do to convince military planners of the air force's potential.

There was no lack of sound thinking on the subject. Liddell-Hart in Britain, de Gaulle in France and Sikorski in Poland all prophesied accurately the nature of future warfare. But the military establishments of Europe (with the notable exception of the German) would not listen. Staffs were full of time-servers, First World War veterans and political appointees, and they were incapable of grasping the future needs of the army, let alone the air force. In the 1930s the conviction gradually gained ground that the paramount function of the air force would be the bombing of cities in order to subdue the enemy, a conviction fuelled by the examples of the Italians in Ethiopia, the Germans in Spain and the Japanese in China.

Poland's likely enemies – Germany and Russia – were far too large to be bombed into submission, even if enough planes could have been procured. The Poles therefore concentrated on the provision of support for military operations and defence of strategic objects, as well as reconnaissance and liaison. What none of the air staffs appreciated before 1939 was the fact that the sky was a battlefield in its own right, and that the war would henceforth have to be won in the air as well as on land and sea.

The plan drawn up for the Polish Air Force in 1921, by a French general on loan to the Polish Defence Ministry, envisaged 16 fighter squadrons, 32 light and 2 heavy bomber squadrons. He arranged the purchase of French planes and superintended the opening of two factories working under French licence. In 1924 General Władysław Sikorski became Minister of Defence, and he wanted to see the air force develop into a separate service distinct from the army. He proposed a twelve-year plan that would boost its strength to 200 squadrons, with a total of 2,306 warplanes. But he did not get the opportunity to put it into practice.

He lost his job after Piłsudski's *coup d'état* in May 1926, and it was then that Colonel Rayski took over as head of the air force. He found a depressing situation. A great deal of money had been spent in the early 1920s on buying French planes that were obsolete by the time they were delivered. Rayski also realized that Sikorski's plan for expansion was economically unsustainable, even if, as Sikorski had intended, more than 25 per cent of the military budget were devoted to the air force. The air force had not come out on Piłsudski's side during his coup, and this lessened its already feeble influence. In the event the figure would be less than 10 per cent. This meant that Poland would never be able to equip her air force from abroad with up-to-date planes.

Rayski's solution was to develop a native aeronautical industry. He invited the Czech firm of Skoda to install an engine factory in Poland, brought existing factories into government ownership, and set up the Polish Aircraft Works (PZL) in 1932. The first plane that went into mass production there, the P–7, entirely designed in Poland, was a serviceable fighter. Its successor, the P–11, was the most up-to-date fighter in the world when it went into production in 1934. This was followed by the P–24, faster and better armed, which earned money through export to Greece, Bulgaria, Rumania and Turkey. The PZL works were also producing the Karaś bomber, while other factories had developed a reconnaissance plane, the R–XIII, and a light liaison craft, the RWD–8. All these planes were of Polish design, and several more were on the drawing-board or in prototype. The PZL Łoś heavy bomber, which went into mass production in 1938, was an outstanding machine, and others, including the Jastrząb, a fine modern fighter, were expected to go into production in 1940–41. The idea was that by 1942 the Polish Air Force should have at its disposal a high-quality modern bomber and the latest fighter.

The trouble with Rayski's programme was that it was too ambitious. Between 1935 and 1939 Germany spent an average of $100 per head of population equipping its air force, Great Britain spent $46, France $25, and Poland $2. With such a level of funding, it was impossible to carry out all the plans, and one project always had to take precedence over others.

Timing was also a factor. In the late 1930s all efforts were concentrated on developing the successful Łoś bomber and a new fighter for the next generation. Since this was going to replace the old generation of fighters, the air force was not issued with the updated P–24s and P–40s, which were being produced only for export. As a result, Poland's fighter force was, in 1939, equipped with a completely outdated plane.

In March 1939 Rayski tendered his resignation, after a bitter attack by General Józef Zając, the Inspector of the Air Force. He had offered to resign several times before, whenever his budget was cut to unacceptable levels, but his resignation had not been accepted. To accept it now, as the clouds of war hung heavily over Poland, was madness. His successor set about replacing personnel and changing structures, rather than devoting himself to last-minute preparations for war.

On the afternoon of 19 March 1939 Lieutenant Witold Urbanowicz, one of the instructors at Dęblin, was sitting in his office staring out of the window. He noticed a flight of planes coming in to land, and was surprised to see that they were not

Polish machines. It was a group of Czech pilots. Hitler had invaded their country, and rather than surrender to him, these men had brought their planes to Poland, asking to be allowed to fight alongside the Polish Air Force. One of them, Sergeant Jozef František, had tucked a pair of tough hiking boots into his cockpit. 'Something tells me that Hitler won't stop at taking over Czechoslovakia,' he told Urbanowicz, explaining that their next fall-back position would be a long walk away.

A few days later Great Britain and France offered their guarantee to defend Poland, and a few days after that Hitler unilaterally renounced the Polish–German Non-aggression Pact. This galvanized the Polish Defence Ministry into action. But it was poorly co-ordinated action. Planes were purchased abroad, including 160 Morane fighters from France, and 14 Hurricanes, a Spitfire and 100 Fairey Battle bombers from Britain, to be delivered in August 1939. A deal was struck to buy Curtiss 75 Hawk fighters from the United States. But the Polish aircraft factories were not mobilized into intensive production, and in May 1939 a consignment of P–24 fighters was exported to Rumania instead of being diverted to the starved Polish squadrons. The Fairey Battles ordered in Great Britain were inferior to the Polish Łoś bombers, a number of which were being exported to Bulgaria in 1939.

On the evening of 31 August 1939 the Polish Air Force had a total of 392 combat planes with which to defend its airspace against a *Luftwaffe* force of 1,941 planes poised to invade Poland, with another 1,000 in reserve. The figures themselves are almost irrelevant, for the two airfleets were of different generations. The German planes were often twice as fast, four or eight times better armed, and able to fly higher than the Polish craft. When, in March 1939, the squadron commanders were shown identification pictures of German aircraft with details of their armament and speed, they gasped with horror.

To make matters worse, the Germans had a plan – to bomb airfields, troop concentrations, bridges, railways, stations, cities, roads, and anything else they found in their way. The Polish Air Force had none. Its only role was to support the army groups to which its units were attached. The Poles had invented a system of sector-homing to intercept enemy aircraft, a forerunner of the highly effective system developed a year later in Britain, but it was under-equipped. The 800 observation posts scattered about the country found it difficult to get their spottings through to the relevant squadrons via a combination of field-telephones and the civilian network.

On 27 August the Polish Air Force mobilized its reserves. Some 10,000 men reported to the main bases, where they found only skeletal staffs and jumbles of liaison and sporting planes. The operational squadrons, totalling 1,065 air and 5,031 ground crew, had flown off to secret airfields in the countryside, so as to avoid being bombed on the ground; but arrangements for getting fuel, ammunition and spare parts to them were inadequate, to say the least. They represented a very flimsy line of defence, and nothing stood behind them.

3

Black September

IT HAD BEEN one of the most glorious summers in recent memory, and the weather showed no signs of breaking. A holiday mood lingered on despite the gathering signs of war. The front-line units of the Polish Air Force waited on their secret field bases, for the most part flat stretches of pasture with a couple of huts and perhaps a barn or two on the edge of a wood, in which the planes could be hidden to avoid detection from the air. German spotter planes regularly flew over the country taking photographs, but as the Polish fighters could not reach their altitude, they soon gave up trying to intercept them. The airmen lounged about in the shade of their planes enjoying the beautiful weather, or explored the local villages and towns for female company and recreation.

Few had any conception of what was about to hit them. 'I went to war entirely convinced that it would end in the defeat of the enemy, that our aces would give the insolent *Luftwaffe* a thorough drubbing, and that within a few weeks, or at worst a few months, I would return home in triumph, take off my uniform, and get down with gusto to my interrupted artistic work,' wrote Bohdan Arct, a twenty-five year old graphic artist and a reserve officer with 5 Wilno Air Regiment. He had opted for the air force because he thought it would be nice to learn to fly. His optimism was by no means exceptional.

While they realized that their planes were no match for the German machines and knew they would be outnumbered, the airmen trusted in their own skill and that of their mechanics, and felt, with the optimism of those who have never been through a war, that these qualities plus sheer determination would somehow see them through. 'In our enthusiasm, we paid scant attention to the shortcomings of our outdated P–11s,' recalled a pilot. 'I faced the future with confidence, and I was ready for anything,' Lieutenant Skalski of 4 Toruń Regiment's fighter squadron recalls. 'That which was about to begin intrigued and excited me, and I secretly hoped that it would begin as soon as possible . . . In spite of everything, I made light of German power.' He was not alone. Nobody anywhere in Europe had the slightest inkling of the might of the German war machine or of the deadly efficiency with which it was to be directed.

Nor did anyone apart from the Germans understand how to use air-power to effect. Just as with tanks in 1916–17, the tendency was to disperse aircraft over the whole theatre instead of using them in massed formations. Five of the Polish air regiments, each with a fighter squadron of two or three flights, a bomber squadron of two flights, a squadron of reconnaissance planes, and one training squadron, were assigned to an army group. The Warsaw Air Regiment was kept back as the high command's tactical reserve, and only this mustered enough planes to be able to deliver significant blows.

In the early hours of 1 September some 1.8 million German troops poured into Poland from three sides. Hundreds of *Luftwaffe* planes preceded them, and at 4.30 a.m. three Junkers 87 Stukas dropped the first bombs of the Second World War – on the deserted Poznań airbase. Polish fighters were scrambled, and sometime around seven o'clock in the morning Lieutenant Władysław Gnyś of 2 Kraków Air Regiment shot down two Dornier 17 bombers, the first air kills of the war.

The German bombers, closing in from East Prussia in the north, Germany in the west and Slovakia in the south, attacked thirty airfields in the hope of destroying the Polish Air Force on the ground. They inflicted enormous damage and destroyed dozens of training and sporting aircraft, but did not hit a single front-line plane.

They then turned their attention to the cities. Shortly before seven in the morning a fleet of 80 bombers escorted by 20 Messerschmitt 109 fighters bore down on Warsaw from the north. It was intercepted by 54 planes of the Fighter Brigade, the high command's tactical reserve, which downed several bombers and three fighters. The German raid was broken up and turned back before reaching Warsaw, but at 4.30 that afternoon a second wave of bombers, this time escorted by several squadrons of Messerschmitts, broke through the Polish fighter screen and managed to bomb the capital. By the end of the first day all major Polish cities had come under aerial attack, as had dozens of smaller towns, railway junctions and bridges. Marauding fighters and dive-bombers swept the countryside, strafing roads, vehicles and even peasants working in the fields. The Polish Air Force was powerless to stop this.

The very sight of the sleek German planes with their retractable undercarriages and protective glass domes infuriated the Poles, in their old-fashioned fighters, with their high-slung wings, toy-like fixed undercarriages and open cockpits, which filled with acrid smoke every time the pilot fired his machine-guns. Only squadron commanders had radio contact with the ground, and all communication between the planes of a flight was done through hand-signals. 'The only thing we were left with after this encounter was a profound bitterness,' Skalski noted after his first attempt to intercept an enemy formation. 'In our mind's eye we could only see the beautiful modern shape of the enemy's fighter planes.'

Unless the Poles could position themselves high up in the path of oncoming German planes and dive onto them, they had not a hope of engaging them, for they could not keep up with, let alone catch, them. Even the German bombers were much faster than the Polish fighters, and, if cornered, could climb high out of reach. The fighters were twice as fast, and better armed. The Polish fighters had only two machine-guns, while the Messerschmitt 109 had four machine-guns and two cannon in front, and the Me–110 had an additional two machine-guns in the rear. When the Poles did manage to get near them, it was terrifying. 'They passed me from one to the other like a couple of footballers pass a ball,' explained one pilot of the Kraków squadron who got into a dogfight with two Messerschmitts. 'I would escape from two guns only to come up against six, and then back to two again.' The German planes were also well protected with armour.

The Polish P–11s did have one advantage. They were far more manoeuvrable than the German fighters, so the Poles did have a small chance of victory. This put their skill and dash at a premium. Only by very clever manoeuvring could they hope to get into an attacking position, only by disregarding the inequality in numbers could they engage the enemy planes, and only by diving on them and delivering broadsides at very close range could they hope to penetrate their armour plating. In these circumstances the pilots' skill and training told, as did their determination. Their own nickname for the bumbling P–11s was 'bees', and they were gratified to discover from captured German airmen that by the end of the first week the *Luftwaffe* had by a strange coincidence begun to refer to them as 'wasps', on account of their aggressive tenacity.

In spite of the fundamental hopelessness of the situation, the Polish airmen relished the fighting, which represented a chance to test their own skill and mettle. And during the first couple of days they contrived to maintain the universal delusion of the glory and chivalry of war. Lieutenant Skalski's first kill was a Henschel 126, which crash-landed in a field. He immediately landed his own plane beside the wreck and went over to assist the German pilot, who was badly wounded. He enlisted the help of a peasant woman who had been picking potatoes nearby, and began to bind the German's wounds. 'As I lifted the man gently with my left arm, supporting myself on the ground with my right, so as to enable the woman to pass the bandage round his back, the German, who had been keenly observing our ministrations, suddenly bent his head and kissed my hand. I recoiled with surprise. For a brief moment our eyes met. My eyes could not have expressed anything but astonishment, but in his I could see real gratitude.'

Several other Polish pilots landed to inspect the planes they had downed and similarly ensured the safe removal of the German airmen to hospital. But when they saw German fighter pilots fly round in circles to machine-gun Poles who had baled out and were parachuting to the ground, and when they began to see evidence of the slaughter of civilians that attended the German doctrine of total war, their attitude hardened. By the end of the first week, Polish pilots too began machine-gunning Germans who had baled out. A blind hatred took over, intensified by the rage engendered by their gradual realization of their own impotence. This hatred fortified their resolve and added the desperate edge to their purpose that was to turn them into some of the fiercest and most determined fighter pilots of the war.

Along with their illusions, the fighter pilots were quickly obliged to ditch pre-arranged procedures and to adapt to the situation. Wacław Król was stuck on the German border with a flight of four

P–11s when war broke out. The first they heard of it was the sound of German planes flying overhead. They could not make contact with base, and a couple of hours later the flight commander was shot down. This left three planes, six pilots and a small ground staff. They shot down three German planes on 1 September, and fell back by easy stages over the next days, guided by their own appraisal of the situation. They could not count on reliable information from anywhere, so they kept one plane up in the air patrolling, while the others sat on the airfield ready for take-off, the pilots strapped into their cockpits and sweating in the broiling heat. At the slightest sign of enemy aircraft they would take off and gain as much altitude as possible so as to be able to bear down on the intruder. But mostly the Germans had passed by the time they were high enough to begin their attack. 'It was enough to drive one crazy,' commented one pilot of the Kraków squadron. On 3 September Król's flight joined up with the rest of the squadron, which had worked out much the same tactics. By 6 September the squadron had shot down ten German planes, at a cost of three of its own pilots and five machines.

Similarly encouraging results were repeated elsewhere. The twelve planes of 4 Toruń Air Regiment's fighter squadron accounted for more than twenty German planes, losing eight of its own in the process. Lieutenant Skalski's flight intercepted sixteen Dornier bombers on 2 September and shot down nine of them without any losses. The Fighter Brigade, based on small airfields dotted round Warsaw, scored exceptionally well. Between 1 and 6 September it downed 43 German aircraft and badly damaged another 29, some of which certainly went down as well. But the cost was high: 2 pilots killed, 2 missing, 17 wounded, and 38 planes put out of action. The 3 Poznań Air Regiment's fighter squadron downed 31 German planes in the first week, losing only one pilot, with five wounded and one missing. The squadron's commander, Mieczysław Mummler, shot down three Germans, but his record was beaten by Skalski of the Toruń Regiment, who notched up six kills.

This level of success could not be sustained. By 6 September the Polish fighter units had lost 50 per cent of their planes, and there were no reserves to draw on. Pilots who managed to crash-land or parachute to safety were of no further use. Many planes which returned to base badly holed by German machine-gun or cannon fire could not be properly repaired, for all the resourcefulness and ingenuity of the ground crews, and flying them became increasingly risky – one airman could see the strain on his propeller, which had been bound up with wire. The exposed undercarriages of the Polish planes were vulnerable to machine-gun fire, and many a pilot who had successfully survived a dog-fight was obliged to crash-land. Planes with retractable under-carriages could land on their bellies with little risk, but crash-landing with a fixed undercarriage usually meant ending up on one's back in a heap of wreckage.

Apart from being obsolete, the P–11s were also very old, and therefore prone to metal fatigue or other malfunctions. The syn-chronizers that permitted the machine-guns to fire through the propeller were worn and prone to deregulate themselves with frequent shooting, with the result that a pilot could shoot off his own propeller in mid-air. A lieutenant of the Warsaw Kościuszko flight went out on his first mission on the morning of 3 September, but it also proved his last of the campaign. As soon as he had gained the requisite altitude he tested his machine-guns, whereupon the whole plane was engulfed in flames and he had to bale out. Another experienced pilot went up for the first time on 4 September and quickly bagged a Messerschmitt fighter, but on his return to base his engine seized up, and it was 1940 before he flew again. 'Sick at heart, we could only sit beside our useless aircraft and continue to pray for replacements to arrive,' wrote a pilot who had shot down a German on his only sortie.

Although the *Luftwaffe* had failed to hit the front-line units of the Polish Air Force on the ground on 1 September, they had wreaked havoc with the principal airfields, destroying supplies of spare parts and equipment. The large-scale bombing of roads, railways and towns further disorganized delivery of supplies and even fuel.

This affected the bomber squadrons even more than the fight-ers. Like the fighters, they were attached to army groups, with only the Bomber Brigade in reserve. They were used mainly to bomb enemy columns, but rarely in large enough formations for this to have any serious effect. Only sorties by several flights of bombers together could hope to delay a column for more than a few hours, or cause serious damage to German armour. To make matters worse, the bombers were also requested by military commanders to make low-level raids over advancing German formations in support of Polish ground forces, and these were very wasteful in planes. The crews themselves showed an excess of zeal, making strafing flights over enemy positions after they had dropped their loads, and the bombers were easily shot down by ground-fire as they did so.

With eight German armoured columns tearing into Poland from three sides, the Polish defences were quickly thrown into disarray. By 6 September the original plan of defence was a shambles. Overstretched air units were pulled back, but no adequate provision had been made for such a withdrawal. On 7 September, Król's flight of the Kraków Squadron was withdrawn to the Lublin region, where they found themselves without liaison, without further orders, and without fuel. On the same day Skalski and the remnants of his squadron fell back to the line of the Vistula, and others followed suit. In some cases, there was nothing left to withdraw. 'We have no more front-line machines, and our radio station is smashed,' noted an officer of the squadron defending Łódź. He and his tired men could only watch helplessly as the German planes passed overhead, shed their load over the city, and then flew back. 'I could not even throw a stone at them,' he complained bitterly.

'Before the war and during its first days we were blindly keen to fight and to win,' writes a pilot of the Warsaw Kościuszko flight, 'but after a few days we began to realize that something was badly wrong.' The frustration of the airmen was beginning to turn into anger as they saw to what extent the military establishment had failed them. It was not merely a question of the shortage of machines – that after all was a consequence of Poland being a relatively poor country. Even the parlous supply situation could be blamed on the disorganization caused by German bombing – although this should have been foreseen, and depots could have been dispersed more intelligently. The real problem went far deeper, and was the result of the military authorities never having understood the role of the air force, and of their seeming incapacity to appreciate its potential or its limitations.

As the Germans advanced into Poland, army staffs began to bombard the air force commanders with requests for tactical support which were entirely unrealistic. Captain Zbigniew Laskowski, commander of the Toruń Fighter Squadron, was ordered to strafe a German Panzer column on 2 September. He was an outspoken man who knew his mind. The son of a wealthy landowner, he had been disinherited by an angry father for giving up his agricultural studies in favour of becoming a pilot. He now rudely told his superior that the order was ludicrous, explaining that the machine-guns of his P–11s could do no damage whatsoever to German tanks, but that his planes could be easily brought down by rifle fire at such altitudes. 'Even if, as you seem to imply, this mission would not inflict any losses on the enemy, it should, and certainly will, make a great psychological impact,' came the reply. 'The only impact will be that my flight will be wiped out,' shouted back Laskowski, slamming down the receiver of the field telephone. He was right. He led the flight of nine planes himself. An hour later five of them limped back to base in tatters. His was not among them. His command was taken over by Captain Tadeusz Rolski, who received a similar order a couple of days later. He too argued vehemently against it. But the military commanders were adamant, and he had to carry out the senseless order, which cost him 30 per cent of his effectives in one mission.

The attitude of the military commanders is understandable. They were desperately attempting to stem the tide that was swamping their feeble defences, and were having their efforts set at nought and the morale of their troops eroded by constant attacks from the air. They wanted to see some Polish planes overhead, and so did their troops. The argument that such inappropriate use of the air force was wasteful was seen by them as airmen's cant.

Relations between army and air force were not improved by the lack of co-ordination between the air force and the anti-aircraft defences. Rayski had vainly attempted to get the anti-aircraft artillery subordinated to the air force, and the consequences of his failure to do so were immediately felt. The gunners had never been given recognition charts of Polish and German planes, and it was no easy task to spot the markings on a plane in the brilliant sunshine that continued unbroken throughout September. They therefore fired at any plane that came overhead, and interfered in dogfights, with catastrophic results. 'Everyone was shooting at us: Germans and Poles alike – the Poles often more accurately,' recalls Skalski. Wacław Król claims that on 8 September alone the Kraków fighter squadron lost four of its planes and two of its pilots to Polish anti-aircraft guns. A pilot who survived several dogfights with German fighters says he only realized what fear was when he was sent in an unarmed RWD–8 to deliver an order to Lublin. 'I was almost taxiing along the ground, in order to avoid the Krauts flying around above, but of course the ground forces felt it their sacred duty to fire at the RWD–8, since it was obvious to them that this particular "enemy bomber" was the most threatening,' he recalls. Having been winged by Polish artillery, he made a forced landing, whereupon he was arrested by an officious lieutenant in charge of a transport column, whom it took 16 hours to convince that he was not a German spy. Paranoia about spies was universal.

The swarms of German aircraft prowling over the country bombing and strafing everything in sight produced a reaction of blind terror to any flying machine, and Polish ground forces would open up at any plane with everything they had, without bothering to check its identity. These German tactics also begot a savage desire for revenge. German pilots who baled out could expect to be bludgeoned to death by angry peasants armed with pitchforks and scythes. Even downed Polish pilots had to be extremely careful. They were usually assumed to be Germans as they parachuted to the ground, and some narrowly escaped being lynched. One showed his uniform and his papers, but the angry peasants refused to be convinced, and ordered him to sing a number of Polish prayers and hymns before they let him go. Even once the locals were convinced that they were Polish airmen, they often got little sympathy, and were insulted and accused of standing by while the country was being devastated.

The bitterness of the airmen came to a pitch in the second week of September. Against all the odds, they had done remarkably well, and they had learnt a great deal about aerial combat. They were eager to carry on the fight to the last plane, and they assumed, when they were ordered back to eastern Poland, that they would be reorganized and thrown back into the fray as soon as possible. But the Polish high command was beginning to lose control of the situation, and now relinquished any grasp it had had of air strategy. Pulling back all front-line units east of the Vistula, far from improving the supply situation, only worsened it. A number of damaged but still repairable planes had to be left behind. Ground crews, following the planes in convoys of lorries carrying fuel, ammunition and spares, got stuck on the over-crowded roads and only rejoined their units after a few days, during which the planes were inoperational. Worse still, the with-drawal to the east had not been planned, and when flights and squadrons reached the indicated airfields, they found nothing there. They would scour the neighbourhood for fuel of any sort, while their ground crews worked through the night fixing and patching damaged planes, then loaded up their equipment and set off to rendezvous again at some other point. 'We are moved from airfield to airfield, we cannot find our planes, and sometimes we are separated for several days,' noted one fitter. With the flood of military and civilian traffic clogging the roads, and the frequent German air attacks, it was a wonder they ever managed to join up with their squadrons. All became adept motor mechanics in the process of fixing their defective lorries. But every time they did find their planes again, there were fewer to service. 'On every airfield we would hold aeroplane funerals,' he goes on, 'as the mechanics plundered whatever was serviceable for their own planes, like a poor family at the wake of a rich relative.'

The men were beginning to feel the strain. Most of them had not had a change of clothes or a proper meal for ten days. 'From the operational point of view, our activity was coming very close to zero,' commented Skalski, whose flight was stranded on an improvised airfield on a country estate near Bełżec. 'We felt bitter, but our spirit was not broken,' he recalls. They spent the days of enforced idleness discussing their experiences. 'On a completely unknown field base near Bełżec a new fighter tactic was being born, together with new methods of combat, which we would put to good use in battle one day, but not over Poland. We were the first cadre of fighter pilots to feel the huge might of the modern German Air Force on our necks. Being in the front rank we gained experience at a bloody cost, and we were the first to draw conclusions from it. Gloomy conclusions they were.'

They at least had had an opportunity of fighting the German invaders, a satisfaction denied to the majority of the Polish Air Force. The many thousands mobilized at the end of August reached their regimental air bases just in time to see them bombed. The bases had minimal protection and no proper shelters. The anti-aircraft guns at the Lida base had no sights. The hangars contained only light liaison planes or civilian aircraft. Enthusiastic ground crew rummaged for old P–7s to fix up, and attached machine-guns to sporting planes. They need not have bothered.

Bohdan Arct had reported to the air base at Lida and was put in command of a liaison platoon consisting of four pilots and forty ground crew, with three RWD–8 planes, one car, one lorry, one revolver and one rifle at its disposal. He saw his three RWD–8s as well as a feverishly resurrected P–7 destroyed on the ground on the morning of 1 September. The next day he was given three more planes and seconded to support the Łódź Army Group. At his first refuelling stop, he discovered that there was not a drop to be had. He pressed on towards Łódź, but ran dry and had to land in a field. He found a Polish cavalry detachment and borrowed a horse from them to go in quest of fuel. But the recently requisitioned horse bolted with him and returned to its farmstead. After many adventures, including having one of his three planes shot down by Polish fire, he reached Łódź. There he was kept hanging about without orders for two days before discovering that the air staff attached to the Łódź Army Group had evacuated without letting him know. He took off himself when he saw German tanks in the distance, but was soon shot down by rifle fire from a retreating Polish infantry detachment. He reached Warsaw, by motor bike, on 6 September, having lost six planes and contributed precisely nothing to the Polish war effort. From Warsaw he was sent on a couple of liaison missions, which made him feel more useful. He also acquired new skills. On the night of 8 September he had to fly to Brześć with no compass, and was told to set a course 'two fingers to the left of the moon'. Astonishingly, he got there. During another mission, he had to take off from a field fifty yards away from two German tanks. Although they failed to hit him, he was soon brought down by the rifles of a Polish infantry detachment, and was finally grounded. He obtained a lift in a requisitioned hearse, and then stumbled on his platoon's lorry, which he had last seen in Łódź – four hundred miles and seven days earlier.

Most of the pilots of the reserve and the cadets of training units were condemned to an even more passive role, as there were no planes of any sort for them to fly. 'They had joined the air force, they had learnt to fly, they had trained in gunnery, all in preparation for this very moment, and it had come,' explains Urbanowicz.

From 3 September onwards the air staff began issuing instructions that units not involved in fighting should withdraw to south-eastern Poland, where they were to regroup and await further orders. As Urbanowicz was preparing to evacuate his cadets from Dęblin by road, he called at the officers' mess to pick up some clean shirts. The whole base was pitted with bomb craters, and the fine residence was a wreck, a gaping hole in one wall and all the windows blown out. But the old orderly was at his post, saluting him as he entered the empty building. Urbanowicz told him to leave. 'Where can I go, sir – and what for?' he replied. It was a nice question.

They did not have much in the way of transport, so while those that had been wounded in the first bombing raids were loaded on to the scarce lorries, the rest set off on peasant carts or on foot. On 5 September all other flying schools, repair units and reserve pilots were also ordered to withdraw.

A general retreat to the south-eastern corner of Poland began. The Polish high command hoped to be able to concentrate and regroup its forces in this area. Britain and France were expected to launch an attack on Germany from the west, which would take the pressure off Poland and might enable the Poles to reorganize their forces, re-equip them from Rumania, with which Poland had a long-standing military alliance, and launch a counter-offensive.

The entire Polish Air Force was by now down to 120 planes, about 30 per cent of its original strength, but it still had hundreds of pilots. The first shipment of 14 Hurricanes and 36 Fairey Battles had been loaded in Liverpool in August, but had wasted much time sailing for Gdynia on the Baltic and then, when the Germans attacked that, being rerouted to the Rumanian port of Galati on the Black Sea. Another transport loaded with fighters from France was about to dock in the same port. On 10 September the personnel of the Dęblin officers' school and a total of 200 pilots with technical staff were ordered to go to Rumania to take delivery. By 14 September some 6,000 air force personnel had converged on the area along the Rumanian frontier. The remnants of the fighting units were to be regrouped on the comparatively safe airfields in south-eastern Poland and provisioned with fuel from oil-producing Rumania. But under pressure from Germany, Rumania had decided to ditch her alliance with Poland and adopt neutrality. The French ship was refused the right to unload its cargo, and the English transport, which had just passed through the Straits of Gibraltar, was again rerouted. The Poles knew nothing of this.

While this withdrawal was going on, the remnants of 3 Poznań and 4 Toruń Air Regiments and the Fighter and Bomber Brigades were still fighting in support of a Polish counter-offensive to the west of Warsaw. The fighter squadron of the Poznań Air Regiment, now down to six of its original strength of twenty-one planes, flew mission after mission in support of the troops fighting it out on the ground, losing four more planes, but clocking up, on 16 September, its thirty-sixth air kill of the campaign. The remaining bombers of the Poznań and Toruń Regiments and the Bomber Brigade also supported the counter-offensive until they were ordered back on 16 September. Some units never received the order, as liaison had broken down. Others did, but could not comply, as they did not know which airbases were still in Polish hands. Warsaw had been encircled on 14 September, and German spearheads had cut right through the country. The last ten planes of 3 Poznań Regiment tried to break out, but they were either shot down by anti-aircraft fire or ran out of fuel.

On 17 September the Polish Air Force scored its last kills of the campaign, a Dornier bomber and a Soviet fighter – that morning the Red Army had invaded Poland from the east. This unexpected stab in the back rendered all further resistance useless. The same afternoon all units were ordered to cross the Rumanian border, so they could carry on the fight somewhere else. The air force was ordered to fly out all available machines.

About 100 war planes and 50 civilian craft, all that remained of the operational force, flew over the frontier that day, landing mostly at Cernauti, the pilots still hoping to find English and French planes waiting for them. Only when they arrived in Rumania did the realities of the situation begin to sink in. 'The vision of Hurricanes and Moranes, the vision of continuing the fight, grew strangely pale,' writes Skalski. 'The naked truth rose before our eyes – it was the end.'

The fighter squadron of 3 Poznań Air Regiment, commanded by Mieczysław Mummler, which had started the war with 21 planes, was down to 2. It had acquitted itself well, shooting down 36 enemy planes at a cost of one pilot killed, one missing, and five wounded. The unit, including its ground crew, was in good order, and only needed planes in order to continue operations. When on 17 September they received the order to cross the Rumanian frontier, Mummler flew out one of the two last machines, while the remainder of the squadron made up a column and set off in lorries and cars to join them. When Mummler landed at Cernauti a few hours later, his machines were surrounded by barefoot Rumanian soldiers toting guns tied together with bits of string, who were none the less aggressive for all their lack of martial appearance. This came as a surprise to the two airmen, who still believed Rumania to be an ally. After some initial unpleasantness, they were ordered to fly to Galati. There they saw other Polish planes, and thought that what they assumed to have been a misunderstanding would be cleared up, only to find themselves taken from their planes and placed under arrest. Wacław Król also recalls bursting into tears as he was led away from his plane, his last tangible link with Poland. By that evening, they were interned in a makeshift camp at Focsani.

The units which had no planes were in a worse situation when the order to evacuate to Rumania reached them – often by roundabout means. Some columns reached the frontier post at Zaleszczyki in good order, only to find the road crammed with tens of thousands of people and hundreds of military trucks and private cars, all jostling each other frantically in order to escape capture by the Germans or the Soviets. The Rumanians had unaccountably closed the border crossing, and a huge traffic jam formed. Eventually, the Rumanians relented. In the night of 17/18 September, the defeated Polish forces drove or trudged across the frontier. 'It was a horrible moment,' wrote one senior airman. 'I don't know whether I shall ever manage to eradicate it from my memory. We all had tears in our eyes. Some kissed the white-and-red barrier, others kissed the ground or even the border guard's sentry-box. Some of the men were sobbing loudly, some were on their knees praying.' Almost everyone scooped up a lump of earth or a pebble, or picked a flower or leaf as a last memento of their motherland. 'I have never seen so many people weeping,' remembers a bomber pilot. From time to time a shot would be heard, as someone who found the shame of defeat unbearable and the future too horrible to contemplate took his own life.

The exodus continued over the next few days, as various units that had become dispersed reached the frontier. The Dęblin cadets had become separated. In the second week of September ten of the pilots had been selected to fly a collection of P–7s, some of them unarmed. They lost eight of the machines but did manage, almost incredibly, to shoot down one Messerschmitt 109, and the remaining two planes flew out to Jassy in Rumania on 17 September. The other cadets had made their way towards the frontier in lorries or on foot, but some were cut off by the advancing Russian pincer movement and forced to double back, while one group was captured by a German forward column. These managed to escape – one of them by dressing up as a schoolgirl – and by the end of the third week in September most of the fledgling pilots were safely across the border.

The campaign was still not over for some. One bomber pilot

refused to comply with the order to evacuate. He went on harrying the advancing Germans in his Karaś until he ran out of fuel a few days later. As Skalski pointed out, 'you cannot fight a guerrilla war in the air'.

Warsaw, surrounded entirely by the Germans, continued to hold out, as did the military strong-point at Modlin to the north, and the small garrison of the Hel peninsula outside Danzig. The Polesie Army Group in eastern Poland was still fighting hard – against Russians as well as Germans – and did not lay down its arms until 6 October.

There were airmen with each of these forces. Those stranded in Warsaw had formed a small unit which used patched wrecks and sporting planes to carry out reconnaissance and liaison flights and to drop the odd bomb or grenade on the encircling Germans. Others took over the anti-aircraft defences and desperately struggled to ward off the now unfettered *Luftwaffe*. On 25 September no fewer than 420 German bombers preyed on the capital unopposed, and it was clear that the city could not hold out much longer. That evening a Polish plane landed in Warsaw bringing orders to the garrison from the high command in Rumania. It flew out again under the cover of darkness, bound for neutral Latvia. The following night, 26 September, a number of senior airmen collected together the nine remaining airworthy planes, and made a dash for Hungary. The airmen left behind continued to fight as an infantry battalion in the trenches, opposing the German tanks until the city surrendered on 27 September.

The last operational flight of the Polish Air Force in 1939 took place some days later, on 4 October, when a couple of reconnaissance planes attached to the Polesie Army Group, patched with sticking-plaster requisitioned from a local chemist's, flew out in support of its beleaguered troops, dropping hand grenades on German infantry and shooting from the cockpit with side-arms: a fitting image with which to close the campaign.

4

Balkan Farce

CONSIDERING THE SPEED of the *Blitzkrieg*, the unexpected Soviet invasion and the attendant chaos, the Poles had managed to save much from the defeat. The government and high command had withdrawn to Rumania, followed by tens of thousands of soldiers of all arms. They had also managed to safeguard a number of national assets. A large part of the navy and merchant marine had got away, as had the civilian planes of the Polish airline LOT. Thanks to General Rayski, jobless since his resignation earlier that year, most of Poland's gold reserves had been flown out in a variety of planes during the last days.

In all, about 80 per cent of the Polish Air Force's pre-war effectives, as they stood on 1 September, survived the campaign and managed to escape capture by the Germans. In sometimes tortuous ways, 9,276 of them crossed the border into Rumania, and some 900 into Hungary. Another 1,000 or so made their way to the neutral Baltic states of Lithuania or Latvia, while about 1,500 were captured by the Soviets – and promptly sent to labour camps.

Those who had crossed into Rumania found that they had entered a different world. It was a beautiful but poor country. The population was extremely welcoming, offering bread, cheese and wine to the Poles and helping them on their way. The military detachments they came across were made up of scruffy, sometimes barefoot men, led by elegant white-gloved officers eager to show off their French. The police were largely illiterate, but carried impressive sabres which they would unsheathe, somewhat uncertainly, at moments of perplexity or crisis. The attitude of the police and the military towards the Poles varied from extreme cordiality to open hostility, and their treatment of the escapees was highly erratic. As they crossed the border the Poles had been ordered to throw down their arms, but many of the airmen held on to their pistols and daggers, which they concealed about their persons. As they marched further into the country, they encountered other Rumanian units. One roadblock would wave them through with a smile, the next would search them, confiscate their side-arms and impound their vehicles. But the Poles soon discovered that ingenuity and above all bribery could get round most obstacles.

Lieutenant Urbanowicz and a party of cadets were arrested and frog-marched towards a railway station on their second day in Rumania. As they waited for a putative train, they saw a pig being chased frantically down the road by a Rumanian officer and two soldiers. The cadets joined in, and captured the pig, which, it turned out, had just been acquired at great difficulty and expense by the officer for his forthcoming wedding. He was so grateful to the Poles that he gave their police guards a dressing-down and sent them packing. He then invited all the cadets to a bar where, after many toasts had been drunk to the health of King Carol, he resolved to help them further by giving them an official pass. He drew up an impressive looking document to which he appended a number of seals, and explained to Urbanowicz that 'this document is both very important and completely ineffectual; it depends to whom it is shown and how much is given as a bribe.'

Most of the airmen had crossed the border in orderly fashion with their units, and their officers did all they could to keep them together and disciplined. This proved none too easy. In most cases the escapees had been directed or escorted to internment camps which were as poorly guarded as they were primitive and uncomfortable. The beaten-earth floors and bug-infested pallets held little attraction for the men, who sneaked out in the evenings and found themselves more comfortable accommodation in the beds of single women in the locality. As it was so easy to slip out undetected for the night, it was only a matter of time before some of the more enterprising decided to take their future into their own hands. They wanted to get to France or Britain in order to continue the fight against Germany, and while in many cases they had only the haziest idea of how to get there and which countries along the way might be hostile, many decided to set off at once, rather than wait for instructions that might never come.

Wacław Król and four other pilots escaped from the internment camp at Focsani, traded in their uniforms for civilian clothes, changed their remaining currency on the black market, and set off for Bucharest, hoping to get information and passports at the Polish embassy there. Many others did likewise, and Rumania was soon crawling with young men dressed like scarecrows, jumping on and off trains and avoiding patrols.

On the whole, none of this was as risky as it might sound. Civilians were exceedingly well-disposed and helpful, prepared to hide the Poles in their houses and pretend they were members of the family. The Poles soon found that the best way of getting through on a train was to find some lady travelling alone, take the seat next to her and engage her in conversation. If a police patrol came through the train, it was as a rule assumed that the man sitting next to her was a secret lover, and no questions were asked. This often had the added advantage of yielding a bed for the night at the end of the journey.

When they did get arrested, it was hardly more serious. A policeman could always be enticed into a bar, where, after many toasts to Polish–Rumanian friendship and less decent aspirations, as well as a more or less discreet transfer of *lei* into the policeman's pocket, the matter would be resolved in amicable fashion. One Polish officer managed to buy his freedom by exchanging his boots for the policeman's worn-out pair. Once in a while, a policeman or military officer turned out to be an implacable Nazi sympathizer, particularly in the larger towns, where there were plain-clothes Gestapo agents and members of the Fascist Iron Guard keeping an eye on things. In Bucharest itself the police were more alert, so the airmen had to dodge about as they made for the embassy.

Some of the more sophisticated officers had arranged things better. One major of the Kraków Air Regiment had contrived to drive out to Rumania in his sporting Lancia, the pride of his life, and used it to great effect picking up girls in Bucharest. One of his colleagues from the regiment managed to get his wife out of Poland, and they ended up in a camp in southern Rumania. A local grandee who came to see the camp liked the look of the wife and insisted on removing the couple to his country house. There they spent a relaxing few weeks playing tennis, riding and dancing, the only problem being that the generous nobleman offered to look after the officer's wife 'for the duration of the war' – and even offered him money so that he could keep a mistress in Paris the while, which made it all the more churlish to have to refuse. Others managed to sell their military vehicles before these were confiscated, bought themselves smart clothes and settled down to enjoy the legendary delights of Bucharest nightlife, while waiting for further orders.

The Polish government had reconstituted itself in Paris under the premiership of General Władysław Sikorski, who was also the new Commander-in-Chief. This was good news for the air force, which Sikorski had always valued highly. The other good news was that, as they contemplated the prospect of a long war, both the British and the French air forces became aware that they lacked sufficient reserves of trained men. The British Air Attaché in Warsaw, Group Captain A.P. Davidson, had a high opinion of the Poles. He had been carrying on talks since May on the subject of borrowing some navigators, of which the RAF was short. Now that the war was on, all air force personnel would come in useful, and the idea of forming up Polish air units in Britain was being discussed before the evacuation to Rumania had begun. The British and French legations in Bucharest had been instructed to help with the onward evacuation of the 90,000-odd Polish military personnel, and to give priority to airmen. The diplomats of both countries unofficially pressed the Rumanian authorities to take a relaxed attitude to internment, and the Rumanians were generally willing to help, surreptitiously. German diplomats and military observers, not to mention a swarm of agents scattered over the country, kept a close watch on the goings-on, and protested vehemently that the Rumanian government should observe its obligations as a neutral state – that is, intern all foreign military personnel. But they had an uphill struggle, what with the laxity of the Rumanians and the ingenuity of the Poles.

General Zając, the commander of the Polish Air Force, assembled a special staff and set up a clandestine evacuation centre with an office in a private apartment, where the principal work surfaces were a dining-table, a grand piano and a huge double bed. They made up lists of all the airmen in the respective camps, and sent them orders and money, using for the purpose three girls who had already proved their worth in the air. On 1 September Barbara Wojtulanis, a member of the Warsaw Aeroclub, had turned up at the Mokotów airfield at a moment when there was nobody available to deliver an important order, so the base commander sent her off with it in her sporting plane. Soon she and her two colleagues, Zofia Turowicz and Anna Lęska, were regularly flying liaison missions for the staff, and they flew out of Poland with it on 17 September.

In Rumania they played a key role as couriers, since it was easier for them to travel around the country than for suspect male civilians. But they were often arrested and ill-treated, and theirs was not an easy job. The Polish Embassy issued passports and identity cards in which the airmen were described as students or priests. These were taken, along with enough money to bribe camp commanders and guards, to the camps themselves, while other pay-offs had to be delivered to various officials at border posts and ports.

Those airmen who had already slipped out of the camps and arrived in Bucharest were also given papers and cash, and ordered to assemble at Constanza, Balcic, Efori or some other port on the Black Sea. Others were directed to Split in Yugoslavia or Piraeus in Greece. Others simply decided to go it alone and set off, by train, by peasant cart or on foot, through Yugoslavia and northern Italy. One officer of the air force intelligence section was picked up by his colleague based in France, who came to fetch him – and elements of the Enigma decoding material he was carrying – in a Paris taxi.

Despite being allied with Germany, the Italians turned a blind eye to these peregrinations – although General Zając himself was taken off a train at Fiume and detained on suspicion of being a Jew. He was only saved by having a rosary and his Polish decorations in his pocket. Everyone had been instructed to divest himself of every scrap of evidence of ever having belonged to the Polish forces, and most complied. One pilot remembers wrestling with his emotions for some time before flushing his silver eagle, the equivalent of British 'wings', down the lavatory of a Bucharest hotel. But some held on to souvenirs – quite perversely in several cases: one pilot took the propeller off his RWD–8 which had crash-landed near Cernauti, and contrived to lug the two-metre-long lump of wood all the way to London (where it still stands in a corner of the Sikorski Museum).

Similar evacuation operations were implemented on a lesser scale in Hungary, Latvia and Lithuania. The Hungarian authorities were friendly and courteous. Poles were interned in comfortable camps with lax security that did not tighten in spite of

escapes of up to 50 prisoners a day. One camp lost 405 airmen
in less than three weeks, and still the guard was not reinforced.
One group of 70 escapees actually hired Hungarian buses to take
them to Yugoslavia.

The Baltic states were another matter. Lithuania was not well-
disposed to Poland, while Latvia, though friendly, was wary. The
planes escaping from north-eastern Poland landed at Dyneburg,
and were immediately surrounded by Latvian gendarmes with
drawn sabres. Latvia was under heavy pressure from the Soviets
not to let the interned Poles out, so any evacuation was more of
an escape, facilitated by Polish agents and the British Consulate.
Individual men or groups had to slip through to Sweden by boat,
then on to Norway and Denmark, from where they made for
France and, later, directly for Britain.

The Rumanian evacuation was by far the largest, and the most
complex, for the obvious, Balkan reasons. Arrangements would
be made, and then the officials in question, having come under
German pressure, would renege on them. Groups of airmen
would suddenly be held up or arrested, and only large quantities
of *lei* would smooth the path once more. Nor was it easy to keep
the impatient and increasingly bitter young airmen in order.
They felt let down by a government and high command that had
prepared so ill for war, and they were often insubordinate. They
would go off on their own, invent different schemes, or cause
trouble by continuing to fight the war. While hanging about at
the port of Balcic, two cadets of the Dęblin school noticed a distinctly un-Rumanian-looking individual snooping around the
docks, so they tailed him. They followed him to a small villa on
the outskirts of town, and caught him transmitting in German
from a radio in the cellar. Assuming him to be a spy, they killed
him.

By the beginning of October the Rumanian Black Sea ports
looked as though they were benefiting from a late-season tourist
boom. Balcic seethed with young men hanging about its cafés
drinking and listening to gypsy music. The Hôtel Moderne in
Constanza overflowed with raffish types bent on sampling the
local delights. On 15 October some 800 airmen embarked on a
Greek-flagged coaster, the *St Nicolas*, in the port of Balcic. The
Rumanian troops overseeing the embarkation knew perfectly
well who these 'students' were, having been briefed from
Bucharest to turn a blind eye to this exodus – and showered with
several briefcases of *lei* by Polish Consular officials. They never-

theless searched the airmen's battered suitcases and bundles, weeding out anything of value, and occasionally refusing to let one of them through. One officer turned back after showing a passport in which he figured as a student, rejoined the queue and produced another, in which he was described as a priest. This did not cut much ice either, and he was turned back once more. He waited an hour, then joined the queue again. This time he showed his driving licence, and he was waved through. Then, expectedly, the Rumanians put their foot down, declaring one group of a hundred or so to be suspect. After accepting more *lei*, their commander agreed to let his troops literally look the other way as soon as the *St Nicolas* had cast off, and the remaining airmen were able to dive into the sea and clamber aboard the ship as it nudged its way towards the harbour mouth.

The *St Nicolas* was not new to such cargo, having in the past transported Jewish immigrants to Palestine. But it made no concessions to the comfort of its human passengers. It consisted of one huge hold, normally used for transporting pigs and sheep; the airmen could just fit on board by lying like sardines one next to the other on the old mattresses that lined it. Thus they spent the next week, passing through the Bosphorus and sailing down the Turkish coast.

On 21 October the *St Nicolas* sailed into Beirut, and the by now bedraggled and filthy airmen were astonished and a little embarrassed to find themselves disembarking to the strains of a French military band drawn up smartly on the quayside. They were each given a bottle of cold beer and a packet of Gauloises, then taken to the Foreign Legion barracks, where they found showers, food and beds. The mattresses were crawling with bedbugs and the airmen, maddened by the forced inactivity of the past week and excited by their new surroundings, made scant use of them. Many prowled around the exotic city, stopping to stare at palm trees, natives and the French colonial troops – most of them had never seen coloured people before. Some even came across Poles serving in the Foreign Legion, who took them on a tour of the nightspots.

The next morning the airmen were put aboard a passenger ship, the *Ville de Strasbourg*, which set sail for Marseille. They were wonderfully fed and plied with wine, but most of them were violently seasick, and relieved to reach Marseille on 30 October. Here, still looking more like tramps than soldiers, they had to disembark and parade while a military band played the Polish

and French national anthems, before being led into the
Customs hall, where a banquet had been laid on by the Mayor of
Marseille. After a deal of food, drink and speeches, they were put
aboard buses and transported to Sallon airfield outside
Marseille. Wacław Król, though already a blooded pilot, was still
the son of a Polish peasant, and he stared out of the bus window
at the French countryside in disbelief – he could not see a single
horse-drawn vehicle.

On 5 November a second ship took a similar consignment of
airmen from Constanza to Malta, where they were transferred to
the luxurious SS *Franconia* for the onward journey to Marseille.
'Can you imagine how we felt?' wrote one of the bedraggled officers. 'Suddenly we walked into a fairy world of crystal chande-
liers, snow-white table-cloths, gleaming table silver and were
greeted by immaculately-dressed stewards whose eyes never
betrayed by so much as a flicker what they must have thought of
us.'

Such overt evacuation could not be kept up for long. With
increasing German diplomatic pressure and the rising influence
of the Fascist Iron Guard, Rumanian officials had to be more cir-
cumspect. Their prices went up and the difficulties multiplied.
The treatment of the remaining Polish internees took a change
for the worse. They were moved to better guarded and less
comfortable camps in the Dobrudja, and treated harshly by the
Rumanian military police. Worsening conditions and food shortages brought on sickness. The large camp at Babadag lay in a
region notorious for malaria, which took a heavy toll of the prisoners. Escape became difficult, and the organization of large-
scale evacuation even more so.

Nevertheless, the network set up by the Poles in Bucharest had
gained much in experience, and the evacuation continued,
albeit at a slower pace. It was still only via the Black Sea that it was
possible to organize the movement of larger groups. A Greek
vessel sailing under the British flag and a French coaster ran a
shuttle service between Balcic and Syria or Malta. Smaller groups
of officers were smuggled out on cruise ships which took them to
Alexandria. By the spring of 1940, when the Rumanian officials
completely ceased to co-operate, there were only some 400
Polish Air Force personnel left in the camps – and 390 of these
somehow managed to dribble through to Britain by the autumn
of 1940.

The resourcefulness of these men matched their indomitable

desire to fight the Germans. A group of three mechanics developed their own method for frontiers: they approached the Italian frontier on the Yugoslav side and 'admitted' to the Yugoslav border guards that they were Italians who had entered Yugoslavia without a visa. Horrified at the prospect of filling in forms, the border guards simply pushed them into Italy. When crossing from Italy into Switzerland a week later, the three confessed to the Italian guards that they were Swiss and had strayed into Italy over the mountains without their papers. In no time at all they found themselves being shown across an unguarded stretch of the Swiss frontier by the Italians. By this stage France had fallen, so they employed the same ruse to return to Italy, where they stole a fishing boat and made for Spain. It took them eighteen months to get from Poland to Britain.

Soldiers as well as airmen trapped in German- or Russian-occupied Poland also tried to make their way to France or Britain. Many tried to get through to Hungary over the Carpathian mountains, but winter came early in 1939, and with temperatures as low as 40° below freezing, all too many either died or had to have limbs amputated as a result of frostbite. Some took the shortest route and managed, by walking across Germany and Belgium, to rejoin the Polish ranks in France. Others went east. One escaped from a Soviet gulag and reached Persia by crossing the Karakum desert. One travelled to Odessa and stowed away on a Turkish ship bound for Istanbul. Several others crossed the whole Soviet Union and reached Britain via Japan and the United States.

5

French Fiasco

'FOR MYSELF, AS for' other Polish soldiers, the time we spent in France was one long stream of disillusionment,' writes Bohdan Arct. By the end of November 1939 several thousand Polish Air Force personnel had been reassembled at Sallon, at the large airfield of Lyon-Bron, and at Le Bourget to the north of Paris. The problems started soon after their arrival. The airmen, particularly the young pilots, were champing at the bit, desperate to get airborne. After the heat of the September fighting, when every second seemed precious, they found inactivity hard to bear. Their worst fear was that the war might end before they had been given a chance to get their own back on the Germans. Yet the French seemed to be in no hurry. Railway stations and public places were plastered with posters contrasting France and Britain, and their combined colonies, with an insignificant Germany. '*Nous vaincrons parce que nous sommes les plus forts*', ran the caption. The phoney war was in full swing.

Waiting was not made any easier by the physical conditions. The camps at Sallon, Bron and Le Bourget were hardly luxurious. Septfonds, however, was worse. Run up to accommodate Spanish Communist refugees from Franco, whose company the Poles did not relish, it consisted of long huts with earth floors on which thin straw pallets were laid for sleeping. 'As for the French authorities, one got the impression that they did not really know what to do with us,' wrote an inmate, a young man from Poznań who had always wanted to be in the air force and had escaped from Poland at great risk in order to pursue this dream. 'We felt like intruders.'

Conditions were hardly better in the camp at Istres. The airmen were installed in barracks previously occupied by Senegalese colonial troops, who clearly deserved little consideration in French eyes. There were no panes in the windows, and there was only straw on the concrete floors, no furniture. The request for a stove was peremptorily refused. The men were allowed to make use of the facilities of the French military base next to the camp, but they had to pay for each shower they took and were not allowed to read the papers in the mess. 'We did not have any amicable relations with the French officers,' recalls Urbanowicz; 'they treated us as though we were enemy prisoners of war.' Another pilot puts it more brutally: 'They treated us like white niggers.'

Although the escapees were given a small amount of pocket money, this did not permit them to pass their time pleasantly in Lyon or Marseille, and they were anyway too ashamed of their appearance to enjoy strolling about the boulevards. They were still dressed like Rumanian tramps, some with trousers stopping half-way down their calves and jackets that hung down to their knees, others with sleeves that ended just below the elbow. Their clothes were not only scruffy, they were filthy as well. Poles like to cut a dash, and these young men found it profoundly humiliating to be seen in the streets in such a guise.

They were overwhelmed at first by the delights of French cooking, the wine and the strong *caporal* cigarettes, but the novelty began to pall, and their rations were drastically reduced. They found themselves longing for a hunk of Polish sausage, a bowl of *bigos* (cabbage stew), and vodka – a sure sign of growing homesickness. 'The worst are the unexpected thoughts of home that assail one suddenly, bringing on a mood of total despondency,' noted one of them in his diary.

At first the French civilians, particularly poor people, showed great enthusiasm for *'les braves Polonais'*. There were also official attempts to keep the Poles happy. One or two local committees sprang up to bring them cheer. French 'godmothers' were recruited to send the young airmen parcels and invite them home for weekends. Some of these sent samples of their own lingerie with the chocolates and cigarettes before inviting the airmen to come and stay. Women were on the whole more accessible and better disposed, while men displayed indifference and

even hostility. The Poles found themselves being accused of
having started the war, or at least of being its cause – and the war
was regarded in France as a major nuisance. Another poster to
be found all over France read: '*A bas la Guerre; Vive la Paix!*'

The men therefore spent most of their time sitting about in
the primitive barracks, trying to learn French and going over
their wartime experiences. As they compared notes, they began
to realize how well they had scored against the Germans, even
with their pathetic resources. In fact, in the course of just over
two weeks Polish fighters had shot down 126 German planes for
certain, with another 10 probables and 14 badly damaged. Only
36 Polish fighters had been brought down by the *Luftwaffe*.
Reflection on the September campaign and endless discussion
tended more and more to end in indiscriminate accusations
against the Polish high command, and indeed against all authority. Their present enforced inactivity seemed to confirm the
feeling that they were being let down by their superiors.

Although they could not know it, a great deal was being done.
The Polish government, now in Paris, had set up shop in the
Hôtel Régina at the corner of the rue de Rivoli and the rue des
Pyramides, and while many of its personnel were trekking across
the world, the Polish Air Force headquarters on the second floor
was planning their future. This was not as easy as the airmen
imagined. 'Our talks with the French are not always pleasant,'
General Zając noted in his diary on 13 October, soon after reaching Paris. On 25 October 1939 a meeting was held between high-
ranking Polish, French and British officers at the French Air
Force headquarters to decide how the Polish Air Force should be
used.

Sikorski favoured moving the whole lot to Britain, on the
grounds that the Polish airmen had some experience of British
aero-engines and that they rated the RAF higher than the *Armée
de l'Air*. 'Great Britain would provide a better chance of everything being carried out in a more businesslike way than France,
where the bureaucracy is terrifying,' as Zając put it. The French
demanded that at least half the airmen should remain in France
and join the *Armée de l'Air*. The British, who in any case lacked
accommodation for all of them, were uncertain as to the value of
the Polish airmen. They feared they might prove unreliable, they
assumed that they had been demoralized by their defeat in
September, and they did not suppose them to be good enough
fliers to make fighter pilots. They therefore declared themselves

prepared to take 300 air crew and 2,000 ground staff, who would be allotted to Bomber Command.

Negotiations then struck another reef. Sikorski wanted his men to serve in independent units, but the British view was that these 'would be almost impossible to control and administer'. He also insisted that the Polish Air Force must remain a sovereign force under Polish command. The British declared this to be out of the question, and stated that the Poles could only serve as members of the Royal Air Force Volunteer Reserve (RAFVR). While negotiations on this point continued, three RAF officers toured the Polish camps, looking for volunteers. This provoked heated discussion among the airmen. Would they get airborne quicker if they went to Britain, or if they stayed in France? Which had the better planes? Which was better organized?

These were all open questions, as the Poles had little knowledge of either country or its air force. After observing French officers and troops for a week or two, Tadeusz Schiele, a nineteen year old volunteer who had crossed the Carpathian mountains and walked to France on his own, decided that they would not last long against the Germans. 'How different was the manner of the British,' he wrote. 'We took an immediate liking to them.' Many decided to go to Britain, if only to get out of Lyon-Bron or Le Bourget, where the atmosphere had gone from bad to worse.

Conditions in the camps remained appalling, with little or no heating, sparse bedding, Gallic sanitation and minimal washing facilities. The men had still not been given uniforms, and the clothes they had acquired in Rumania were wearing out. Their shoes were falling apart, and they had no overcoats. They had no money, so they could not buy food with which to supplement the less than adequate rations the French handed out. It was all a far cry from the military bands on the quayside. But above all it was the boredom and the uncertainty that got to them. Nobody seemed to know what was going on. Their frustration was vented in increasingly mutinous tones. Rumours circulated to the effect that senior officers were drawing huge salaries while the lower ranks starved. There were protest meetings in the camps and demands that all senior officers be cashiered.

Recreating an army after the September defeat was not as difficult as recreating a political leadership and a new command. All those associated, either politically or militarily, with the defeat were tainted. Many who had axes to grind blamed others for the defeat. General Rayski, for instance, found himself cold-shouldered and refused a post when he turned up in Paris and volunteered to serve in any capacity. In this acrimonious climate, ridiculous rumours spread and wild accusations flew. General Zając himself was accused of hiring out air force personnel as 'mercenaries' to England, where they would have to swear an oath of allegiance to the king.

Zając listened to the delegations of young subalterns who came to see him in Paris with their grievances and aspersions, and went down to Lyon-Bron to try to reason with them. But he was heckled and insulted, and concluded that 'they are very badly brought up, both from the general and the military point of view'. He was not exaggerating. 'There were mutinous outbursts, discipline collapsed entirely, and a day did not pass without some incident,' recalls one of the inmates. 'Demoralization has reached alarming levels, behaviour towards officers, particularly older ones, is terrible,' another noted in his diary, adding that a couple of majors who tried to restore order in a lunch queue were pelted with stones. 'With the French, it is mutual hatred,' he also noted. 'Knives have been out.'

It was not until 4 January 1940 that an agreement was concluded with the French military authorities. The plan was to form three Polish fighter squadrons: one from the remains of the Warsaw Air Regiment, the second out of the Kraków and Poznań regiments, and a third which was to be sent to help the Finns in their war with the Soviets. The airmen began to be issued with uniforms – in the navy blue cloth of the *Armée de l'Air*, but cut in the Polish style, and with Polish buttons and insignia – and morale shot up at once. Some of the men could be seen hugging and kissing their new side-arms.

The first complement of sixteen pilots selected to go and train at the fighter school at Montpellier arrived there on 7 January 1940. They were in paroxysms of excitement when they saw the Morane fighters they would be flying. The course was to last three months, and they were to spend the first two on two-seater trainers. In the event, they showed themselves to be such good fliers that they were put on the Moranes directly and the course cut down to one month. The French were so pleased with them that they decided to reward them with a skiing holiday in Mégève. But the pilots did not want holidays, they wanted to fight. They relapsed into despondency when they were sent back to Lyon-Bron. There was nothing for them to do here, but at least, with smart uniforms and some money, they could while away the time picking up girls in Lyon.

At the end of March the Montpellier pilots finally got their own planes, with the Polish Air Force chequer on the fuselage. General Sikorski came down to Lyon-Bron to see them off. The whole base paraded, attended an open air Mass and listened to a speech by Sikorski, after which the pilots climbed into their machines and staged a fly-past before going to join the French units they had been posted to.

The 1 Polish/145 French Warsaw Fighter Squadron also became operational. The Finnish plan had been scrapped, but the French had now decided to increase the number of Polish squadrons to four fighter, three reconnaissance and three bomber, and by the beginning of May most of the personnel for these were in training. Once it was discovered that the Polish pilots did not need the intensive programme of the Montpellier school, they were allowed to train on their own base at Lyon-Bron. The bomber pilots were sent for training to bases at Blida in Algeria and Marrakesh in Morocco, and the navigators to Rabat. Engineers were assigned to aircraft factories in various French cities. Ground crews and technicians were sent to a number of bases, the largest of which was the air park at Maison Blanche in Algeria. Bohdan Arct felt he had travelled a long way as he stood to attention at the 3 May Polish National Day parade in Blida, while a black Spahi band blared its way through the Polish national anthem.

By the end of May 1940 the Polish Air Force in France numbered a total of 7,000 officers and men, with 86 operational planes. 'The sheer joy and relief of being airborne again was like that which must be felt by caged birds suddenly finding freedom,' writes one of the pilots. But although they were now uniformed, paid and kept busy, their sense of frustration was only partly allayed, and their attitude to the French had not improved. 'The French watched us with interest, but kept their distance,' one officer recalls. 'Our relations with them were correct, but not notably cordial. The homes of the local people were closed to us; all we had were the cafés and the streets.' French girls seemed happy enough to flirt with the airmen, but clearly felt no particular warmth towards them. There was certainly little warmth in the richly dressed lady who drew up outside a café in a gleaming chauffeur-driven limousine, and, after observing the group of airmen sipping their drinks for some time, crooked her little finger at Król and whisked him off.

More surprising to the Poles was the attitude of the French airmen. 'Our French colleagues behaved correctly towards us on duty, but with coolness and evident condescension, and outside duty there was no contact between us,' noted one of them. Attitudes varied. Another pilot found his French colleagues 'highly cordial'. When the Montpellier group arrived to join a French fighter group at Luxeuil, near the German border, they were greeted in the mess with champagne and embraces, and relations remained good.

The Poles were also unpleasantly surprised by the quality of the French *matériel*. 'The Bloch 152, with its two cannon and two machine-guns, looked just the ticket,' wrote a pilot of the 1/145 Warsaw Squadron. 'It wasn't British, but it looked a whole lot better than our P–11s. What optimists we were – we didn't realize that it was just a heap of scrap-metal, a decorative sight in the air, not a fighting tool.' Much the same was true of the other machines the Poles were issued with. 'Caudron's Cyclone refused to climb,' according to one of them. The engine frequently over-heated, and pieces fell off in the air.

Nor were the Poles impressed by the standard of servicing. 'How good it is to have Polish mechanics,' wrote a pilot who was serving in a mixed Franco-Polish flight. 'Your cockpit, when you get into it, is as neat as a drawing-room. Everything shines and glints; there is no question of finding the smallest scrap of rubbish tucked among the equipment. Quite another matter when you get into a French-serviced machine. When you bank the plane in the air, a shower of rubbish assails you. That is why one should always clear out a plane that has been serviced by a Frenchman. You go up to two thousand feet and then, at full throttle and with the cockpit open, you dive down to a thousand in a few seconds. In that brief moment, as you hang upside down, you see a curious sight: a stream of screws, rubber washers, bits of string, lumps of mud, all fly past you. Once, a spanner hit me in the jaw so hard it hurt for three days.'

What really bothered the Poles was the French attitude to the war. 'We had experienced the war in Poland, and we knew that it had nothing in common with the war of 1914–18,' explains Rolski. 'They were sunk up to their ears in the old ideas, and lis-tened to our accounts with barely concealed disbelief.' While waiting for a ship in Beirut, he and a couple of other officers had met General Weygand, who was Commander-in-Chief of French forces in the Middle East. Weygand quizzed them about German tactics. 'He listened attentively, but one could see that he put everything we said through the sieve of his own opinions and only retained the few morsels that fitted in with these.'

These attitudes were reflected in the *Armée de l'Air*'s dispositions. The Poles who were assigned to the front-line base at Luxeuil wondered why the French did not make raids across the border, and were told that there was no point, since the Germans were too weak to attack, and that the war would soon be over. 'The French idea of a war-ready airfield was peculiar, to say the least, and this made us very anxious,' noted Król. The pilots were all billeted in the nearby town, and did not put in an appearance at the airfield until ten in the morning. Meanwhile their planes sat on the grass in neat rows, entirely defenceless against enemy attack. Mummler and Król told the Frenchmen that they should camouflage the planes and keep a contingent of pilots in readiness for take-off from an hour before dawn. General Zając, who had noted the same arrangements elsewhere, warned his French counterparts that their airfields were not properly camouflaged or defended, but met only withering condescension.

All the worst fears of the Poles were confirmed when the Germans attacked on 10 May. At Luxeuil, 25 planes were destroyed on the ground. 'I told them this would happen,' Mummler fumed. 'They should have known that the Germans would attack at dawn, just as they did in Poland. Who has ever seen a war where pilots arrive at the airfield when the sun is high?' The Poles were all the more horrified at the French insouciance, because to them every plane seemed terribly precious. In fact, there was no shortage of machines in France, and 20 new Moranes were delivered a couple of days later. But these too were left out in neat rows for the Germans to bomb.

'They had pilots and planes in plenty, any losses could be replaced immediately, yet they somehow could not, or would not, get to grips with the enemy,' complained Król. Returning from patrol with four French colleagues, he sighted a lone Heinkel bomber, and suggested they attack it. The response of the flight leader was, 'You can do what you like – we're going home'. Król duly veered off and shot down the Heinkel. When he returned to base twenty minutes after the others, he found them all sitting in the mess drinking champagne.

'Our patrol, consisting of three aircraft, encountered twelve Messerschmitt 110s in the air,' recalls another pilot. 'Some 6,000 feet below a squadron of French Curtisses was on patrol, but not a single Frenchman interrupted his routine work in order to help us Poles.' The three Poles shot down four of the Messerchmitts, but when they returned to base the commanding officer refused to credit them with the kills and reprimanded them for taking unnecessary risks. Similar stories abound.

The plan to form the Poles up into separate squadrons had been abandoned, and they were mainly dispersed in flights of three to six planes attached to French units all over the country. Only 1/145 Warsaw Squadron was kept together, defending Lyon, but this was equipped with the defective Caudron Cyclone, which was grounded by an order from the French air ministry. The Poles would have none of it. 'We felt it was better to fly in coffins than not to fly at all,' as one of them put it. They managed to shoot down ten German planes in a week in these coffins.

There were plenty of good planes available. The Montpellier flight stationed at Luxeuil was re-equipped with Devoitine 520 fighters, which were excellent, and another flight was given American Curtiss 75s. 'The French could have given us Curtiss or Devoitine machines, which were burned some time later in the depots at Bourges and Toulouse,' fumed a pilot of the Warsaw Squadron. 'It is difficult to forget and forgive them this; we could have forgiven them everything else,' he added, alluding to the insults and the cold-shouldering.

A large number of Polish pilots were dispersed in groups of half-a-dozen and given the task of defending factories or strategic objectives. These 'chimney flights', as they were dubbed, were given poor planes and a boring task, but they achieved some successes nevertheless. In all, 150 Polish pilots flew operationally during the French campaign, and they downed 56 German planes at a cost of 13 of their own number.

The French early-warning system broke down on the first day of the German attack. Just as in the Polish campaign, there was little co-ordination, and just as in the Polish campaign, they kept being ordered to fall back. The Poles could hardly believe the chaos. 'They seem to be setting up in competition with us,' one of them quipped. The Germans entered Paris on 14 June, and four days later the ageing Marshal Pétain signed the armistice which brought Franco-German hostilities to an end. The French heaved a collective sigh of relief and set about celebrating the 'peace'.

The Poles were scandalized. On 18 June Rolski, who had cobbled together a squadron which had just been issued with new planes at Clermont-Ferrand, was told by the French base commander that the war was over. The French airmen repaired to the mess to crack open the champagne. Expecting the Germans to arrive at any moment, Rolski and his 16 pilots flew off to an airfield south of Toulouse.

The Polish government had left Paris, and on 19 June General Sikorski made a radio broadcast instructing all Poles to make for the ports of Brest, St-Malo, La Rochelle, Bordeaux, St-Nazaire, Bayonne or St-Jean-de-Luz, where ships were standing by to take them to Britain. General Zając, his staff and a large number of airmen embarked on the Polish ocean liner *Batory* at St-Jean-de-Luz, despite the attempts of the local French forces to intern them. Other Polish liners and cargo ships picked up soldiers and airmen at different ports. For some units it was a dash against time, as the Germans were streaming southwards and westwards. And the French authorities were not always helpful. One Polish flight based at Bussac-Forêt airfield near Bordeaux was placed under arrest by the French commander, but over the past weeks they made friends with the Senegalese troops who guarded the base, and these freed them. Many of the Poles helped themselves to arms abandoned by the French soldiers, and even dragged heavy machine-guns aboard the transport ships.

Most of the operational units were by this stage too far south to make the ports on the west coast. A later broadcast mentioned Port-Vendres on the Mediterranean as an evacuation point. Here, too, there were attempts by the French to prevent the embarkation, but in the end some 2,000 men were taken off in British vessels. Those who were too far east, and cut off by the Italian invasion, bolted for Switzerland. One airman crossed the Lake of Geneva in a rowing-boat, climbed under the Pullman coach of a train in Lausanne bound for Yugoslavia, and by way of Greece and Turkey reached British Palestine.

Many naturally thought of escaping by air. Very few were far enough north to attempt the flight direct to England, and there was the added risk that they would be flying over German-occupied territory. Only Captain Zdzisław Henneberg made the Channel crossing successfully with two of his pilots. The Montpellier squadron, now reunited at Perpignan, found the airbase in a state of chaos, as most of the French officers had taken leave to celebrate the peace. Resourceful to the last, the Polish pilots pretended that they had lost their pay-books and managed to get the base paymaster to give them three months' pay. They located some maps and raided the workshop for inner tubes of lorry tyres, which they blew up and placed in their cockpits, just in case they had to ditch in the sea. They took off for Algeria, and eventually landed in Tunis. Here they were received coolly and their planes were impounded. They set off by train for Algiers and Casablanca, where they hoped to get a ship for England.

Rolski, whose squadron had their planes impounded at a base south of Toulouse the day after receiving them, was also determined to get to Africa. He located two small passenger planes on the airfield, and organized his men for various tasks. One lot went on a discreet scrounge for fuel, while the other went in search of tyre tubes and provisions. He himself scoured local bookshops, but only managed to find a school atlas. On the night of 23 June they wheeled the planes silently out of their hangars and up to the end of the runway. They started their engines both at once and made a dash for it. When Rolski's plane landed at Oran, the engine spluttered to a stop before he could taxi off the runway – he had used the last drop of fuel.

Various other airmen stole planes and flew singly or in small groups to Africa. Mirosław Ferić stole a Morane, and by the time he was over Majorca he realized that he was running low on fuel. It was too late to turn back to France, and if he landed in Spain he would be interned. 'I made a quick decision: to fly on,' he wrote. 'At that moment I said to myself: "Long Live Poland!" No, its's no exaggeration, it's the simple truth.' He just made it over the African coast before his engine cut out. Another pilot spent two days making secret preparations, but when he crept into the hangar at night to wheel the plane out, he found several French officers already in it – they had got wind of his intentions, and wanted to go to Africa with him. Another managed to fly to Maison Blanche in Algeria. 'There we found noise, shouting, and complete chaos,' he writes. 'A jam of planes, black men, Arabs, Frenchmen, Poles, Czechs, all shouting, quarrelling, indignant and perspiring. Nobody blames themselves, everyone blames someone else, everyone has a different plan to save themselves and Europe.'

The pilots of the Polish bomber-training base at Blida in Algeria were meanwhile plotting to steal planes and fly to Gibraltar. But the distance was too great at one hop, and they could not count on friendly refuelling facilities, so they went by train to Casablanca.

Once again, thousands of Polish airmen were on the move. In

one of his broadcasts, Goebbels dismissively referred to all these Polish servicemen trying to get to England as 'Sikorski's Tourists'. Certainly, in spite of being taken aback at first by the exoticism of their new surroundings, they were fast becoming seasoned travellers. One group which ran out of cash raided an army bedding store and hawked sheets door-to-door. Others explored the kasbahs of Oran and Rabat, and soon discovered what bargains could be struck in the souks. It was a strange experience for many of them. One pilot who had managed to get hold of some money was chauffeured around Algiers by a former White Russian general, and around Oran by a Spanish Communist exile. They drifted into Casablanca in whole units or in small groups, and the first arrivals found places on British transport ships. A number of French officers who had decided to go to Britain to fight at the side of General de Gaulle wanted to board them too, but were being prevented by the French authorities, so the Polish airmen dressed them up as Poles and smuggled them past the harbour guards.

The ships sailed for Gibraltar, where they waited to form up a convoy, but more airmen kept appearing at Casablanca. There turned out to be two Polish ships in the harbour there, one a naval supply-vessel, the other a square-rigged sail-training ship. Neither had crews, so the airmen set about making two up from among themselves. They persuaded a couple of Danish sailors with whom they had made friends to come and help them, and in one of the sea-front bars found an old captain of the Tsarist merchant marine. He had not been to sea for twenty years and was hardly ever sober, but he was the only one they could find who knew anything about navigation, so they persuaded him to take command. The two craft weighed anchor, and joined the convoy off Gibraltar. During the onward journey the supply-vessel was left behind, but it wallowed into Liverpool some days after it had been given up for lost, with several hundred starving pilots in its holds.

A few hundred airmen were stranded in Algeria, and some were imprisoned. Most of these contrived to escape, and the last group was taken off a deserted beach by a Polish naval cutter as late as December 1941. Those who reached Casablanca after the departure of the last transports took whatever ships they could, and some found themselves embarking on extraordinary voyages. One boarded a tramp steamer that took him to Mexico, whence he made his way via the United States and Canada to

England. Another coasted down to Dakar, where he took ship for Brazil, whence he too went north to Canada.

They were determined to continue the fight at any cost, but were beginning to have grave doubts as to whether any of the Allies felt the same way. For a century and a half, France had been the fall-back position from which defeated Poles could continue the fight for freedom. If they had not always received effective support, they had always met with great cordiality and total solidarity. This generation too had hoped to fight their way back to Warsaw from France, but 'the ground vanished under our feet', as one of them put it. And if the traditionally stalwart French had proved such poor allies, what could they expect of the British, to whom they were linked by neither history, culture nor religion? Britain was the last ditch. The question on everyone's lips as the airmen hung over the rails of the pitching transport ships was whether the British were prepared to fight.

Mist and Regulations

SITTING ON A dirty collier ploughing its way across the Bay of
Biscay, Bohdan Arct summoned up in his imagination the full
extent of his knowledge of Britain, towards which fate was now
steering him. 'We knew about Shakespeare and Sherlock
Holmes,' he writes. 'We had heard of the notorious English fog.'
Beyond that, he had a mental picture of aloof aristocrats, eccen-
tric old ladies, retired colonial colonels and insensitive businessmen, and believed that 'the typical Englishman differs little in
temperament from a fish'. He was also gloomily convinced 'that
you might spend a lifetime searching, but that you would never
find a beautiful woman the length and breadth of the country.'

Rolski's thoughts as he leant over the rail of his docking ship,
peering through the mist and drizzle, were more practical, but
hardly more optimistic. 'My mind was still reeling from the
desperately heroic Polish shambles, and the insouciant French
shambles. It was therefore with some apprehension that I awaited
the first symptoms of some third variety of shambles – a British
shambles.' He and his colleagues were all the more surprised by
what they found.

The first Polish airmen in Britain were those who had opted
for the RAF shortly after reaching France, and they had begun to
arrive at Southampton on 8 December 1939. In contrast to
France, there were no military bands and no reception committees on the dank quayside. They were given a cup of hot tea and
a sandwich, put aboard waiting trains and taken directly to RAF
Eastchurch, near Sheerness. The station commander was Group

Captain A.P. Davidson, the former air attaché in Warsaw, who knew some Polish. He greeted them cordially but without ceremony, and they were installed in comfortable barracks.

The very next day, however, some particularly British irritants were visited on them. They had to parade, endlessly, while roll-calls were taken. They then had to start filling in forms. Then followed a series of medicals. Then came English lessons and an introduction to King's Regulations, a mystification to them. Then nothing. The war appeared no less phoney on this side of the Channel, and the British, like the French, seemed to be in no hurry. 'It should be remembered', Air Marshal John Slessor later wrote, 'that in spite of the fate of Poland, we had not really taken the measure of the German threat.' The RAF needed pilots, but it was not yet desperate, and its top brass held the view that the Poles must have been 'demoralized' by their defeat at the hands of the Germans. Underpinning this view was a feeling that, however splendid they might be, they were a rung or two lower on the ladder of civilization. It was therefore deemed desirable to let them settle down and to induct them gradually into the ways of the RAF.

But the Poles wanted to fight, not settle down. And their impatience only served to confirm the British in their Darwinian views, as the waiting brought out the worst in them. Successive batches of airmen arrived at Eastchurch at three-weekly intervals from December 1939 to February 1940, and there were soon an increasingly disgruntled 2,000 or so Poles milling about the place with nothing to do. They complained about conditions, and most of all about military dispositions, on which they all reckoned themselves to be experts by now. They vented their discontent on their own officers and on the British, whom they referred to as 'ostriches', since they seemed to be hiding their heads in the sand where the German threat was concerned. 'The naïvety of the British drove us to distraction,' recalls one of them.

Air Marshal Hugh 'Stuffy' Dowding, who came down to Eastchurch to greet the Poles, was not impressed by their attitude. He delivered a polite welcoming address and finished by asking, somewhat rhetorically, whether there were any questions. Witold Urbanowicz stepped forward and demanded to know when they would start flying. Dowding replied coolly that they would start their training in good time. This did not satisfy Urbanowicz, who declared that they had not come all this way to sit around learning English.

When General Zając arrived at Eastchurch at the end of
February for an inspection, he took a similarly dim view. He was
warmly received by Davidson and his British colleagues, but
found the Polish airmen, particularly the subalterns, rude and
mutinous. He was informed that there had been quarrels and
incidents, and that discipline had all but broken down on occasion. Twenty young hotheads had refused to swear the oath to the
king that was necessary on joining the RAFVR.

The British officers at Eastchurch felt daunted by the Poles.
The language barrier was not confined to language itself. Spoken
Polish is a language of rapid communication, reliant to a large
extent on mood and inference, while English is far more precise,
requiring attention to every word. As soon as they had mastered
a few words of English, the Poles would frequently deduce what
they assumed to be the sense of an order without considering
every word, and dash off to do quite the wrong thing. The British
response – to speak slower and louder – was of little help.
'Rebuking a Pole was a waste of time,' writes a British officer. 'He
would appear to understand, give a magnificent salute and then
go away and default again.'

It was partly a clash of two different military traditions. The
Polish habit of saluting everyone, on station, in town, in restaurants, irritated the British officers, who found that they could not
cross the airfield or walk down a street without acknowledging
several dozen salutes. 'They were always giving you salutes even
if it was their despatcher handing you a cup of coffee,' recalls an
RAF officer. 'The heel-clicking that went on was terrific,' remembers one RAF fitter, 'and they had a funny way of bowing stiffly,
from the waist up, like tin soldiers.' In contrast to this
punctiliousness, the Poles had a matter-of-fact attitude to regulations, based on their being a republican and, in effect, a
volunteer force, and this did not sit well with the hierarchical
deference that underlay British military culture. 'Whilst on the
one hand there exists a distinct class feeling between officers and
airmen and the former often treat the latter with a lack of
consideration unknown in our own Service, on the other hand,
officers fraternize with airmen, walk about and play cards with
them,' reported a clearly baffled and somewhat shocked
Davidson.

Another Polish trait that worried and annoyed the British was
the Poles' propensity to quarrel among themselves. Some perceived affront would give rise to dissensions which the British

observed uncomprehendingly and helplessly, and would eventually be resolved by a Tribunal of Honour, which had superseded duelling. The members of such a tribunal were elected, and when the British first noticed Poles confabulating in corners, canvassing and arguing, they deduced that a political coup was brewing.

Zając gave instructions for a number of initiatives to distract the men at Eastchurch and nearby Manston, into which they had overflowed. In March the base started its own band and put on amateur dramatics. A swimming competition and a football tournament used up some of the excess energy, and visits were organized to the British Museum and the BBC in London. A Polish Air Force newsletter was started. This kept the airmen informed about international events on the one hand and appealed to their better instincts on the other. 'Let us be gentlemen!' the second issue harangued the men. 'Let us look at the English, let us observe them, let us study their better qualities and appropriate them. We are not tourists who do not need to adapt themselves to the manners of the country. We are soldiers of the Polish forces, and the eyes of all Englishmen are upon us.'

Matters again improved when the men were issued with uniforms – the officers were fitted by deferential staff from Austin Reed who came down to Eastchurch for the purpose. They were normal RAF uniforms, with the word 'Poland' embroidered on the shoulder. 'We changed our skin. Our appearence altered, and so did our state of mind,' as one airman put it.

Now that they had proper uniforms and the weather had improved, the men started going out, and again they found a pleasant contrast with France. As they drifted about nearby Ramsgate and Margate or went sightseeing in London, they met with astonishing cordiality from the civilian population. People were 'embarrassingly friendly', in the words of one pilot. Seeing the 'Poland' flashes, they would walk up to airmen in the street and invite them home. Bus conductors refused their fares, waiters settled their restaurant bills for them, and they only had to walk into a pub to be offered free drinks.

This was the more remarkable since Poland had not enjoyed a good press in Britain during the pre-war years. 'Beyond the fact the Poland existed, that it lay between Germany and Russia, that Piłsudski, Paderewski and Chopin were Poles, the average Englishman knew absolutely nothing,' writes one RAF officer. 'He imagined it was some hundred years behind his own country, that its inhabitants lived in a state of superlative ignorance, with the result that his naïve questions, like "have you trams in Warsaw?" or "have you cinemas in Cracow?" were sometimes exasperating to the Poles.'

Those who did think they knew something of the country nourished a general impression of a booted, strutting, anti-Semitic regime and a primitive society. Socialists viewed it as little better than Fascist Italy or Spain. Mass Observation soundings recorded a low level of esteem for Poland, even after the German invasion. But the presence of the defeated yet unbowed young men seems to have stirred the popular imagination and cut through such prejudice at street level.

Seeing their shoulder-flashes, girls would accost the airmen with a 'Hello, Poland!' which they found unnervingly forward, but such confusion did not last long. Reticence or polite banter were simply not possible when 'you very beautiful' and 'I love you' were the only phrases they had mastered (by rote-memorizing of *Ju weri bjutyful* and *Aj law ju*). One girl recalls that introductions always made her think of the 'Me Tarzan – You Jane' scene. 'The verb may not be in the proper mood, but the soldier doesn't worry about that, so long as the girl is,' as the *Sunday Post* put it.

'The blackout was a natural ally in the first contacts with girls', and a park bench afforded total intimacy, according to one pilot. Soon, the more sophisticated had mastered advanced pick-up lines such as 'You go me pictures yes?' But any further communication was usually carried on through the good offices of the RAF adjutants and language instructors. 'I was never allowed a half-hour's peace without somebody wanting me to write their love-letters for them or translate those received from their English girl-friends,' writes one, Sergeant Alexander Gray. A colleague of his hit on a labour-saving device. 'Our English teacher on the base wrote out a series of letters for us, some inviting a girl to a cinema or a dance, others more intimate,' explains one of the Poles. 'So, depending on what you wanted to do with a girl, you'd go up to him and say "Teacher, letter number three please".' The first wedding between a Polish airman and a local girl took place at Manston that spring.

'Matters of rank, prestige and, above all, "having a good time" have become predominant,' Davidson added to his already disapproving report on the state of affairs at Eastchurch. 'Both Polish organization and discipline leave much to be desired and the experience of the last three months suggests that without extensive British control it will be impossible to form efficient Polish Air Units,' he wrote. 'Neither Polish officers or NCOs have the authority with their men necessary to create discipline as known in the British Air Force.' This was hardly surprising in the conditions of enforced idleness.

The reason why nothing was happening was British confusion and dithering. An Air Ministry document identifies the problem as stemming partly from 'the multiplicity of Air Ministry branches dealing with details of principle and organization', but most of all from an 'inability to obtain authoritative decisions'. Behind these lurked the problem that the RAF did not have enough planes for the Poles. The verbal agreement had been that the Poles would be formed up into two Wellington bomber squadrons, but it now turned out that there were no Wellingtons available, and the best the Air Ministry could come up with were some old Fairey Battles. They were too embarrassed to admit this, and sheltered behind delay. There were also lingering doubts. 'Group Captain Davidson said that the Pole was an individualist, and that an aircraft like the Wellington, with a crew of six, was not really suited to their temperament,' ran a confidential minute.

Eventually a batch of pilots was sent off to Redhill for training. Another went to a special Polish Operational Training Unit (No. 18 Polish OTU) at Hucknall in Nottinghamshire. In June, 18 OTU was transferred to Bramcote, near Nuneaton in Warwickshire, which was to be the cradle of the Polish bomber force. Morale shot up at once.

The Poles were overwhelmed by the civilized routine of the RAF station. 'After the splendours of French cuisine, it was not so easy to accustom oneself to what our English colleagues ate,'noted one of them. But he warmed to the unheard-of luxury of early morning tea served in bed by a deferential batman who ran a bath and cleaned his uniform for him. Another novelty, and something of a treat, was the presence of WAAFs on the stations.

These well turned-out, cheerful girls milling around the station gladdened the hearts of the men. 'It is above all thanks to them that the Poles not only quickly mastered the essentials of English, but also discovered the English people from the nicest possible angle,' in one pilot's words. While some were full of military virtue, most of them were flirtatious, and many were quite determined. 'The WAAFs are on the offensive,' noted Wacław

Król in his diary. 'I have received a one-kilo packet of chocolate from one of them, with the message "From the one who loves you" – but which of them can it be?' He was to discover the answer a couple of days later, when a Scots girl of twenty slipped into his room at night.

The presence of the WAAFs also provoked a number of inter-Allied conflicts between Poles and RAF men, and there were some ugly confrontations. On one base where a Pole and a Briton had come to blows, the entire WAAF complement on the base took sides. 'The Polonophile party confronted the conservatives, who had, it appears, expressed themselves unflatteringly about our men,' records a squadron chronicler. 'The bloodletting among the weaker sex must have been considerable, as the camp doctor complained of being overworked, and even the hairdresser and the tailor seem to have profited from it.' All this made life on a RAF station far more interesting.

But the greatest morale-boost was getting down to work. The Poles, who thought they knew all they needed to know, got a shock. They gazed and listened with fascination and mounting respect as their British instructors initiated them into the wonderful world of radar, beacons, sector-homing and other navigational aids. It was a far cry from making hand signals to one another from the cockpit.

There was a great deal of tedious hard work involved. 'Everything here was back to front,' noted Zumbach. 'In Poland and France, when you wanted to open the throttle you pulled; here, you pushed.' Even the parachute-opening toggle was on a different side. 'We had to reverse all our reflexes.' They also had to learn to judge everything in feet instead of metres, miles instead of kilometres. 'Training them on British aircraft was not an easy job,' recalls Neil Wheeler, a flight instructor at Bramcote.

There was also a lingering doubt at some levels of the RAF about the reliability and trustworthiness of the Poles, and it was thought best not to give them too much information about the workings of inventions such as radar. 'It hurt to discover that we were the object of suspicion when all we wanted to do was shoot down Germans,' recalls Zumbach. Most of them were not so much hurt as exasperated by the British routines. 'We were pushed into a fog of alien regulations and a thicket of instructions, which we could not understand, and sometimes did not even want to grasp,' one airman complained. Even regulations concerning the making of beds were different.

But they soon began to appreciate the purpose of the routines and the efficiency of the British in general, and 'the contrast with France was enormous,' according to one. Progress was nevertheless far from smooth, vitiated by a myriad misunderstandings, disagreements and lapses in discipline. A notice in Polish posted at Hucknall by the station commander is characteristic.

> You are here in order to train for battle with the Germans according to our methods, and not in order to fool about or argue with each other. Our personnel, our equipment and our time are being devoted to your training. If you do not take account of this with due respect, we shall take no further interest in you or your training. If you cannot take yourselves in hand in a disciplined way, we cannot make anything of you.

At the heart of these problems lay a lack of agreement at the top on the very status of the Polish Air Force in Britain. Sikorski's talks with the British in the autumn of 1939 had been inconclusive. He was determined that Polish soldiers, sailors and airmen should form their own units and remain a separate and sovereign allied force subject only to the Polish government-in-exile. The British pointed out that it was unconstitutional to have foreign troops stationed on British soil. They were adamant that all Polish airmen must join the RAFVR. Negotiations continued over their precise status while the men arrived in Britain and commenced training, adding an extra layer of uncertainty to their lives – it has to be appreciated that these men were being expected to place complete trust in Sikorski, a figure they did not know very well, and in Britain, a country they knew not at all.

It was not until 11 June 1940, a day after the Germans launched their offensive against France, that a formal agreement was signed. It was a compromise, and it did not satisfy the Poles. It stipulated that the Polish Air Force could form two bomber squadrons, at the Polish government's cost (a loan would be extended by the British government). They would be subordinated to British station commanders, quartermasters and paymasters, and subject to King's Regulations. They would swear two oaths – one to their own government and one to the king. The Polish Commander-in-Chief would have the right to visit the units, and a Polish Inspectorate would liaise with the British command. Promotions would be agreed jointly, on the recommendation of the British station commanders. Pay would be the same as that of RAF personnel. The men would wear RAF uniforms, with the Polish Air Force eagle on their caps and the 'Poland' flash on their shoulders, but no other distinctive insignia. They could paint a small chequer on the fuselage of their planes along with the British markings, and the Polish Air Force flag could fly beneath that of the RAF on station.

The most unsatisfactory aspect of the agreement as far as the Polish airmen were concerned was the matter of rank. All officers were demoted to the rank of Pilot Officer (equivalent to Second Lieutenant in Poland), and only after retraining and posting would they be given higher rank. But they would lose this, and the pay that went with it, if they were given an inferior posting. In Poland, squadrons and regiments had often been commanded by officers who no longer flew and some of whom had never been pilots (the captain of a Polish bomber was not the pilot but the navigator). But in the RAF it was a cast-iron principle that only pilots could lead an operational unit. So a number of senior officers suddenly became subalterns, with very dubious chances of promotion. This caused distress and bad blood, particularly between the young pilots, who were rapidly promoted, and the senior officers, who were left jobless, underpaid and humiliated. An early casualty was General Zając, originally an infantry officer, who was replaced as head of the Polish Air Force by General Stanisław Ujejski, an experienced pilot. The only group who were happy with the arrangement were the ground crews, who were similarly demoted, to the rank of Aircraftmen Second Class, but were now paid several times as much as they had been in Poland.

The Anglo-Polish agreement did at least provide the basis for action, which was generally welcomed. The Polish Air Force Depot was moved from Eastchurch to Blackpool, and intensive training began. On 1 July the Polish Air Force flag was hoisted on station at Bramcote, as 300 Mazovian Bomber Squadron came into being, followed on 26 July by 301 Pomeranian Bomber Squadron. Each had a British as well as a Polish commander, and a British adjutant and technical advisers. And, of course, they were subject in all things to the dreaded King's Regulations. When King George VI went down to Bramcote on 20 August to visit the squadrons, he conversationally asked the commander of one of them what he found most difficult to adjust to in Britain. 'King's Regulations, Your Majesty,' came the immediate reply.

Although a large proportion of the 2,164 Polish airmen who had arrived in Britain by the end of February 1940 were fighter pilots – and many more wanted to be – there was as yet no provision to create Polish fighter squadrons. The British view was still that the Poles had had the fighting spirit knocked out of them by defeat, and that while they could prove useful in bombers, they would lack the nerve and dash necessary for good fighter pilots. There was also an entrenched prejudice that the Poles were incapable of the high degree of discipline and teamwork required in fighter squadrons.

But the loss of several hundred of its best pilots incurred by the RAF at Dunkirk and in the defence of France left Fighter Command with no choice. By the end of May, Air Marshal Dowding had a shortfall of 450 pilots. He tried to make it up by poaching pilots from Bomber Command and Coastal Command, by absorbing volunteers from Canada, South Africa, Australia and even the United States, and by inducting trainees who had in some cases no more than ten hours' flying in a warplane behind them. But losses continued to mount over the next weeks as the *Luftwaffe* began to make probing raids across the Channel. Dowding would need more than 300 replacements a month, something the RAF could not produce. Whether he liked it or not, he would have to use some of the Polish (and Czech, Dutch, Belgian and Norwegian) fighter pilots to fill out his ranks. At the beginning of June a couple of dozen Poles were taken in for retraining as fighter pilots, to be fed singly or in pairs into undermanned RAF units. There was still no question of forming up separate Polish fighter squadrons.

The fall of France altered the situation dramatically. On the one hand, an invasion of Britain by the Germans became a serious possibility and there were simply not enough pilots to deny the Germans control of the skies. On the other, thousands of Polish airmen, some of them with recent combat experience in France, were on their way to Britain, along with tens of thousands of soldiers. The *Arandora Star*, loaded to the gunwales with Poles picked up at St-Jean-de-Luz, docked at Liverpool on 24 June, turned round and went back for more. The Polish liners *Batory* and *Sobieski* reached Plymouth a couple of days later, and the various colliers and coasters bringing further contingents sailed into Southampton, Portsmouth, Falmouth, Glasgow and other ports over the next two weeks. The soldiers were sent to Scotland, the airmen mostly to Blackpool.

Of the 6,863 Polish Air Force personnel stationed in France in June 1940, 6,200 had been successfully evacuated. Having just witnessed the disgraceful capitulation of the French, they were astonished and delighted to find in Britain a defiance that had hardened under the imminent threat of a Nazi invasion. 'We marched through the streets of Liverpool in fours, and the British shouted "Long live Poland!" and held their thumbs up,' writes one of them. 'Every moment new cheers greeted us. Why? What for?' They must have presented a mock-heroic spectacle, with their tattered blue uniforms and the odd assortment of side-arms they had picked up, marching in tight ranks and singing martial songs. One of the Warsaw Squadron pilots who disembarked from a Dutch coaster at Plymouth a few days later was no less astonished. Everyone made V-signs and smiled at them. 'Simple workmen threw their lunch-packs and packets of cigarettes in through the train windows to us, and spoke to us in what was for us a still incomprehensible language.'

There was much about Britain that was incomprehensible to the Poles. The airmen were on the whole not highly cultivated, and very few had ever been abroad before. And if the past few months had made them consider themselves experienced travellers, the first impressions of England dented this confidence. 'Everything here is different, unusual,' one noted in his diary after three days. 'Everything is so clean and prosperous.' The very scale of things put them out. The weather was another, not very pleasant, surprise. 'If it's as misty as this in summer, what on earth will the autumn be like,' wondered one airman on landing at Liverpool in June. Those who had spent the winter at Sheerness quickly filled him in. Although the temperature never fell anywhere near as low as it did in Poland, the damp often made it seem much colder. And, unlike Polish ones, English houses were not built to exclude the cold or the damp, and heating was virtually nonexistent.

The worst shock for some was the food. And it came early, with the soggy white fish-paste sandwiches they were offered on disembarkation. Strongly brewed milky tea was the next shock, rapidly followed by warm beer. 'British cookery consists of recipes for making the worst dishes from the best produce on earth,' wrote one pilot. Their criticism of British food went beyond the usual north/south differences that made it so unpalatable to, for instance, the French. Poland, like Britain, was a northern pork-and-cabbage culinary culture. But the Poles could not understand why the cabbage had to be boiled out of existence. Speculating on how mutton could be made to taste so awful, one airman reckoned that it was boiled all night, then cut into the thinnest of slices so it could dry out entirely while it cooled, and then 'singed to freshen it up'. He was fascinated by custard, 'a thick, glutinous, improbably yellow paste with the recherché flavour of washing powder', and cited it as the nadir of British cuisine. Opinions on this point varied considerably. 'In the disgusting gamut of English cooking, the most disgusting of all must be what they call sausages,' noted another. But some actually found the food perfectly good. 'The food is first-rate, though quite different from ours or from French food,' commented one.

On first acquaintance, the British themselves surpassed all the national stereotypes nurtured by the Poles. 'If ever a man from Mars has visited Earth it is unlikely that he felt less at ease than I did,' writes one young would-be pilot, who could not get over the 'totally alien way of life'. 'Luckily, the English seem to come into their own in such circumstances,' he continues. 'Having no illusions about the mental capabilities of foreigners they patiently used hand signals and loud monosyllables to repeat instructions many times.' The imperturbable calm they displayed in every situation seemed downright 'exotic' to one airman. 'These people don't seem to have any nerves at all,' he commented.

Just as striking was the quiet efficiency with which arrangements were made. 'After what we'd been through in Poland and France, it was difficult to comprehend how this place could be so calm,' says a future bomber pilot. 'I envy the British their ability to organize themselves so well, without any shouting,' wrote another. 'British organization is excellent,' noted a third in his diary two days after disembarking; 'everything happens quickly and efficiently, in spite of the fact that the British have enough problems of their own.' The evacuation and accommodation of the troops from Dunkirk had been no easy task. The additional one of dealing with tens of thousands of non-English-speaking foreigners, many of them undisciplined, and each of whom had to be screened as a possible spy infiltrated by the Germans along the way, was a tremendous strain.

Once the military installations in and around Blackpool had been filled, billets were found for the remaining 4,000 airmen in hotels, boarding-houses and bed-and-breakfasts in town. It was a somewhat brutal confrontation with British working-class culture. Few people were taking a seaside holiday that year, and the windswept resort was exceptionally cheerless. The Air Ministry had provided a bevy of language teachers and civilian instructors – including such unlikely people as the self-proclaimed aesthete Harold Acton, who astonished them by wandering about in the full kit of a Chinese mandarin, complete with pigtail, and the later Oxford Professor of History, Richard Cobb. But the airmen were still left with nothing to do most of the time. They spent the pocket-money they received on fish and chips and beer. They loafed about the esplanade and the pier, playing the machines, presenting an unedifying picture in their tattered uniforms. They made their first acquaintance with what they called 'real Anglo-Saxon boredom' and the horrors of an English Sunday. 'Any Pole who can learn to more or less put up with the English Sunday will be able to bear almost anything else with ease,' noted one of them.

'The inhabitants are extraordinarily kind to Poles, maybe because they don't know us very well yet,' noted Arct in his diary. 'They accost us in the street, invite us into pubs for a whisky or a beer, try to teach us the language. As for the women, one just cannot shake them off – which is not a matter for dismay.' His earlier preconceptions had given way to wonder. 'How come there are so many pretty girls in England?' he wrote, recalling that he had been brought up to believe that every Englishwoman was flat-footed and flat-chested. 'Romance is in the air at a northern resort where several thousand Polish airmen are in training,' reported *Reynold's* newspaper on 27 October 1940. 'Local girls have been acting as guides, companions and language tutors to the young Poles and now many of the friendships have turned to romance.' The report added that 'the Poles have quite ousted the boys of the RAF and the British Army in the affections of the local girls', and also commented with some amusement on the fact that some of the more enterprising bars and restaurants had printed menus in Polish.

The adjutant of the Blackpool base was bombarded with complaints from locals, relating mostly to alleged indecent advances to women, drunken brawling, and cheating the machines on the pier. One of his officers who happened to speak English was engaged on an almost continuous round of hotels, pubs and boarding-houses, with the mission of placating ruffled landladies and managers. A couple of pilots anxious to improve their diet had taken their French army rifles out into the countryside and

gone rabbit-shooting, which ended in them being arrested by the
local police as German fifth-columnists. But these minor misdemeanours did not poison the atmosphere. One great talent of
Blackpool was an almost limitless ability to handle vast numbers
of people with a minimum of fuss. Within a couple of days, most
of them knew the words of 'It's a Long Way to Tipperary' and
'Roll out the Barrel', as a result of spending hours nourishing
Anglo-Polish solidarity in various Blackpool pubs.

'We are now united, for better or for worse,' Churchill
declared on 19 June to Sikorski, who had transferred to London
with his whole government and staff. And this fortuitous alliance
was about to be tested in the heat of battle. Some six dozen Polish
fighter pilots were already being put through a brief refresher
course in flying on two-seater planes, given basic training in
ground control and navigational aids, and allowed to try out a
Hurricane or a Spitfire, prior to being sent to RAF squadrons.
The rest of their training was done in the squadron itself, often
in the course of operations, a recipe for potential disaster.

As they walked into the messes of front-line RAF squadrons
singly or in pairs during those summer months of 1940, these
pilots entered a completely different Britain. It was a far cry from
the bed-and-breakfast, fish-and-chip culture they had come to
know at Margate and Blackpool. It was public school, Home
Counties, cricket Britain, and on first acquaintance it was for-
bidding. The atmosphere in the messes was cliquey, and suspicious of the newcomers. The young pilots, some of them mere
boys, who risked their lives daily were often in the grip of a deep-
seated terror – which they kept down and covered up with layers
of boisterous and prickly humour. Czesław Tarkowski 'felt a bit
out of place, and very shy' when he and another Pole joined 85
Squadron at Church Fenton. The commander, Squadron Leader
Peter Townsend, did everything to put them at their ease, but he
could not conceal a natural diffidence. 'Our English superiors
and colleagues treated us with marked respect, but at the same
time kept us under observation, with a cool curiosity,' writes one
of the pilots. But Stefan Witorzeńc, who joined 501 Squadron,
did not notice anything of the sort. 'I felt quite at home from the
start,' he says.

British officers tended to accentuate the 'colourful' aspects of
the Poles' behaviour when, often years later, they came to write
their memoirs. Hence the stories of bizarre Polish celebrations,
of exaggerated hatred for the Germans and of reckless indisci-

pline. Certainly, the Poles were keen to uphold national honour when the bottles came out, but they found their match in most RAF pilots. And they refrained from machine-gunning German pilots who had baled out when it was explained to them that this was bad form – Germans who jumped over England would be captured and might provide useful intelligence. It is true that some pilots still finished off parachuting Germans by flying directly over them; the slipstream would cause the parachute to cannon and the man would fall to the ground like a stone. But the general impression conveyed of recklessness and indiscipline is ill-founded.

Squadron Leader Robert Stanford-Tuck, who took over command of 257 in the middle of the Battle of Britain, found the four Poles in the squadron 'competent enough, but very independent'. Once in the air, he complains, 'they became hurtling bolts of fury, beyond all reason and authority'. This kind of view was common mostly to those who never flew with the Poles, and it gained general currency in the post-war years. It fitted in with widely held perceptions of romantic, hard-drinking Poles and made a good story. Also, and perhaps significantly, it allowed the British to heap deserved praise on the Poles while at the same time holding something back. British pilots interviewed by the American journalist Dorothy Thompson in 1941 explained that the problem with the Poles was they tended to behave like 'a suicide squad'. 'Our business is to carry out the operation and get home, and use common sense as well as courage,' one of them continued. 'The Poles are all courage. They are terrific.' The inference was clear: the Poles were as good as they could possibly be, and it was not their fault they lacked the British virtues of steadiness under fire and common sense.

'The casualties in the [Polish] fighter squadrons were high, partly because of the natural dash of the pilots and partly because their individualistic outlook often led them to break away from their formations to carry out an attack in which they would be swamped by superior German numbers,' wrote Air Marshal Sir Philip Joubert in 1946. One has only to look at the casualty ratios to see that this is nonsense. And it is also contradicted by people well placed to do so. One Briton who commanded a Polish squadron for six months poured scorn on the view that 'the Polish pilots were so enthusiastic that they became reckless with their own lives', and went on to say that all pilots who were on duty the following day refrained from drinking and went to bed early. Another British pilot who served with Poles for long periods confirmed that the Pole 'never allow[ed] himself any daredevilry' unless there was a good reason for it.

The Poles were, in fact, extremely careful of their lives, their planes and their reputations, particularly when serving side-by-side with Britons. But they were often impatient at what they saw as English 'slowness', and they found it hard to accept certain RAF tactics and practices.

Karol Pniak, who was posted with two other Poles to 32 Squadron at Biggin Hill, was appalled at the British flying formation. This consisted of four ranks of three planes each in very close order. On patrol, the middle plane of the last rank would drop behind. This was known as a 'weaver', and supposedly covered the rear. Time after time the squadron would land without having spotted the enemy, but minus the weaver, who had been picked off quietly by a German marauder without anyone noticing. Using this tactic, the squadron lost twenty-one men in three weeks. On his first sortie Pniak, who was flying in the last threesome, dropped back to cover the weaver, and was severely reprimanded by the squadron commander after landing. 'As a pilot I had ten years' experience, a fairly high level of training, and some thirty operational wartime sorties in the September 1939 campaign behind me,' writes Pniak. 'That is why I could in no way accept the commander's opinion, and I struggled in my poor English to explain that their way of flying was useless and dangerous.' It is not difficult to imagine the reaction to such effrontery.

Pniak's was not an isolated criticism. 'Apart from its defects, this formation had no positive features whatever,' wrote Skalski, who was with 501 Squadron. It did have one positive feature, namely that it helped to keep units from getting separated in cloud or mist, but it was not suited to combat. Rolski complained that the tight formation meant pilots had to devote more attention to the hazard of colliding with each other than to looking out for the enemy, and it reduced visibility. Bohdan Arct termed it 'simply suicidal'. There were to be many acts of persistent insubordination and heated rows on this point alone.

By the beginning of what came to be called the Battle of Britain, on 10 July, there were more than forty Poles flying in RAF fighter squadrons. On 19 July Antoni Ostowicz, serving with 145 Squadron, downed a Messerschmitt 110, the first Polish kill over Britain. The same pilot was also the first Polish loss over

Britain, when he was shot down on 11 August, having downed two more Germans in the interim. On the same day Michał Stęborski of 238 Squadron went down over the Channel, and on the following morning 145 Squadron lost its second Pole. By 13 August, 'Eagle Day', on which the Germans launched 500 bombers and 1,000 fighters in what they hoped would prove a decisive onslaught, there were more than fifty Poles in the air. Most of them were stationed along the coast, in the thick of the action, and they were rapidly breaking down prejudice by daily shows of prowess and reliability. By the end of August several, such as Antoni Głowacki of 501 at Gravesend, who shot down five German planes in a single day on 24 August – an RAF record – were beginning to be regarded as 'aces', and the renown of such pilots as Pniak, Ostowicz, Skalski of 501 Squadron, Henryk Szczęsny of 74 and Urbanowicz of 145, spread beyond the units in which they were serving. 'All the squadrons that had Polish pilots posted to them formed an equally high opinion of them,' as Squadron Leader Crook of 609 Squadron put it.

Crook's was a typical auxiliary squadron, made up mainly of public-school chums, the sort of 'long-haired weekend aviators' that RAF regulars looked down on. They were brave and dashing, but often inexperienced, and so keen on scoring a 'kill' that they abandoned caution and fell easy prey to seasoned *Luftwaffe* pilots. When not in the air, they would sit around drinking Pimm's and discussing cricket scores. There was little in common between them and the two Poles, Nowierski and Ostaszewski, who joined them. Luckily 'Novi', as he was dubbed, shot down two Messerschmitts on his first sortie with the squadron, who promptly decided that they were 'grand chaps'. Crook, an experienced pilot who suffered to see so many young men pass quickly through his ranks, took the same view. 'They were certainly two of the bravest people I ever knew,' he wrote, adding that they were exceptionally skilful pilots who helped him staunch the flow of young blood with their experience.

Equally appreciative of these qualities was the commanding officer of 253, who was rebuilding a squadron that had been decimated at Dunkirk. On 16 June 1940 two Poles joined it at Kirton-in-Lindsey. 'The spirit in the squadron, which was then rising to commendable proportions, received an added impetus by the arrival of these two officers, whose enthusiasm and determination was unbounded,' he wrote. Their value lay in the combination of qualities they displayed, and he stresses that they fought 'with an abandon, tempered with skill and backed by an indomitable courage'.

Some squadrons were quite simply swamped. By the end of the summer, 32 Squadron at Biggin Hill contained seven Poles, two Czechs and one Belgian, out of a total complement of twenty. Its commander, Squadron Leader Michael Crossley, had to take a philosophical view. 'I don't believe in interfering with bad habits,' he would say. It was a wise attitude. One of his Poles, Jan Falkowski, formerly a flying instructor at the Dęblin school, had been piloting an unarmed RWD–8 on a liaison mission in September 1939 when he was attacked by a Messerschmitt bent on shooting him down. By sticking close to the ground and forcing the German to follow him through a variety of man-oeuvres, he contrived to make his enemy crash into the ground. Such a degree of flying skill was not going begging in the summer of 1940.

Nor was what one British squadron leader termed the 'almost incredible audacity' of the Poles. Skalski, badly burned the second time he was shot down during the Battle of Britain, absconded from the hospital in which he was recovering and rejoined 501. He was left with such a terror of fire that he could not bear to light a cigarette, but he did not admit this to his British commanding officer. He insisted on going operational, even though his leg was still so badly burned that he could not run during a scramble and therefore had to sit in his plane for hours waiting for the signal.

Once the original diffidence was broken down, relations between the Polish pilots and their British colleagues grew memorable. As the Germans had announced that all Poles would be shot on capture, Polish airmen were issued documents with an English identity – but these were not the names used in the messes, where Tadeusz became Teddy, Jacek became Jacky, Włodzimierz became Jimmy and Zbigniew Wysiekierski was just 'Whisky'. Imaginative new varieties of pidgin evolved, and the Poles were soon shouting 'Tally-ho!' along with the rest.

With the exuberance born of having survived one more day, they vied with one another in the horseplay of the mess. At first, there was a degree of misunderstanding. 'It seems unbelievable that grown-up and sane people can, with the help of only a small quantity of alcohol, play in such a carefree way,' noted one Pole in his squadron diary; 'they're like grown-up children.' Making an ass of oneself and debagging one another have never formed part of the social culture of the Poles, who tend to take themselves seriously and can be highly touchy on points of personal dignity. General Zając was outraged when he was forced to play blind-man's-buff with a waste-paper basket on his head in the Eastchurch mess, and then tossed in the air. Younger men took it more in their stride. 'Sometimes, particularly when alcohol went to the head, there were some quite sharp confrontations, but I can only remember very few of them,' notes another. Once they had understood the spirit of the games, the Poles joined in with gusto. 'I believe that their youthful spirits infected us,' comments a squadron chronicler; 'we felt younger in their company.'

Ludwik Martel, who served with 54 Squadron before being posted to 603 City of Edinburgh Squadron, still enthuses about the experience. 'Relations were fantastic,' he says. 'I felt so well in my English squadron – it was actually a mixture of Englishmen and Scots – that I twice refused to be transferred to a Polish unit. I felt so happy among these comrades, I can honestly say that I never had such relationships ever again in my life . . . It is impossible to describe how charming they were, how kind. They never left me on my own. If I went for a walk, one of them would always come up and ask how I was. My most cherished memories date from 1940 to 1941, when I was in an English squadron.' Bolesław Drobiński, who flew with 65 Squadron based at Hornchurch, is similarly effusive, and he too refused to be transferred to a Polish squadron. Such feelings seemed to grow in intensity the closer one came to the front line. Czesław Tarkowski, who was moved from 85 to 605 Squadron at Biggin Hill, a cratered and pitted station that knew little rest, was virtually mobbed on arrival. 'Poles were much loved,' he noted meekly. 'Every squadron wanted to have a Pole serving in it,' confirms Karol Pniak, who was with 32 and later 257. 'When they started forming Polish squadrons, my British comrades did everything to keep me with them.'

The creditable conduct and above-average results of these pilots, their growing popularity with their British colleagues and commanders, as well as the continuing attrition of pilots, strengthened Sikorski's bargaining position. So, curiously, did a change of position by Dowding, who was now 'extremely apprehensive about the infiltration of foreign pilots into British fighter squadrons', as a conversation with the Minister for Air on 29 July revealed. 'Apart from the language difficulty, he is uncertain as to the effect that this will have on the morale of his squadrons.'

He consequently pressed 'very strongly' for the formation of separate Polish squadrons.

On 5 August a fresh agreement was signed between the British and Polish governments. All Polish airmen ceased to be members of the RAFVR and became part of the Polish Air Force, which was recognized as sovereign and swore allegiance to the Polish government only. The Polish Air Force was to remain subject to the RAF in matters of organization, training, equipment, discipline, promotions and operational use. The Polish Inspectorate was to manage personnel matters, while liaising with the RAF, and the men were to wear Polish buttons and cap-badges, and Polish as well as British insignia of rank on their tunics. The Polish Air Force ensign was to fly beside the RAF flag on station. The Polish Air Force was to be expanded to four bomber squadrons, two fighter squadrons and one army support squadron, with their own reserves. The possibility of further expansion was left open, and the numbers 300 to 309 were accordingly reserved for Polish units (the Czechs were to start numbering at 310). On 22 August Parliament passed an Act enabling the new agreement to come into force, as it was unprecedented in British history and created a constitutional anomaly. But events had already anticipated the agreement.

On 13 July 302 Poznań Fighter Squadron was formed at Leconfield near Beverley in Yorkshire from the nucleus of 3 Poznań Air Regiment and 1/145 Polish Squadron in France, under the command of Mieczysław Mummler and Squadron Leader Jack Satchell, assisted by two British flight lieutenants. On 2 August, 303 Kościuszko Squadron was formed at Northolt outside London from the remnants of the Kościuszko Flight of 1 Warsaw Air Regiment. It was commanded by Squadron Leader Ronald Kellett and Zdzisław Krasnodębski, who had led the Fighter Brigade in September 1939.

British caution clashed with Polish impatience across 'the language barricade' as these units struggled to get airborne. The British intelligence officer of 302 spoke some Polish, but the others were at sea. 'We got by,' recalls one of the flight lieutenants, 'with a mixture of English and French, sign-language, and that ultimate British resource – shouting.' The British squadron leaders and flight lieutenants were supposed to be in command, but the Poles had a tendency to regard them as little more than instructors who were getting above themselves. They were in the unenviable position of having to lecture mature pilots as though they were novices. The pilots of 302 Squadron, for instance, belonged to a unit that had shot down 31 German planes over Poland and 12 over France, and were, in the words of one of their British instructors, 'terrific pilots, more experienced than us'. They did not take kindly to being lectured on tactics. They would make comments to each other in Polish over the radio while being given flying instruction, which often drove the British instructors into a blind rage.

But the British ranks were being thinned mercilessly in the daily round of attrition with the German fighters. Between 8 August and 18 August, the RAF lost 94 fighter pilots killed and 60 wounded – twice as many as it could replace. All remaining reservations were dropped. On 27 July 302 Poznań Squadron had been given their Hurricanes. On 14 August they became operational and joined 12 Fighter Group in East Anglia. Six days later, they downed their first German over Britain, a Junkers 88 bomber crossing the east coast. The following day they shot down another two enemy planes. Their colleagues of 303 Kościuszko Squadron were still training, but their day was about to dawn.

7

The Legend of 303

ON THE AFTERNOON of 30 August 1940, 303 Kościuszko Squadron, still undergoing training at RAF Northolt, was carrying out an exercise in escorting a group of Blenheim bombers. As the twelve Hurricanes hovered above the Blenheims, a formation of German planes came in sight. Squadron Leader Kellett, the unit's British commander, wanted to get the vulnerable Blenheims and his own planes out of the battle zone. Pilot Officer Ludwik Paszkiewicz, who had noticed the enemy planes first, reported his wish to attack them over the radio, and, apparently receiving no answer, he took matters into his own hands and peeled off from the formation. He went for the nearest of the German planes, a Dornier 17, which he shot down with a single burst of his machine-guns. Having chased off the others he returned to Northolt, where he landed a little after the rest of his squadron. He was ordered to report immediately to Kellett, who gave him a thundering reprimand in front of his fellow pilots for leaving the formation without authorization. Kellett then privately congratulated Paszkiewicz on his skilful attack, and announced that on his personal recommendation the squadron had been posted operational as from the next day. Thunderous cheers greeted the news. The pilots had been getting desperately restive as they watched the other squadrons stationed at Northolt, one British and one Canadian, go up on operations every day. They were also at loggerheads with some of their British superiors.

The squadron had started forming on 2 August around a

nucleus of old hands from 1 Warsaw Air Regiment, many of whom had clocked up several kills in Poland and France. They included Zdzisław Henneberg, who had brought his whole flight safely to Britain after the fall of France; Josef František, a Czech who had joined them in Poland and fought with them in France, knocking out eleven enemy aircraft by the time he reached Britain; Urbanowicz, transferred from RAF 145 Squadron; Zumbach; and others.

Grouped together in their own squadron, the Poles were not on their best behaviour, like those posted to British units. 'They were a complete law unto themselves,' in the words of a British fitter stationed at Northolt. 'Nobody could control them.' Their clannishness and cockiness put backs up and irritated those less concerned with their flying and fighting skills than with having to live and work alongside them. 'The Poles were a funny bunch, actually,' remarked the same fitter. 'We used to get along. . . . *reasonably* well, but there was no real love lost between us.'

There was even less love lost between the Poles and the detachment of Irish Guards assigned to the base, and their differences flared dangerously on at least two occasions. One was at a dance in Ruislip, when a disagreement over dancing partners turned into a pitched battle after which a number of guardsmen had to be hospitalized. The other was sparked off by an altercation between drunken Polish ground crew returning to base and guardsmen checking their passes. 'Machine-gun fire from the south-east corner of the aerodrome!' barked the tannoy in the operations room, to the consternation of the station commander, Group Captain S.F. Vincent. 'I became thoroughly alarmed, thinking of parachute attacks, fifth columnists or something equally serious,' he writes. When he went outside his own ears confirmed his alarm. 'I'd been out to the cinema one night and I heard the rattle of rifle and machine-gun fire – what the heck's going on?' recalls the British fitter. 'I wasn't very far from the entrance gate, and all merry hell let loose there! There was the Guards and the Poles having a proper firefight.' Both sides soon ran out of ammunition, and Vincent managed to restore order. He also managed, miraculously, to hush up the incident, thereby avoiding a string of enquiries and commissions, but he had the Irish Guards replaced by the Coldstream Guards.

Group Captain Vincent was a regular officer in the RAF who had seen action in the First World War and, at 43, was now decidedly on the old side. An enthusiastic flier, he understood the feelings of pilots, and he was not wedded, like some, to minute observance of regulations. But he did have certain responsibilities, and he had been given the firm instruction that 'until all the Poles learn to speak English properly, they stay on the ground'. The primary concern was that if they did not understand English, the pilots could not be directed to an interception point or vectored home over the radio. Vincent did what he could. The pilots were given bicycles, told to don radio transmitter sets, and made to cycle around Uxbridge football pitch in perfect flying formation, responding to every order they received to turn one way or the other. 'I could not declare them operational until they could understand English better, so they hated me!' writes Vincent.

Squadron Leader Ronald Kellett, 303's commander, was more popular. A small, jovial figure known throughout the service as 'Boozy' Kellett, he was an Auxiliary who despised most regular RAF officers and liked to tell them so. And he could afford to. His father owned a coal-mine in Durham, he had been brought up in a stately home, and he made a respectable living as a stockbroker. He was also a very experienced flier. He delighted the Poles – and annoyed the regulars – with his magnificent Rolls-Royce and his subversive attitude.

He had been less than enthusiastic when he heard of the command he had been given, and his spirits had sunk further when the two hundred or so Poles turned up at Northolt in their tattered French uniforms. But he was a natural leader and most considerate of his men. When he discovered that their pay had been held up in the red tape and the chaos, leaving them penniless, he reached into his own pocket and paid his unit himself for a couple of weeks.

He had two flight lieutenants, Athol Forbes and John Kent, an intelligence officer, an adjutant, an orderly-room corporal and three senior ground crew NCOs to help him turn these Poles into a fighting unit. The fact that they considered themselves to be one already did nothing to help him. To make matters worse, Kellett, Kent and Forbes did not get on together.

Kellett himself and Forbes spoke fluent French, which permitted them to communicate with some of the Poles. Kent, a Canadian from Winnipeg, was 'thoroughly fed up and despondent' about his new job. He was a very competent officer, but he was arrogant and tended towards bossiness, which did not endear him to many. He was also ambitious, and probably resented being placed under the command of an Auxiliary. 'All I knew about the Polish Air Force was that it had lasted about three days against the *Luftwaffe* and I had no reason to suppose that they would shine any more brightly operating from England,' he writes. He spoke no French at all, so he concentrated on learning a few key words of Polish, which earned him the sobriquet of 'Kentowski'.

Kellett was less concerned with linguistics than with the pilots' skills. One pilot remembers him pointing to a plane and uttering the word 'Hurricane', then flapping his arms like a bird and saying 'Fly', and then pushing the pilot towards the plane. Kellett quickly realized that these were excellent fliers; but, being new to it, they often left the radio switched on when not using it, which jammed the frequency, or forgot how to use it at critical moments. More worrying was that, with little experience of retractable undercarriages, they sometimes forgot to lower them when coming in to land, and being unused to closed cockpits often forgot to open and lock the covers before landing (a precaution against being trapped in a burning machine). They soon got the hang of their Hurricanes, and although only the most rudimentary communication had been established, the squadron was needed in battle. English or no English, the Poles felt that they were ready, and in this they were not mistaken.

On the squadron's first operational day, 31 August, six planes went up on patrol and returned to base having shot down four Messerschmitt 109s, with two more unverified. The pilots were euphoric, not least at the ease of fighting in proper machines. 'I caught up with him easily,' one of them scribbled in the squadron scrapbook that evening. 'He grew in my sights until his fuselage filled the whole luminous circle. It was certainly time to fire. I did so quite calmly, and was not even excited, rather puzzled and surprised to find that it was so easy, quite different from Poland, where you had to scrape and strain until you were in a sweat, and then instead of getting the bastard he got you.'

Telegrams of congratulation poured in. 'Magnificent fighting 303 Squadron,' ran that from the RAF Chief-of-Staff. 'I am delighted. The enemy is shown that Polish pilots definitely on top.' As a treat, the pilots of 303 were given a day off – the very last thing they wanted. The RAF believed it was good for the psychological health of pilots to spend as much time as possible off the station. There was some justification for this with respect to British pilots, who could go home to their families. Polish pilots posted to RAF squadrons were often taken home by their British colleagues or relaxed with them at suburban tennis clubs, but the pilots of the all-Polish squadrons were isolated and had nowhere to go. They regarded it as a punishment rather than a treat to be grounded, particularly on 1 September, the anniversary of the German invasion of Poland.

On 2 September they were in action again, over the Thames estuary and Dover, downing two German planes, with another two unverified. Along with a signal of congratulation, they earned themselves a light rebuke from Air Vice-Marshal Sir Keith Park of 11 Fighter Group. 'The Group Commander appreciates the offensive spirit that carried two Polish pilots over the French coast in pursuit of the enemy today,' it read. 'This practice is not economical or sound now that there is such good shooting within sight of London.' The British were still nervous of 'Polish hot-headedness'.

The squadron went on notching up successes without any losses. On 5 September they shot down seven more planes and damaged one and on 6 September they repeated the same score, this time losing six of their own planes, but the only pilot hurt was Kellett. This meant that it was Forbes who led them on the following day to head off a massive German raid on London, which Göring termed 'the historic hour when our air force for the first time delivered its blow right into the enemy's heart'. He had come to the Headquarters of the *Luftwaffe* 2nd Fleet at Cap Gris-Nez to take personal command.

It was also an historic day for 303, which was scrambled in mid morning and sent round the north of London towards the docks. There they encountered a formation of 40 Dornier bombers with an escort of Messerschmitt fighters. Forbes failed to spot the bombers, but the pilots behind him took matters into their own hands and dived into the formation. By the time Forbes had caught on and turned, it was to see 'the Dorniers fall out of the sky like partridges out of a covey, sometimes two at a time'. The remainder turned back and made for France, while the squadron veered to meet the fighter escort. The total bag for 303 was 14 enemy planes shot down for certain, with a further 4 probables – a record for any RAF squadron in a single day. It had been bought at the cost of two planes, and again the only casualty was a Briton: Forbes was slightly wounded. The Poles were in seventh heaven and, even though they hardly drank at all in those days of permanent readiness, they were intoxicated with the joy of being able to get their own back on the Germans after so long, and the Northolt mess resounded to the sound of Polish singing.

Congratulations from the staff and the government were flooding in daily. When the car arrived with the sixth message from Downing Street, Kellett had had enough, and he sent back a note to the effect that, as words were losing their power, a more appropriate token of appreciation would come in the shape of a case of whisky – which duly arrived. But the extraordinary successes of 303 had also raised eyebrows, and the Northolt intelligence officer was asked to investigate whether the Polish claims were not on the wild side (this was before cameras were fitted to run when the guns fired). Kellett and his two RAF flight leaders insisted that, if anything, they erred on the side of caution. As well as being highly competitive, the pilots of 303 had a healthy dose of the Polish characteristic of jealousy of one another's achievements, and none of them could get away with claiming a kill unless it had been witnessed and certified beyond doubt by at least one colleague. But Group Captain Vincent was suspicious.

The next time 303 was scrambled, he took a plane up and followed them. The squadron met a large enemy formation over the London docks. Two Hurricanes immediately climbed high above, while the rest hung back, with Vincent behind them. Then the two lone planes dived almost vertically onto the Germans, spitting fire and making as if to collide with them, which forced the bombers to break formation. 'The Poles behind jumped in on to the scattered individuals and suddenly the air was full of burning aircraft, parachutes, and pieces of disintegrating wings,' records Vincent. 'It was all so rapid that it was staggering.' He tried to join in himself, but each time he fixed on a German plane it disintegrated before his eyes as a Pole got there first, and he returned to Northolt feeling old and musty. 'I told Wilkins [the intelligence officer] that what they claimed they did, indeed, get!'

That day, 303 had repeated their record of 14 certain kills, but this time at the cost of their first real losses, as two pilots were killed in the afternoon sortie. One of these, Flight Sergeant Wójtowicz, found himself on his own against six Messerschmitts. The population of Westerham spilled out onto the streets to watch as he destroyed two of the enemy planes before being sent to the ground in flames himself, and on the next day the Town Council sent a message of thanks and condolence to Northolt.

A remarkable aspect of the Battle of Britain was that a high proportion of civilians could actually see it going on. As the citizens of southern England were in a sense living on the battlefield, they could even participate, when a pilot crash-landed or parachuted to the ground. This helped to create a very special brand of solidarity between combatants and non-combatants. But it held hazards for any Pole who might come down to earth in such a way: they could never be quite sure of the reception they would get on the ground, as they were often taken for Germans. Franek Surma's parachute caught in a tree just outside a pub in Kent, and a group of Free French who had been drinking in the pub almost lynched him for a '*sale Boche*'.

Zdzisław Krasnodębski, the Polish commander of 303, was just setting his sights on a German bomber when he was himself attacked from behind. 'Suddenly the glass on my dials was splintering and the fuel tank, holed by shells, burst into flames. I wanted to jump, but I could not undo the straps,' he writes. 'There was a moment of resignation, but the will to live triumphed and I managed to undo the straps, open the cockpit and bale out. Remembering my unpleasant experiences in Poland, I refrained from opening my parachute, so as to get out of the fighting as quickly as possible and not make a target of myself [. . .] As I approached the ground, I thought that my adventures were over, but this turned out to be premature, for out of the bushes and buildings spilled the figures of Home Guards, brandishing guns, evidently hoping to bag a German. Luckily their English sang-froid held out and they did not shoot.'

Krasnodębski was so badly burnt that he was rushed to hospital, but on the whole parachuting airmen were kept by the locals as long as possible and lionized. In this way, they got to know a remarkable cross-section of English society. Czesław Tarkowski dropped on to the top rung.

'I was floating down, looking at the countryside. Fields and meadows, large old oak trees. Despite frantic efforts, my parachute caught on the top branches of one of these. People with pitchforks and staves ran up. One of them, armed with a shotgun, was screaming "*Hände hoch!*". "Fuck off," I answered in my very best English. The lowering faces immediately brightened up. "He's one of ours!" they shouted in unison. Hands reached up to help extricate me from the extremely uncomfortable position I was in.' He was escorted to a vast fourteenth-century house, the likes of which he had never seen before. 'The walls were covered in oak panelling, the darkened portraits of forebears looked down attentively, and a maid in a mob-cap led me into a large drawing-room,' he continues. 'When they found out I was a Polish airman, they did everything they could for me. I was scorched and dirty, so I was given the opportunity to wash and my clothes were cleaned up. A young woman put some ointment on my burning and raw face . . . At lunch, my host made sure that my glass was never empty, and the twenty-year-old wine with which I was plied warmed and relaxed my aching muscles. It went to my strained and still reeling head.'

He was installed in a comfortable armchair, where he slept until he was picked up by a sergeant from his base. 'The shock, the alcohol and the sunny afternoon meant that I sat in the car in a complete daze. I looked at the surroundings through a mist.' At a set of traffic lights, he noticed someone waving a stick and shouting insults in German. 'Madam, it's one of ours – its's a Polish pilot,' the driver explained. The old lady's face fell. She reached into her purse and produced a florin. 'There was no time to resist, so I returned to base with a gleaming florin.'

Another airman penetrated a less aristocratic, but no less exclusive world, as Richard Cobb relates:

My sister's father-in-law's tennis club was a respectable institution, that is to say, members were admitted to it not according to the quality of their tennis, but of their speech. The first essential . . . was that the aspiring member should 'speak nicely'; if he did, one would assume he was a gentleman and a fit person to play ball with. My sister's father-in-law always played a 'foursome' with the unmarried sister of a vicar, 'a gentleman who kept dogs', and his wife . . . The 'foursome' was of about fifteen years' standing, not the sort of thing in fact that Adolf Hitler could interrupt.

On this particular Saturday, the doggy gentleman and his wife and my sister's father-in-law were all on the court punctually at 3 p.m., but there was no sign of the vicar's sister. At 3.30 they were still standing on the court; it was most annoying, such a thing had never happened in fifteen years. Up above, all sorts of things were happening, and now and then aeroplanes fell out of the sky like dead flies. But the three were much too angry to pay attention to the weekend visitors from across the water. How were they going to have their game? How was my sister's father-in-law going to get through till Wednesday without his exercise? The doggy man swore and swore, and his wife started getting irritable. 'It's too bad, Archibald,' she said, 'it really is too bad, war or no war.' There was a war. A parachute was coming down, with someone swinging from it. The wife was the first to notice it. 'Archibald, look, look, one of those Germans is coming down, surely he won't land here, it's private property!' But he did, parachute and all, in a tree by the ladies' dressing-room, where he remained hanging. The three would-be tennis players were puzzled what to do. My sister's father-in-law, a resourceful man, eventually decided. 'Look here, we'll go to the foot of the tree and ask him who he is. If he's a German we'll leave him up there and phone Police Constable Snodgrass. If he's one of ours we'll cut him down and give him tea.' So they moved over to the tree and shouted up, 'Hello there! Who are you? *Sind sie Allemanisch*, or whatever it is? You know – *sie wissen was* I mean? *Understanden sie?*' 'Ask him if he is a Nazi,' said the wife triumphantly. '*Sind sie Nazi?*' 'B—— fools Nazis,' came distinctly from the branches. 'Me Polish man!' 'Oh, good chap, b—— good chap!' said the doggy man. 'Let him down.' Then my sister's father-in-law had an idea and the three whispered together. 'But he's not a *member*,' objected the wife. 'To h—— with that,' said her husband vigorously. So they cut him down. 'Do you play tennis?' he asked, and the airman replied, 'Pardon, yes, thank you, I am quite all right.' So they lent him some white flannels and took him to the gentlemen's dressing-room.

When the RAF car came for him, the remaining three staggered to deck-chairs. They'd never had such a game. The wife gasped: 'Such a nice man, so strong, and how polite!' My sister's father-in-law murmured: 'What a game! I don't think I'll play next Wednesday.'

In the club minutes you can read: 'August 23rd, Polish officer, introduced by Mr and Mrs ——.' That's how a Pole came to this little town and entered the English Holy of Holies, a lawn tennis club which was strictly closed to all but 'nice people'.

Lower down the social scale, the experience could still prove interesting. One pilot came down in a south London back garden and fell at the feet of a girl, whom he married two months later.

The knowledge that there were Poles up in the sky over London touched a chord in the population, and the fame of 303 began to spread. The press related tales of the bravery and skill of the 'cavaliers from a conquered land'. Fan mail poured in from all over the country. A school in Ruislip had a whip-round and sent 450 cigarettes 'for the brave Polish fighters'. A girls' school in Glasgow sent them ten shillings. The Borough of Willesden, which had collected money to fund a Spitfire, stipulated that it should be flown by a Pole. The *Daily Telegraph* printed poems sent in by enthusiastic *literati*: 'Gallants, who here patrol the sky, And strew the land with wrack of raiders,' one bard began.

'We had a fantastic time,' remarks one pilot. 'We were continually mobbed, and we were also very much in demand among English women.' For a girl at this time, to be seen on the arm of a fighter pilot was a triumph. 'I just cannot begin to describe the effect that "wings" had on a girl then,' confirms Joan Wyndham, a WAAF stationed at Stanmore. Besides wearing two sets of 'wings', the regulation British ones and the Polish pilot's eagle, the Poles enjoyed an additional glamour based on novelty value and the romantic aura with which people endowed their nation.

One day 303 returned to base after an operation, but without Flight Lieutenant Antoni Wczelik. Next day, his crashed plane and a Messerschmitt he had evidently shot down were located. The German pilot was apprehended, but there was no sign of Wczelik. Two days later he was officially posted missing and his gear was packed up to make room for a new pilot. But that evening he gaily marched into the Northolt mess. He had parachuted on to a golf course, to the consternation of some elderly gentlemen in the middle of a game. He was dragged off to the club house and plied with drinks. By the evening he was so drunk that he was taken home by a lady whose husband happened to be on active service overseas, and who refused to let him go for two days.

The only ones who had mixed feelings about the successes of 303 were the pilots of 302, who had been patrolling the east coast for the past two weeks without sighting a single enemy plane. Their frustration built up into frequent rows between their commander Mieczysław Mummler and his British counterpart, Squadron Leader Jack Satchell. Satchell was a regular officer, and although he was thirty years old, he was young in spirit, more so than Mummler, who belonged to the old school and could not catch the spirit of 1940. Satchell's flight lieutenants were younger and less experienced than their Polish pilots, and one of them, Nigel Farmer, was by common consent a poor and therefore dangerous pilot. The only thing that made up for this was that 302 was stationed with 242 Canadian Squadron, commanded by the legless Douglas Bader. Poles and Canadians vied with each other in horseplay, and having no legs did not prevent Bader from leading his men when the evening's entertainment consisted of building a barricade of furniture down the centre of the room and then fighting a battle over it.

302 Squadron's chance to prove themselves came on 15 September, arguably the most crucial day of the Battle of Britain, when massed German attacks on London succeeded one another and virtually swamped the fighter squadrons sent up to meet them. As if sensing the importance of that Sunday, Winston Churchill had gone to the headquarters of 11 Fighter Group at Uxbridge, and spent the whole day in the operations room following the course of the battle.

303 Squadron was scrambled in mid morning and again at about 2 p.m., when, along with one other RAF squadron, it had to head off a raid by some 400 German planes. The fact that only 24 Hurricanes could be sent up to meet such a force is eloquent testimony to the shortage of fighters on the British side. To bolster the thinning defences of the capital an extra fighter wing, consisting of 302, a Czech, a Canadian and two RAF squadrons, was seconded from 12 Group to help. This wing was led by Douglas Bader, who was already immensely popular with the Polish pilots, and as it took off from Duxford to go into action, Bader shouted 'You'll be in Warsaw soon!' over the radio. The pilots of 302 were determined to show their colleagues what they could do, and shot down ten German planes, with another five probables, at the cost of two planes and one of their own pilots killed.

But they could not match 303, which was involved in frantic dogfights 4,000 feet above London. With dozens of planes weaving about shooting at each other, the pilots had to watch out on every side, and one of them who had baled out 'just prayed that I wouldn't get some piece of burning wreckage on my parachute'. The viciousness of the encounter was such that when the pilots ran out of ammunition they carried on fighting by whatever means possible. A British pilot of 605 Squadron rammed a Dornier bomber with his Spitfire, and another of 607 Squadron brought down two in this way before baling out. Flight Sergeant Karubin of 303, a slight youth of twenty, had done even better, on 5 September. He had shot down one Messerschmitt and was pursuing another when he ran out of ammunition. He continued to chase the German, bearing down on him and forcing him to fly lower and lower. 'I came up very close, and then shaved him,' he explains. 'The terrified mug of the Kraut flashed by, and a split second later he crashed into the ground, throwing up a cloud of smoke and clods of earth. I pulled up higher and circled over the burning remnants of the machine before turning away and taking a course for my base.' But on 15 September, when he tried to repeat the procedure with a German bomber over the Thames estuary, he ended up ramming it and had to bale out of his disintegrating Hurricane. Another pilot of 303 also rammed a German, but he was less lucky and died on the way to hospital. 'I got him, though,' were his last words.

He was the only casualty of 303 on that day, and their total bag set a new record – fifteen German planes shot down and one probable. In all, sixty Polish pilots had been fighting in various units on that day. 'After every such victory one cannot help the thought going through one's head that if we'd had such machines in Poland, things would have been so wonderful and so different,' mused the adjutant of 303, a former member of the Polish parliament.

Churchill declared that the German squadrons had been 'cut to rags and tatters' on that day, as he left the Uxbridge operations room. But it was not just a question of numbers of aircraft shot down. As one British pilot pointed out, the Poles, and particularly the pilots of 303, were particularly effective at breaking up and driving back enemy bomber formations, which was, after all, the object of the exercise. Thus, on 11 September, the 12 Hurricanes of 303 had intercepted a force of 150 German bombers crossing the south coast bound for London and forced them to jettison their bombs over Sussex and turn back for France.

They achieved such successes in a number of ways, but the principle was always the same – to force the Germans to break formation. Standard RAF training dictated that a pilot should open fire at a distance of not less than 150 yards, when all eight of the machine-guns in a Hurricane's wings (which converged slightly) would hit the enemy plane at the same spot, producing maximum impact and minimizing the risk. The Poles would have none of this. With centuries of cavalry tactics in their blood, they believed in the psychological effect of a charge aimed at the

centre of an enemy formation. They also swore by holding their
fire until they were very close, with the whole side of the enemy
plane before them. 'When they go tearing into the enemy
bombers and fighters they go so close you would think they were
going to collide,' wrote Forbes. At this point they would fire a
raking broadside which, even it it did not hit something vital, certainly unnerved every single member of the enemy bomber's
crew. When flying together in formation German bombers could
defend themselves with their combined firepower, but once scattered they were far more vulnerable, so if their formation was
broken up, individual planes would tend to cut and run.

'The great number of German fighters and bombers they
brought down by this method shows that they knew how to make
it pay,' comments Wing-Commander W.B. Austin. But the Poles
did not stick rigidly to any one tactic, and the pilots of 303 continually worked out new variants, with Kellett, in response to
what was a completely novel form of fighting and a novel situation. Any tactic required 'complete trust and perfect timing', and
in this respect the Poles responded well to him. 'It was just
common sense, really,' adds Kellett. 'And besides, once you'd
gone in to attack there was no time to worry about what anyone
else was doing.' A few seconds' pause or hesitation could cost a
pilot his life.

Although Sunday 15 September 1940 is now regarded by
many as the turning-point in the Battle of Britain, this was by no
means obvious to the participants. Huge formations of German
planes continued to raid London in a desperate attempt to
smash Britain into submission. By mid September Poles represented well over 10 per cent of all the fighter pilots defending
the south-east, as British casualties mounted and Poles took their
places. It was nevertheless 303 that continued to steal the lime-
light.

On 17 September General Sikorski came down to Northolt to
visit the squadron and decorate some of the pilots with gallantry
awards. Churchill also dropped in unannounced several times
on his way back to London. On 26 September King George VI
paid 303 a visit. He inspected the base and talked with the pilots,
who were on readiness in the dispersal hut. Suddenly the telephone rang, scrambling the squadron. The pilots dashed for the
door, brushing aside the king with little ceremony, and ran to
their machines. The king watched them take off and wished
them 'happy hunting' over the radio before leaving the base. He

also asked to be informed of the results. The squadron engaged and turned back an invading party over Portsmouth and returned to base safely. The telegram they sent to Buckingham Palace that evening read: '11 shot down for certain, 1 probably destroyed. Own losses nil.' On the next day, 27 September, with an RAF squadron, 303 destroyed 31 German planes in 30 minutes over the Isle of Wight, and notched up its hundredth confirmed kill in Britain. It lost two pilots, including Ludwik Paszkiewicz, who had scored its first kill exactly four weeks earlier. Such losses could not mar the joy of the 303 pilots, and even Group Captain Vincent was dragged into the celebrations, noting that he had never found himself propelled so high into the air without wings before.

Life changed after that. On 28 September the Germans adopted a new tactic. Instead of massive raids against London, they now used their bombers by night, or in very high-level flights. Their fighters swept the skies in smaller groups, engaging and tying down British defending fighters, or carried out low level strafing raids. This meant more work for the defending squadrons, which were scrambled several times a day but often could not make contact with the smaller raiding parties. There were thus fewer engagements, and consequently fewer kills. It was altogether more tiring and less fun for the pilots. It was also dangerous. The RAF's losses continued to mount, causing it to draw on the pool of waiting Polish airmen, with the result that by the beginning of October 1940 there were times when one in five of the British fighters defending London was manned by a Pole.

303 Squadron had clocked up another 26 kills by 11 October, when it was withdrawn from the front line and sent to Leconfield for a period of rest. It had set two new records – for the highest number of enemy planes shot down in a month (more than double the tally of the next highest-scoring squadron), and for the lowest ratio of own losses to successful kills. The squadron's place at Northolt was taken by 302, whose pilots welcomed the opportunity to boost their reckoning. But their expectations were dashed. They were frequently scrambled but rarely made contact with the enemy, and when they did come across a large formation of Messerschmitts on 15 October, they lost two of their own pilots. Three days later they again lost two pilots in battle, while two more killed themselves landing in bad weather.

The Battle of Britain is officially deemed to have ended on 31 October. Of the 2,927 pilots who manned a fighter at any point between June and November, 146 (just under 5 per cent) were Poles. Of the 2,692 German planes deemed by the RAF 'destroyed for certain' (including those brought down by anti-aircraft fire and balloons), 203 (over 7.5 per cent) had been credited to Poles. 303 Squadron had downed three times the average RAF score, and incurred one-third of the average casualties. Excluding the 16 planes shot down by Kellett, Kent and Forbes, 303 accounted for 110 certain kills, 9 probables and 6 damaged, at the cost of 8 of their own pilots. The figures for 302, excluding the 5 aircraft shot down by its British pilots, were 16 definites, 10 probables and 1 damaged, at the cost of 6 own losses. The 89 Polish pilots serving in various RAF squadrons accounted for 77 definites, 16 probables and 29 damaged, and 17 of them lost their lives.

Although these figures proclaim a glorious performance, one must be very cautious before extrapolating any conclusions from them. The Polish individual top score of 17 enemy planes shot down was about half the personal scores of some British 'aces'. On the other hand, statistics show that in the RAF as a whole, 4.9 kills cost one own death, while the Polish squadrons notched up 10.5 enemy planes destroyed for every own pilot killed – a staggering discrepancy. Apart from demonstrating that Poles together work better than Poles apart, these figures would seem to bear out the Polish claim to superior tactics and better teamwork – the last thing the RAF top brass had expected of them.

Dowding and his colleagues had assumed that the Polish fighters would be reckless and irresponsible. Quite the reverse proved to be the case. It was true that they were determined to attack, even if heavily outnumbered. It was also true that they took risks. But they knew what they were doing. 'If I did not have a good position, I did not attack,' writes one. And, as Kellett pointed out, they never threw caution to the winds, but remained highly disciplined in the air. He also makes the point that they were very quick to take in a situation and to act upon it – it was almost instinctive. They were, according to Flight Lieutenant Thomson of 302, 'tremendous individualists'. But it was never a free-for-all, even as they split up into pairs, the one keeping an eye on the other's tail while he was pressing home an attack. 'The readiness to help a stricken comrade was a feature among the Poles that I was to witness on several occasions,' writes Kent. 'One felt safe with them,' adds Thomson; 'they knew their business.' Kellett himself is almost embarrassed by the way the three Poles of his section looked after him in the air, with, as he puts it, an almost 'feudal' sense of loyalty.

Figures and statistics are by nature unfair, and in the case of the Battle of Britain, one is not comparing like with like. The RAF had many seasoned pilots of great skill, but it also contained many chivalrous boys, barely out of school, with great reserves of courage but little training and no fighting experience. The average age of all fighter pilots who took part was twenty, while the average age of the Polish pilots involved was twenty-four – a significant difference. All the Poles had hundreds of hours of flying time on a variety of planes behind them, and most had some fighting experience. The British squadrons had more time in the front line than the Polish ones, which entered the battle at a later stage or, like 302, were largely outside it. This meant that the British aces could clock up more kills, but it also meant that many more inexperienced young pilots were killed, particularly in the first weeks.

The fact remains that the Poles did achieve above-average results, and there are several good reasons for this. Their very strong motivation and their hatred for the Germans meant that they were psychologically steadier and more determined than their British colleagues. They were on the whole older and more experienced, and they employed superior tactics. They had been trained to fly on inferior planes with little in the way of support systems, and as a result 'their understanding and handling of aircraft was quite exceptional', in the words of one British flight instructor. This meant that they were better equipped to get themselves and a damaged plane back to base, or to make a safe forced landing in difficult terrain. They had also had to face a vastly superior enemy in their primitive machines. They were thus able to make the most of their equipment, and while 303 was flying Hurricanes, which were inferior to the Messerschmitt 109, they could nevertheless achieve better results than British squadrons equipped with the far more advanced Spitfire. 'We would have done better if we'd had Spitfires, like the English,' commented one. The Poles had, it has to be remembered, downed Messerschmitts with their P–11s, which had a fraction of the speed and one-fifth of the firepower of a Hurricane. But perhaps their greatest asset was their eyes.

British airmen were trained with a wealth of sophisticated equipment, including radar and constant radio contact with the ground and other planes. They therefore naturally relied on these to tell them where they were and where the enemy was. 'You'd get these chaps who'd go up, lose half their bloody squadron, and they never saw a thing,' as one British squadron leader puts it. The Polish airmen had been through rigorous medicals before being accepted into the air force, including stringent eyesight tests. Moreover, until they reached England they had never enjoyed the luxury of radio or radar, so they relied for their own safety on keeping an eye out on all sides at all times. 'The Poles always seemed to see everything first,' remarked Squadron Leader Crook, who had two of them in his squadron, and he was not alone in noticing this. 'The Poles seem to have an uncanny gift in this respect,' another British pilot told a *Daily Telegraph* reporter. 'They have "spotted" Germans in the distance long before I have been able to see them.' Another, talking to an *Evening News* reporter, explained that 'whereas the British pilots are trained to rely on their radios, and to go exactly where they are told, Polish pilots are always turning and twisting their heads in an effort to spot a distant enemy'. Given the speed with which an enemy fighter could dive out of the sun and attack from behind, this was a tremendous asset.

Another element in the fine showing of the Polish squadrons, intangible yet undoubtedly very important, was the superiority of their ground crews. These were the pick of the pre-war ground personnel, supplemented by LOT engineers and technicians from aircraft factories in Poland. 'I don't believe any squadron had better NCOs or better aircraft maintenance than 303,' wrote Kellett. These men faced a challenge quite different from that faced by the pilots.

'For the pilots, a Hurricane or a Spitfire was not actually such a novelty. A machine like any other, they used to say,' writes one of the mechanics. 'A little practice and you're off. But for the mechanics it was a difficult, a very hard nut to crack. While the engine itself and the body did not present any great problem, the instructions, the names of tools and parts caused major headaches to even the most resourceful among us. At first, we would get new machines in exchange for damaged ones, but as the number of sorties grew, the supply system began to falter and one had to begin to fly "on one's own industry", just as it had been in 1920 and 1939 in Poland, and in 1940 in France. And it was here that the Polish mechanic showed what he could do. With strange use of language and particularly hands, they managed to explain to the stores personnel what the problem was in order to obtain the necessary part. And if the part they needed was not there, they would make it up themselves, because, after all, the pilots had to fly on something.' What helped was the quality of the machines they were put to work on. 'Nothing flashy,' commented the chief engineer of 303, 'but there are no nasty surprises or construction faults either – it's all good sound workmanship.'

He and his men felt a little like 'poor relations' of their British colleagues at first, but they soon realized that they were better qualified and more experienced. They were infuriated by the British habit of knocking off for tea-breaks or for the night, leaving work half-done. They also disagreed with the British rule that all mechanics should work as a team on all the planes. 'The mechanics like to have their own planes to work on, and here you can see our Polish traditions and habits coming out,' writes the engineer. 'It was always the tradition that every plane had its own fitter and his assistant – it did not like or want others. To begin with, when we blindly subordinated ourselves to British ways and abandoned our own, it often happened that numerous doctor-mechanics would endlessly debate how to repair a sick plane.' As soon as they joined their own squadrons, they reverted to the Polish system. 'The return to Polish ways has meant that the planes now have their permanent guardians, tender and sensitive to every minute ailment of their own machine.' These 'guardians' were to be found hanging around their Hurricane at all hours, endlessly cleaning and rechecking odd pieces of equipment.

'There was no caste difference between pilots and mechanics,' writes Król. These are not empty words. He was the son of an illiterate peasant, while many of the fitters were middle-class men with degrees. Yet several British officers have made the point that the Polish officers treated their men 'like dirt', and professed themselves disgusted by it. Kellett recalls having to sort out a mutiny by three ground staff who refused to obey one of the officers of 303. Andrzej Nahlik, a pilot who spent as much time in British as in Polish units, tells a different story. 'The British treated their ground crew with far greater *hauteur*, even with scorn,' he states, adding that there was far more rigid stratification in the RAF between aircrew officers, aircrew NCOs and ground crew. The very idea that an officer was awarded a DFC and an NCO a DFM for the same action struck the Poles as monstrous. Polish ground crew themselves believe they enjoyed a completely different standing from those of the RAF.

The very proportion of ground to air crew must have made a difference: in the RAF it was more than 100 to 1, in the *Luftwaffe* it was about 80 to 1, and in the Polish Air Force it was only 30 to 1. 'Brothers have never been closer than we were,' confirms Skalski's fitter. He recalls a reception where Skalski, the Battle of Britain ace and by then a wing-commander, walked up to him and kissed his hands. The British officers present were astonished and a little shocked at the sight of a wing-commander kissing a fitter's hands. 'Were it not for these hands I would never have shot down so many planes – I'd be dead,' Skalski declared.

'The whole squadron was one family, sharing the joy of victories and successful flights, and sharing in the sorrow of losses,' Król continues. The mechanics would be in a frenzy of excitement as the planes came back from an operation, waiting to see whether they would buzz the airfield or make a victory roll, signifying success. They could see from the torn masking of the machine-guns if the plane had been firing and would run up to their planes, hang on to the wings while they were still taxiing and shout: 'How many?' The pilots would show them on their fingers. According to the pilots, the ground crew took more pride in the squadron's score than the pilots themselves. '"Mine's been firing," hollers one of them, as though it were all down to him,' writes a pilot. 'Such is the unwritten but immutable law, that the machine belongs not to God, nor to the king, nor to the government, but to him, and only to him, an oil-smeared scarecrow in blue overalls.'

The ground staff were just as eager as the pilots to get the machines airborne again. 'Just take a look at what happens when a plane returns from a flight – like a honey sandwich it is instantly covered in busy bees, and you can almost hear the hum of a hive,' writes 303's engineer. The only time they permitted themselves a few hours' sleep was when the planes were in the air. Their dedication was so great that during its whole participation in the Battle of Britain, 303 only went up four times with less than its full complement of twelve planes. When the squadron returned to Northolt after the fighting of 15 September, the ten planes (two had been shot down) were declared write-offs by Kellett. But the mechanics refused to see the squadron reduced to its four spare machines, and after a night of frenzied clanging and banging, twelve planes stood ready for take-off on the runway.

Such hard work meant that the squadron remained at full strength in virtually all operations, which obviously increased its effectiveness and its collective safety. The meticulous attention to detail also minimized the possibility of snapping cables, jamming machine-guns or instrument failure, all of which could easily cost a pilot his life. Above all, the devotion of the mechanics meant that the pilots were utterly confident that their planes were in prime condition and fine-tuned, and such confidence counted for a great deal in battle.

However one reads the statistics, one can see what made Flight Lieutenant Kent call 303 'the finest squadron in the whole world' – to which he added 'profound thanks for keeping me alive and teaching me to fight'. And it is impossible to deny that the Polish airmen as a whole contributed crucially to victory in the Battle of Britain. With only about 400 fighters defending the south-east at any one time, the Polish contribution of between 50 and 100 in action throughout September and October was vital. On 11 September, the Poles accounted for 18 per cent of the enemy aircraft destroyed, on 15 September they accounted for 14 per cent, on 19 September 25 per cent, on 26 September a staggering 48 per cent.

'Our shortage of trained pilots would have made it impossible to man the squadrons which were required to defeat the German air force and so win the Battle of Britain, if the gallant airmen of Poland had not leapt into the breach,' wrote Sir Archibald Sinclair, the Secretary of State for the Air Force. 'What we could have done without the Polish fighter pilots in the Battle of Britain is difficult to contemplate,' wrote Air Marshal Sir Michael Beetham. More telling still is the statement by the far from effusive Dowding, who declared that 'had it not been for the magnificent material contributed by the Polish squadrons and their unsurpassed gallantry I hesitate to say that the outcome of battle would have been the same'.

Fighting On

THE EXPLOITS OF 303 were watched with mounting envy, tinged with pride, by dozens of other Poles training at stations all over Britain. On 24 August 307 Lwów Night-fighter Squadron had started forming at Blackpool, followed four days later by 306 Toruń Fighter Squadron, and on 9 September by 308 Kraków Fighter Squadron and 309 Czerwień Army Support Squadron. By the end of the Battle of Britain the Polish Air Force in Great Britain numbered a total of 8,154 officers and men. Another 930 who had failed to get out of the Balkans before the fall of France arrived by way of the Middle East before the end of the year. By 31 December 1940 the Polish Air Force had seven operational squadrons (two bomber and five fighter) and three more finishing their training. On 1 January 1941, 302 and 303 shed their British officers and became entirely Polish units. The next months were to see the formation of three more fighter squadrons (315 Dęblin, 316 Warsaw and 317 Wilno), bringing the total strength up to thirteen by the spring of 1941.

Sikorski was determined to keep his air force independent of the RAF and, trading on the goodwill built up during the Battle of Britain, he managed to amend the Anglo-Polish military agreement in his own favour in the matter of jurisdiction and ranks. Poles serving in British squadrons were encouraged to transfer to the new units. Most of them did, but a number chose to remain, and in the course of the war no fewer than 290 Polish pilots served some time in one of 80 British fighter squadrons. Sikorski also wanted his pilots to be trained separately. As a result three Polish Operational Training Units (OTU) for fighter pilots were opened, 55 at Usworth, 58 at Grangemouth and 61 at Heston, along with 60 OTU at East Fortune, near North Berwick, where night-fighters trained on Defiant planes.

British top brass welcomed neither the concept of setting up an autonomous allied force in Britain nor the problems involved. Its rapid expansion testifies to the military value of the Polish personnel, to Sikorski's authority, and, not least, to Churchill's personal regard for Sikorski and his deep conviction that the Poles were worthy allies. There were, inevitably, many difficulties, and a certain amount of friction. The situation was a novel one, and the relationship between the Polish command structures and the British was ill-defined. 'Nobody has managed to explain satisfactorily where the Englishman's command ends and where the Pole's begins,' one officer of 307 complained. And this ambiguity vitiated the efforts of the Polish commanders to form their men up into disciplined units.

The ease with which 303 had cohered was misleading. It was made up of some of the best men in the Polish Air Force, it was given first-rate British commanders, it was equipped and sent into action promptly, and the men were conscious of the import-ance of their role. The formation of the subsequent units was to prove more difficult.

Most of them had a sprinkling of seasoned pilots who had seen action in Poland and France, but the rest of the men had been denied the chance to fight, and for them the war was beginning to seem no more than an aimless trek from one base to another. Their frustration brought out the worst in them, and their super-iors often lacked the personal authority to take them in hand. 'Our officers were not trained to be real leaders of men,' wrote the medical officer of 307. 'The air force officer was supposed to be a good flier, but he did not know how to command.' The older officers found it more difficult to adapt to the new conditions in Britain than their younger colleagues. Many of them had left wives and children behind in Poland, and this affected their spirits. Most of them had also had to accept demotion to a lower rank on arriving in Britain, which some found humiliating. Because there was nowhere for them to go higher up in the air force hierarchy, they also effectively blocked the promotion of younger officers. 'British officers cannot understand how one can feel affronted by such a silly thing as one stripe more or less on one's sleeve,' someone noted in the 304 Squadron journal.

To the Poles, it was a matter of deep feeling and apparently limitless preoccupation.

Traditionally, the Polish forces had resorted to fierce disciplinary measures to maintain order, but this was now impossible, as an officer of 316 complained. 'If one could take some of these malcontents firmly in hand and apply Polish discipline to them, we could achieve the desired result, but this is precluded by King's Regulations, a splendid collection of fine rules – which are appropriate only to dealing with a normal, loyal and well brought-up Englishman,' he wrote. 'The Polish soldier is of a completely different psychological construction, and needs to be handled quite differently.' This view was endorsed by the commander of another squadron. 'It is difficult for us to enter into the spirit of the English system, customs and regulations, and I do not think it is possible in the space of a year to remould Poles in the image of perfect British citizens,' he wrote. 'While we try to respect English customs, we would like some of ours to be respected too.'

The clash of temperaments was not calculated to make a resolution of this problem any easier. As a nation, the Poles tend to be individualistic and perverse. 'We cannot stand being ordered about – we won't do anything without a fight,' as one officer of 307 noted in the squadron diary. 'The English are out of their depth; they just cannot understand why we are so difficult at times.' And the difficulty of handling the Poles was aggravated by their psychological state.

It has to be remembered that the majority of the Polish airmen were young men of humble backgrounds, and while their upbringing was generally of a high moral standard, their levels of culture and social education were often very limited. An enduring sense of having been let down by their superiors in 1939 encouraged a cynical attitude to authority, the personal tragedies many of them had suffered and continued to suffer played havoc with their emotional balance, and the uncertainty that attended everything in their lives provoked conflicting waves of apathy and anger. As a result, there was much petty quarrelling, jealousy over ranks and decorations, gossip, criticism of the Polish and British commands and governments, and a great deal of drinking.

Always quick to take offence, the Poles often misunderstood the statements or actions of their British colleagues or superiors, and national or personal pride was often felt to have been

affronted when no such thing had been intended. But sometimes it was. The station commander at Hucknall issued all
British officers and NCOs with side-arms, but refused to arm the
Poles on the base, and would not even allow them to borrow six
rifles for a burial party. The Polish Inspectorate's fortnightly
reports often noted: 'Anglo-Polish relations on this station not
cordial'.

'Those were difficult times for the RAF,' explains Stanisław
Wandzilak. 'They had some magnificent fliers, but out of a
couple of dozen squadrons they suddenly had to create a whole
air force, so they were naturally spread pretty thinly, and often we
were put under the orders of officers who had less experience
than us.' This overstretch in the RAF meant that the station
commanders, flight instructors and technical officers assigned to
training the new Polish squadrons were usually older men,
grounded by age or wounds, sometimes resentful of having to do
such jobs, or pilots who had served their years but never shone.
'I think there were some pretty awful people hanging about in
the RAF before the war,' comments one British Air Chief
Marshal. They tended to be immune to Polish charm and dash.

Similarly immune were the large number of adjutants, paymasters, quartermasters and other bureaucrats who had never
flown. Many of them had joined up recently and were imbued
with the importance of their new rank. They tended to be mar-
tinets and sticklers on minor points of order, and some could not
hide their racial prejudice. Unable to assert their authority, they
could become quite obsessed with the alleged 'uncontrollability'
of the Poles, and they were daily needled in their insecurity by
the slightly subversive and occasionally mocking manner of many
of the young airmen.

One Polish pilot who had smuggled a woman into his room for
the night betrayed himself by asking his batman for breakfast for
two. He was reported to the British station commander, who summoned the Polish squadron commander. Having worked himself
up into a tremendous lather over the heinousness of the crime,
he turned to the Pole and asked what he proposed to do about
it. The Polish commander put on his most concerned look.
'Quite right! Very serious offence!' he said. 'We shall deal with
the man.' The station commander enquired about the form of
punishment to be meted out. 'Very simple,' announced the Pole
with gravity. 'We will shoot him!'

Almost everything the Poles did was bound to irritate or alarm such superiors. To be fair, it has to be said that the Poles often behaved fecklessly, particularly when airborne. Tadeusz Schiele relates how he and another pilot once buzzed a flight of RAF novices training on Tiger Moths by zooming past at full throttle a dozen yards in front: the turbulence caused the biplanes to weave about 'like drunken pigeons'. It must have seemed a capital joke to them, but not quite so funny for the trainees. The Poles were forever skimming the airfield, flying through hangars and performing dangerous aerobatics.

The training of 306 Toruń Squadron (drawn mostly from the remnants of 4 Toruń Regiment) was a case in point. They started forming under the command of Tadeusz Rolski at Blackpool on 28 August 1940, just as the Battle of Britain had entered its phase of greatest intensity. On 3 September they were moved to Church Fenton, where they trained on Tiger Moth biplanes. Their British commander, Squadron Leader Douglas Scott, and his deputy, Flight Lieutenant Tennant, were both killed in crashes a few days apart. In spite of the delays caused by these tragedies, the men were ready to start fighting by the end of the month. Yet no Hurricanes arrived for the next four weeks, and they were not posted as operational until 8 November, when the action was over. They cursed the slowness of the British and heckled their instructors regularly.

308 Kraków Squadron (drawn from the survivors of 2 Kraków Air Regiment) also started forming at Blackpool on 9 September. A week later it was moved to Speke outside Liverpool, then to Bagington near Coventry. Its commander, Squadron Leader Davis, was killed during a training flight, which delayed progress and undermined confidence. They were not posted operational until 1 December, and then given night-fighter duties, for which their Hurricanes were entirely unsuitable (they were difficult and dangerous to land in the dark).

The training of 315 Dęblin Squadron, under Stanisław Pietraszewicz, proceeded smoothly at Acklington in Northumberland, in spite of the soggy airfield and a collection of old Hurricanes, each from a different series. 'I have great pleasure in stressing the kind and cordial attitude of the local British authorities to us, full of heartfelt concern for our well-being,' noted Pietraszkiewicz. The squadron's departure from Acklington was marked by a rowdy party. 'The whole company got completely sozzled, but there was no broken furniture or legs. Our doctor only had to stitch up one head,' noted the commander. 'We got on grandly with the English here – splendid boys!' The sentiment seems to have been mutual. 'Never shall I be as happy as I was with them,' wrote one of the British officers.

But 316 Warsaw Squadron, formed at Pembrey on 22 February 1941, was dogged by every problem. There was a severe shortage of training and ground personnel as well as equipment, and the British commander, Squadron Leader Donovan, was deeply unsympathetic. He found fault with everything, right down to the way the mechanics wore their scarves while servicing the planes. 'Undoubtedly the fault is also partly ours, but he has made himself so thoroughly unpopular that there is no way out,' wrote the Polish commander, Squadron Leader Aleksander Gabszewicz, a Battle of Britain ace. 'This is very sad, because we are the guests of the English.' The conflict became so fierce that it was only resolved by the intervention of the commander of 10 Fighter Group.

Possibly the most disgruntled of all were the men of 307 Lwów Night-fighter Squadron. They were sent for training at Kirton-in-Lindsey in Lincolnshire (and were nonplussed on arrival by the station commander pointing proudly to the 'Polish' flag he had run up to greet them: it represented a Prussian black eagle on a white ground, not the Polish white eagle on a red ground). They were given Defiant fighters, in which the pilot had to manoeuvre so that his gunner could get a shot at the enemy. They resented this new role of 'chauffeurs' and they hated night-fighting, which relied on constant radio contact with the ground, a cause for linguistic headaches and misunderstandings. They continually demanded transfer to fighter squadrons, but were refused. They were moved to Jurby in the Isle of Man and given convoy protection duties, and in January 1941 to Squires Gate near Blackpool with the task of defending Manchester and Liverpool from night bombers. It was monotonous, dangerous and thankless work.

The night-fighter's was a lonely job, demanding great staying power. He would have to take his Defiant up on patrol several times a night, returning every hour or so to refuel. Up in the air, all he could do was quarter the night sky, his eyes peeled for a shadow, a silhouette or a vapour-trail, haunted by the uneasy feeling that he might have let a German bomber slip through a few yards above or below. When he spotted a raider, he would have to manoeuvre with precision in order to allow his gunner the best possible shot, as there would almost certainly be no second chance – even the most unwieldy bomber could easily lose its pursuer in the dark. It was not until 26 March, nearly five months after becoming operational, that 307 Squadron was awarded its first certain kill.

The difficulties of forming the units were exacerbated by the *matériel* shortages. Britain was making up for years of neglect. In spite of Beaverbrook's energetic handling of production there was a shortage of aircraft, and conditions on the rapidly impro-vised airfields were often primitive. The lack of basic creature comforts over long periods was not conducive to good morale. The unfortunate 309 Army Support Squadron was based first at Renfrew, where the pilots lived in wooden huts with broken windows and no washing facilities, then at Dunino near St Andrews, where they slept in tents and queued at a stand-pipe for water. 'The tents, field-kitchens and outdoor life were reminiscent of a gypsy encampment,' noted one of the officers, adding that the men had begun to refer to it as 'the penal squadron'. The fact that the best equipment the Air Ministry could come up with for them were a couple of senile Westland Lysanders did not improve their sagging morale. They received visits from the Polish President, the Duke of Kent and General Sikorski, but no planes. And relations with the British were not what they might have been. 'Our poor Polish commander had a real cross to bear in the shape of the British CO,' someone wrote in the squadron diary.

Matters picked up in the spring of 1941. On 15 April the first Polish Fighter Wing was formed at Northolt, made up of 303, 306 and 308. In August 2 Polish Wing was formed at Exeter, made up of 302, 316 and 317. At the same time, several new types of operation were inaugurated: Rodeos and Mosquitoes, followed by Sweeps, Rhubarbs, Ramrods, Intruders and Spheres. This bouquet of exotic names was used to describe three basic types of operation over northern France: the provision of top-cover for bombing raids, the seeking out of enemy aircraft, and the strafing raid on ground targets by fighters on their own. The last of these, Rhubarbs and Mosquitoes, were very much to the taste of the Poles. 'It's a kind of fighting which is best suited to the Polish temperament, and seems to recall the tradition of our cavalry,' according to Squadron Leader Henneberg of 303. The squadrons would cross the Channel, reach a specified area, and then split up into pairs. They would fly low, preying on German airfields, gun emplacements, troop convoys, railway stations, and any other military objective they chanced upon; on the way back there might be some coastal shipping to attack. The pilots could see the damage they caused, and it was often significant. But these operations were not without danger.

The French coast was heavily defended by German anti-air-craft batteries, airfields were ringed with machine-gun nests, and German fighters occasionally intercepted in force. During the Battle of Britain a pilot who baled out could be up in another plane later that afternoon, but in operations over France he was almost certain to be taken prisoner. These new types of operation also required flying at much higher altitudes, with attendant discomforts, such as pain in the ears and swelling of the stomach. The intense cold often frosted up the cockpit window. The oxygen kits were very crude, and the pilot had to keep regulating the flow with a tap as he climbed or descended. If he forgot to do this, or could not because he was engaged with an enemy plane, he would pass out, with fatal consequences. The oxygen pipe was so narrow that it only required a few drops of saliva to freeze before it blocked. The Northolt mechanics rigged up wider pipes, but the equipment was nevertheless unwieldy. The oxygen dried out the mouth, causing the lips to crack and bleed, while sweat would freeze around the edges of the oxygen mask, adding to the discomfort.

The truly unpleasant aspect of any operation beyond British shores was the possibility of ditching in the Channel on the way back. Air-Sea Rescue did its best, but a pilot could go down unseen, or fail to get out of his plane in time, or be drowned under his parachute, or simply die of exposure before he was located and picked up.

Its first Mosquito raid, on 22 January 1941, was an exhilarating experience for 303. But the risks involved gradually became apparent. One pilot felt an impact while attacking a machine-gun nest, but managed to get home without much trouble. It was only after he had landed that his mechanic pointed out that six inches had been shorn off the end of each of the three blades of his airscrew by machine-gun fire. Another whose luck held flew so low over Le Touquet airfield that he brought 25 yards of power-cable back to Northolt wrapped round the tail of his plane. One pilot of 306 was returning from a Mosquito having expended all his ammunition when he was set upon by two Messerschmitts. He dodged and weaved to shake them off as they pumped bullets into his plane, to no avail. In desperation, he dived steeply towards the sea, followed by the two German fighters. At the very last moment he pulled his Hurricane out of the dive, but the nearest German, whose less manoeuvrable Messerschmitt could not respond, went straight into the water, while the other cried off. The Polish pilot landed safely, but when he got out of his plane his knees gave way, and he collapsed. Many were less fortunate.

Zdzisław Radomski had his arm shot clean off at the elbow in a dogfight over France. Despite twice falling into a faint, he managed to nurse his Hurricane back across the Channel, his left arm lying in his lap, and landed the plane on its belly in a field seconds before passing out from loss of blood. He would never fly again. Squadron Leader Henneberg, who had scored eight kills in the Battle of Britain and enjoyed the Mosquito raids so much, ditched in the Channel on the way back and drowned.

Poor weather conditions hampered operations in the early months of the year, and it was not until the onset of summer that things got into full swing. A whole new set of rules had to be worked out for these operations, as the situation was very different from that over England in 1940. Now that the Poles operated independently in their own wings, they could at last employ their own tactics. Their preferred formation for flying on patrol into enemy territory was in three sections of four planes. The planes in each section were positioned like the fingers of the back of the right hand: the section leader was second from left and a little in front, with his wingman to his left; to his right flew his 'number three', with his wingman to his right and slightly behind. In this way, the leader and the 'number three' were fully covered by their wingmen, while the four planes could bring their combined firepower to bear at the same time. They could also split into twos very easily if attacked. The three sections flew abreast, but at different altitudes, forming three 'steps' with the lowest on the side of the sun. This increased visibility and made it very difficult for enemy fighters to sneak up on any one plane.

But as mature pilots were killed or withdrawn after completed tours of duty, younger ones with little or no combat experience took their places, and had to be assiduously schooled. Any lapse could have fatal consequences. During a sweep over France, 308 was attacked by fifteen enemy planes, and its commander, Marian Pisarek, an experienced and steady flier, gave the order to veer right. One overexcited young pilot thought he knew better and shouted 'Left, not right!' over the radio, and Pisarek and one other were killed in the ensuing shambles. By dint of continually insisting on the necessity of fighting as a unit, listening to orders and keeping together, the older officers managed to bring their squadrons up to scratch and to make sure that such things never happened again. The new arrivals learnt to remain in their pairs, to regain formation after every action, and to look out for any planes that did not. The squadron leaders kept an eye on all their men and detailed pairs off to escort damaged planes back across the Channel.

It was sometimes necessary to teach a cocky novice a lesson, and 'Johnny' Zumbach, then commander of 303 and a man who positively thrived on danger, knew how to do this with a young pilot by the name of Piecyk. Piecyk had been on three sweeps over France and already considered himself an expert, complaining loudly that he had not yet seen a German he could shoot at. In the course of the squadron's next sweep, the following dialogue took place over the radio: 'Piecyk, can you hear me?' 'Yes, sir.' 'Still hoping to see a German, are you?' 'I'd give anything for it.' 'You'd better keep your money – you might need it for your funeral.' 'I'm not leaving this world before I've taken a few Krauts with me!' 'Good, but in that case you'd better take a look in your mirror.' 'Jesus, Mary!' Zumbach had been on the German's tail all along, but waited for the bullets to start flying around Piecyk's cockpit before he intervened and sent the Messerschmitt off with smoke pouring from its fuselage.

In these demanding operations the younger squadrons were at last able to prove their skill. On 23 June 306 shot down six Messerschmitts over the French coast, and on 1 July 308 destroyed five over Lille. Meanwhile 303 was keeping up its fine record, destroying 46 enemy planes over France in six weeks and never losing a single bomber they were detailed to escort. At this point 303 was withdrawn for a rest and its place was taken by 315. This squadron had been having a particularly depressing time carrying out convoy duties from Speke, near Liverpool. In four months it never saw an enemy plane, but lost several pilots in bad weather conditions. On 27 March alone, one crashed on landing, and two more were lost over the sea. Soon after arriving at Northolt, they were able to demonstrate that it had not been their fault. On 14 August, 315 shot down nine Messerschmitts during a sweep over St-Omer.

The other disgruntled squadrons also graduated to more congenial duties during the summer. With the formation of 2 Polish

Wing at Exeter, 316, which had been patrolling shipping lanes leading to Bristol, and 317, which had been doing the same off Liverpool, joined 302 there. Even 307 Lwów Night-fighter Squadron, which had also moved to Exeter, knew better days. At the end of September it was issued with Beaufighters, twin-engined planes equipped with radar. The pilot had four cannon and six machine-guns at his disposal, and a navigator who took care of ground contact. The squadron's task was to protect Exeter and Plymouth, and on 1 November it shot down two Dornier 217s. Three weeks later it bagged a Junkers 88 attacking Plymouth. The German plane caught fire and crossed the sky over the city, blazing brightly. The following day the pilots received a two-and-sixpenny postal order and a letter from a cab driver, thanking them for 'the grandest spectacle' he had ever seen. The squadron's job was still not an easy one, and it suffered several losses, usually on landing in poor weather. But at least it was getting results. On the night of 3 May 1942, it shot down five German raiders over Exeter. The local press outdid itself with headlines such as 'Hats off to Our Brave Polish Boys', and the inhabitants of the city gratefully 'adopted' the squadron, and showed their appreciation in many smaller ways.

In September 1941 the new Focke-Wulf 190 fighter went into action on the German side. Faster and better armed though not quite as manoeuvrable as the Spitfire, it was far superior to the Hurricane. As a result, most of the Polish squadrons were coverted to Spitfire Mark V planes in the course of the autumn. This was a cause for joy. 'I would never have guessed that an hour's flight could bring such anxiety, joy, pride, happiness and emotion,' wrote Tadeusz Schiele, who had just moved from 122 City of Bombay Squadron to 308. 'I wanted to weep and sing with joy.' Władysław Nycz felt much the same after his first flight in a Spitfire. 'I luxuriated in the sensitivity of the machine, in its manoeuvrability,' he wrote. 'I felt so intoxicated by the flight that I was singing, shouting.'

By the end of 1941, all seven of the Polish fighter squadrons had got over their teething troubles, and their record for the troubled year of 1941 showed that the achievements of 303 during the Battle of Britain had been no flash in the pan. Despite most of them having spent much of the year patrolling distant shipping lanes or the Lancashire sky at night, the Polish fighters had accounted for 27 per cent of all air victories scored in 1941 by RAF units operating from the British Isles. And 308 topped the Fighter Command score-board. Only the luckless 309 Army Support Squadron was still kicking its heels in Scotland.

Not surprisingly, the exploits of the Poles were a source of endless gung-ho copy for the press during the last months of 1940 and throughout 1941. Articles with headlines such as 'Plucky Polish Pilots', 'Polish Daredevils,' 'Polish Cavalry of the Air' and 'Polish Demons do it Again' concentrated on the military exploits of the Poles, as did the book *303* by Arkady Fiedler, which came out in both languages and was subsequently dropped into Poland on microfilm, to be printed and distributed by the underground army. But there were also dozens of articles in the press on the perceived characteristics of the Poles, adducing anecdotes to illustrate their strange foreign ways. One, commenting on their extreme politeness and gallantry, told of the airman who offered his seat on a London bus to the conductress.

Then came films. The first, *Dangerous Moonlight*, which was also shown under the title *Suicide Flight*, was made in the spring of 1941. In it, the heart-throb Anton Walbrook plays a Polish pilot who also happens to be a concert pianist. Later that year the Ministry of Information made a short dramatized documentary, *Diary of a Polish Airman*, in which real airmen played themselves. The pilots of 303 had tremendous fun during the filming sessions at Northolt, as it gave them the excuse to show off to their hearts' content. In 1942 Alex Korda's *To Be or Not To Be* also featured 303 in a walk-on role, and one of its pilots in one of the main parts. In the same year, Terence Rattigan's *The Flare Path*, in which a Polish pilot is one of the protagonists, opened on the London stage.

With this amount of publicity, it was not long before London society began to take an interest. In February 1941 the society beauty Jean Smith-Bingham 'adopted' 303 and started giving parties for the officers at the Dorchester Hotel. Betty Norton-Griffiths, 'one of the loveliest women in England', according to the February edition of *Queen* magazine, followed suit, becoming the 'godmother' of 308. Various other ladies adopted squadrons, but the show was stolen by Lady Jersey, alias the film star Virginia Cherril, formerly married to Cary Grant, who became 'Mama' to 315. She took her job seriously, visiting the squadron at Speke, where they held a party for her in the mess – at which they got mightily drunk, judging from the comments scrawled in the squadron diary. She arranged parties for them when they moved to Northolt, and they reciprocated with gallantry. 'Suddenly there was the zooming of an airplane and a Spitfire dived through the clouds and circled the house,' writes a journalist who was interviewing her at her home. ' "That is one of my Poles," Lady Jersey said calmly. "I'm their mother," she continued, with a change of expression on her pretty face.' She not only came to the Christmas Eve dinner, she brought presents. Each of the two hundred or so men in the squadron received a diary, inscribed by 'Mama', and a selection of socks and scarves. She took the trouble to write out each man's unpronounceable name on his parcel. The squadron reciprocated with a scale model of one of their Spitfires and a Polish Air Force eagle. She also, practically, sent the pilots all her laddered stockings to wear in the air, and she also remembered to send parcels to those who had been shot down and languished in POW camps.

Lady Warrender had, much earlier, set up her Polish Armed Forces Comforts Fund, which collected warm clothes for the Poles through appeals in the national press, and also items such as rosaries, crucifixes and missals through the Catholic network. She distributed these from a mobile canteen with Polish eagles painted on the side which had been donated by an American charity.

Much of the interest that focused on the Polish airmen was not so spiritual and disinterested. It became fashionable to have a Polish fighter pilot or two at one's cocktail parties, and positively a triumph to be seen dining and dancing with one. Word got out that Poles were good lovers, and young and unattached ladies in London felt they had to try one out. The airmen took up the challenge and enjoyed themselves, but did sometimes tire of the social whirl, and many were unhappy about being patronized. It was inevitable, given the press coverage, that a stereotype of the 'wild but wonderful', savage yet romantic Pole became fixed in the British consciousness. 'He was good value, old Johnny. One of the very best,' says a British officer about a Polish pilot posted missing in Rattigan's play. 'They're a bit different from us, the Poles, you know. Crazy types, most of them. They're only really happy when they're having a crack at Jerry.' This supposition was thought to be a thrilling challenge to women – it was surely a triumph to unfurrow a brow burning with warlike love of the distant, ravished motherland. 'I love your funny continental ways,' purrs the glamorous heroine of *Dangerous Moonlight*, snuggling up to Walbrook, who is gazing fiercely into the distance as he hammers out the Warsaw Concerto.

The year 1941 had brought two major developments in the war. In June Hitler launched Operation Barbarossa against the Soviet Union, in December the Japanese attack on Pearl Harbor brought the United States in on the Allied side. The first made life dull for the Polish fighter pilots in the second half of 1941 and the first months of 1942, as the *Luftwaffe* withdrew its air fleets from northern France for use in Russia. The second meant that in the course of 1942 increasing numbers of USAAF units, mostly bombers, were brought over to operate from British bases. As a result the Polish fighters were, in addition to their usual work of sweeps over France, providing air escorts for daytime bombing raids by American Flying Fortresses over the Continent.

This type of operation was entirely different from fighter sweeps, and required a new approach. The squadrons had to remain with the bombers while enemy fighters hovered above waiting for a chance to break up the formation and come in for the kill. Early experience in escorting British bombers had revealed the need for iron discipline. An early Ramrod operation, in which 1 Northolt Wing and 2 Exeter Wing were escorting a formation of Blenheim bombers over Arras, speaks for itself.

'After dropping their bombs, the formation turned back towards England. At that moment, somebody from the Exeter Wing shouted through the radio: "Władek, look out, there's a Messerschmitt on your tail." At that, all the Władeks in that wing, and there were quite a few of them, boosted their engines and dived down through the lower squadrons, sowing confusion. In an attempt to avoid collision, 315 descended lower and got in amongst the bombers. The Exeter Wing followed the Władeks and left the formation altogether for a while. But presently 315 returned to its old position covering the Blenheims. Luckily, the Messerschmitts hanging up above did not notice anything and did not attack.'

The really difficult part of the task was to avoid being shot down by German fighters which dived down in ones and twos. The fighter escort were not allowed to turn to attack them, as that would have left the bombers defenceless, which was what the Germans were aiming at. Keeping formation with the squadron and in the right position in relation to the bombers in these circumstances was a nerve-racking business, as another early operation, overheard from the operations room, demonstrates:

Just about halfway between Dunkerque and Lille the first voice spoke:

'Brickbat [315] here – from the sun, behind and above one Me attacking from the left. Watch out! . . . He's gone!' and after a moment: 'You've all drifted too far forward.'

'Carmen [303] here – a little higher, please; you're too strung out and too far forward. In front – an Me. No – it's a Spitfire.'

Another voice: 'Oh, shut up, can't you!'

Another voice: 'Bloody Hell, everyone's gone too far forward, we've left the bombers behind! Mes behind us!'

'Carmen here – watch your backs – we've got nobody behind us!'

'Watch out – Messerschmitts!!! Carmen, watch your backs!'

'Mary [308] here – go higher, keep to the same height as the Carmens! And Brickbats go higher too. – Look out, Messerschmitts behind!!!'

'Carmen here – watch your backs!'

'Brickbat here – fall back a bit, all of you: I'm all alone with the bombers . . . Above right, two Mes attacking!'

Another voice: 'Behind left, they're attacking us – watch out!!!'

Another voice: 'A bit of calm, please, gentlemen!'

There follows a period of silence, but it is soon broken. Carmens, Marys and Brickbats all shout in turn. Messerschmitts appear in twos and threes, then suddenly eight of them swoop down.

A Brickbat shouts: 'Get back, damn you!'

Another: 'Wojtek, stop weaving around like that, or we'll collide.'

Another voice admonishes: 'Carmens, damn you all, get back in position!'

'Brickbat here – you're all shooting forward. Will you please bloody well come back.'

One of the Carmens: 'There's nobody with the bombers, dammit!'

Another voice: 'Are you in the right position? I think I am.'

Carmen, politely: 'Don't keep rushing forward, you bloody idiot.'

Suddenly a decisive voice cuts short the whole discussion: 'Shut your traps, the whole bloody lot of you! You don't half get excited, damn you!'

1. A P-11 getting ready for take-off. The Polish Air Force had 159 of these fighters with which to defend its skies against the 2,000-odd planes of the *Luftwaffe*

2. Aircrew about to go into action, their Łoś bombers barely distinguishable in the background

3. A group of 'tourists' in Bucharest, September 1939. Seated on the left is Krasnodębski, the first commander of 303 Squadron

4. Airmen being evacuated from France, June 1940

5. The joy of getting proper planes at last is clearly visible on the face of this 302 pilot

6. The culture clash and the horrors of fish-paste sandwiches were compensated for by British friendliness in the dark days of 1940

7. 303 Squadron pilots waiting for a scramble at Northolt, September 1940

8. A pilot of 303 Squadron climbing into the cockpit of his Spitfire

9. An armourer of 306 Squadron loading the machine-guns in the plane's wing at Church Fenton. In the background, one of the squadron's Hurricanes

10. Long hours of boredom in the dispersal huts were rarely filled with anything more demanding than draughts – there was no point in starting a long book or a game of chess that would certainly be interrupted and might never be finished

11. The mechanics spent every available moment fiddling about with 'their' plane, even when, as in this instance, it was standing in readiness at its dispersal point

12. Flight Sergeant Henryk Pietrzak of 306 Squadron carried out of his plane on 31 December 1942 – he had just shot down the Polish Air Force's 500th kill since reaching Britain

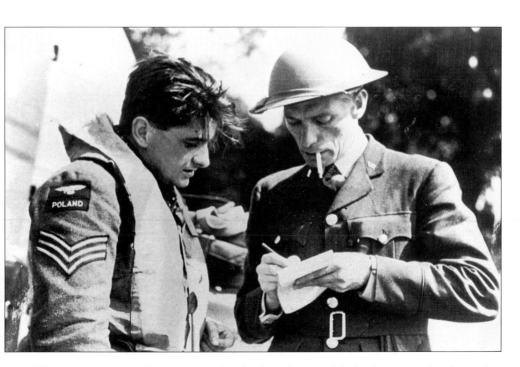

13. The moment a pilot returned – before he could sit down and relax – he had to go through a debriefing with the Intelligence Officer, always British, usually pedantic

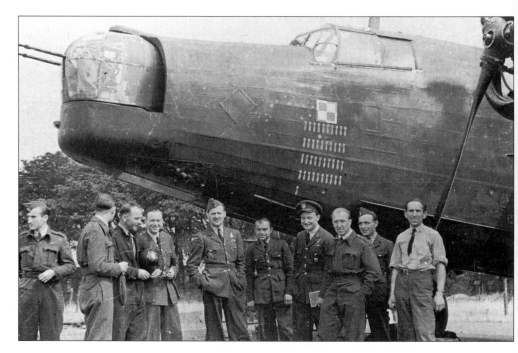

14. The air and ground crew of a Wellington of 300 Squadron. They had just completed their 41st bombing raid. Being cut off from its manpower supply, the Polish Air Force had to send out far older men than the RAF, over and over again

15. Years of flying experience made it possible for this crew to return from the Ruhr in half a plane

16. This young Flight Sergeant of 304 Squadron, at Lindholme in 1941, had finished two tours of duty and been awarded the highest Polish military decoration. He went on to win the DFM and promotion to Flight Lieutenant before being killed, on his third

17. (*above*) Life on some of the bomber bases could be remarkably cheerless, particularly for the ground crews

18. (*left*) Mechanics of 303 at Northolt making Polish sausage for Christmas

19. (*below*) Home cooking on one of the bomber stations

20. The Standard of the Polish Air Force being passed from one squadron to another

21. (*above*) Mascots of one of the fighter squadrons

22. (*left*) Ciapek, the famous mascot of 305 Squadron, who survived most of his crews

23. (*below*) One of the mascots of 317 Squadron. The childishness of the proceedings should not obscure the fact that the pilots in the picture each won a DFC and the one on the left shot down nine German planes

24. Showing a girl one's cockpit was a good ice-breaker, as this pilot of 316 Squadron evidently knew

25. Bomber crews did everything together

26. Assorted mascots of 316 Squadron at Heston

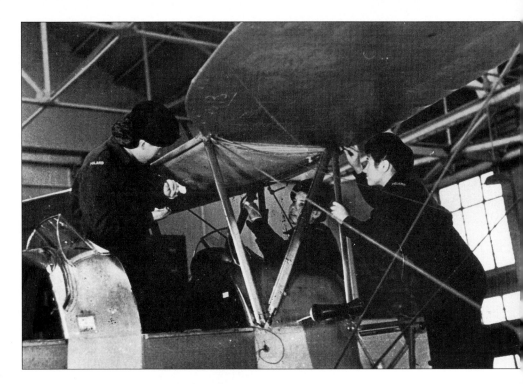

27. Polish WAAFs learning the ropes

28. Many of the Polish Air Force's ground staff were highly qualified technicians, and their skills were deployed in repair workshops and factories

29. Barbara Wojtulanis, one of the Polish ferry pilots

30. A mechanic of 304 Bomber Squadron contemplating a dim future in 1945

Getting the pilots to keep off the air was one of the greatest struggles, but the commanders did finally succeed. An American pilot who flew with 315 the following year noted that he never heard an unnecessary exclamation over the radio – the Americans were even worse than the Poles, it appears – and added that the Poles 'saved their chit-chat for the bar after they got home'.

The Poles also became quite expert at giving close cover to daylight raids by the Americans. The RAF would position two fighter squadrons above the Flying Fortresses and one behind. This proved little more than useless, and bomber losses were unacceptably high. When their turn came to escort the Americans, the Poles of the Northolt wing devised their own plan. As their name implies, the Fortresses were formidably well armed, but they were vulnerable to head-on attack. The Poles positioned one squadron high above and in front, one directly overhead, and the third below and behind. The German fighters were thereby prevented from coming at the Fortresses from the front. Losses on this raid were greatly reduced, and noting the effectiveness of this, the USAAF asked all RAF wings to implement the same tactic. Such a reputation for effective close cover was built up by 302 that it was often detailed to escort royal or VIP flights. When Churchill was flying back from North Africa in 1942, the squadron was withdrawn from its wing and sent to escort his plane.

The Poles took the task of escorting the bombers very seriously, taking a great deal of care to stay with those that had been shot up badly and were losing speed and height. If one went down in the Channel, they would radio for Air-Sea Rescue and circle the dinghy until the men had been picked up. On one occasion, two Spitfires stayed with a Flying Fortress which was in trouble, while two others flew back to base in order to refuel and then returned to take over from the first two, which were by now circling a dinghy with the whole crew in it. They saw a Royal Navy Motor Torpedo-Boat approach, but it veered away, so one of the planes flew over it, making signals and giving the direction towards the dinghy. The MTB ignored its signals and the pilot, usually a phlegmatic man, lost his temper. He dived on the boat and started shooting into the water a few yards ahead of it, until it got the message and turned to follow him.

The Polish airmen were amused to find that many of the Americans in the bomber crews were Polish immigrants or sons of immigrants, and this engendered camaraderie with the USAAF. The renown of 303 had already reached the United States, and the squadron was in regular receipt of letters and gifts from across the Atlantic: in March, a donation of $200 from a parish in Buffalo, in May an embroidered flag from the American YMCA. Mayor La Guardia of New York launched an appeal for books, in Polish and English, for the Polish airmen, and some 4,000 were collected and shipped over. Among the letters was one from Colonel Fauntleroy, one of the two founders of the Kościuszko Squadron, and in March 1941 the other, Colonel Merian C. Cooper, now Chief-of-Staff of the China Air Task Force, paid the squadron a visit.

A special relationship sprang up between 303 and 94 USAAF Combat Squadron, one of the first to reach Britain, which was stationed for a time on the same airfield at Kirton-in-Lindsey. The pilots of the two units got on famously. 'In regard to having a good time, we found that 303 has no equal,' wrote the Americans in their letter of thanks for the hospitality. Lieutenant Earle W. Hille called the Poles 'the best bunch of gentlemen, airplane drivers and fellows I have ever met'.

But it had not been all fun and games. 'We owe more to 303 than can be expressed in words,' wrote another American pilot, and Lieutenant Clark O. Jennings, Jr. called them 'the best damn fighting squadron in the world'. This was no empty flattery. 'This friendship was greatly strengthened during our training,' wrote the commander of the American squadron, 'especially through the many combats between the pilots and the numerous talks here and there; Horbaczewski on deflection shooting, the Polish combat films, Zumbach's instruction on formations, and all the other pilots emphasizing "looking, looking, always looking".' The Polish Air Force in effect trained up quite a number of airmen for the USAAF: several hundred Americans of Polish origin had volunteered for the Polish Air Force in 1940–1, and many of them moved to the USAAF when America entered the war. Frank Gabreski from Oil City, Pennsylvania, joined 315 as a novice pilot and later went back to achieve great things in the USAAF. With 31 kills to his name, he was America's top-scoring ace of the war, and was still flying, as a colonel, in the Korean war. On his first sortie with the Poles he felt utterly humiliated at having failed to see the enemy plane his section leader was telling him to shoot at, but he learned fast, and developed what he called 'the Polish eagle eyes'.

Sound training and alertness were still at a premium. And although pilots were not as hard-pressed as they had been during the Battle of Britain, a front-line fighter pilot's life expectancy in 1942 was calculated by the Air Ministry at two weeks. Many of the fresh pilots coming through into the squadrons by this stage were still in their teens. The feeling that every day was stolen, that it might be their last, had a debilitating effect. It seemed pointless to start reading a book, as the probability of ever being able to finish it was so slight – with the result that the men sat about flipping through magazines that bored them, rather than reading something that might have taken their minds off the presence of death. A Polish journalist visting Northolt noted that the pilots always prefaced their stories with 'before they got X' or 'after Y went down'. 'Deaths are their milestones, marking time as weeks and months do for us,' he mused.

The pilots lived two, sometimes three, to a room, and one of the harrowing aspects of this was seeing room-mates come and go. Survivors were forever packing up the kit of colleagues to whom they had grown close. There seemed hardly any point in making friends. 'Nowadays, when we lose a friend we really feel it, then it was just part of everyday life,' says one. 'Only seven planes might come back from an operation, but our only concern was that there should be twelve ready for action the next day.' Returning to Exeter after a sweep over France, 315 encountered thick fog shrouding the airfield. One pilot was killed and ten were injured as the twelve planes came in to land. A squadron leader remembers the emptiness he felt when, returning from a mission over Dunkirk, his was the only plane of 317 to land back at base. Several awful hours passed before news trickled in of a couple of his pilots who had either been fished out of the Channel or made forced landings on other fields.

The fact of having survived an operation gave little relief. The survivors inevitably felt an unjustified sense of guilt. They became more and more cut off from anyone who was not a pilot by the impossibility of talking about their fear and their experiences, so they bottled up more and more, a source of unbearable tension. Nor did the survivors feel any real sense of security, for nobody knew what the morrow might bring. 'An airman has to keep a grip on his nerves,' noted one of them in his diary as he considered the life-expectancy statistics. 'If it's really to be only two weeks, then one must fit a lot into that short space of time, a lot of wrecking.'

The British pilots at least had the satisfaction of knowing that they were effectively defending their loved ones, while the Poles could only guess at the fate of theirs as they read of Nazi atrocities in Poland. 'The Polish airmen are charming. They have a sense of humour. The officers particularly are alert and witty,' wrote an RAF education officer. 'But most of them have sad eyes. One does not like to ask the Poles about their families.' At the same time, this brought out a burning anger in them, and the determination to kill as many Germans as possible as soon as possible was a potent calmer of nerves and dispeller of introspective broodings.

The Poles' hatred of the Germans entered British folklore at the time of the Battle of Britain, and it was often illustrated with apocryphal stories. On 30 October 1940 the *Daily Mirror* ran a story about a Polish bomber crew on a training flight breaking away from their formation in order to go and bomb Germany all on their own. Despite its absurdity, the story did the rounds of all the major papers, with increasingly silly headlines. The press laboured an image of the Poles as uncomplicated souls rubbing their hands with glee at the idea of doing damage to the Germans. 'Bombing Reich Thrills Poles – We Go Tonight, Yes?' runs a typical headline. The imputed sentiments, supposedly bred out of the British by civilization, were admissible in 'colonial' troops – and they made the Poles popular with the long-suffering British public during the Blitz. 'When you get to the stage when you can't stand the gentility of the BBC or the peace-aims arguments of the intellectuals any longer, there is, at least, one avenue of escape,' ran a piece in the *Daily Telegraph* on 23 February 1941. 'The best thing to do is to go and see the Poles. I am told that the Canadians and the Australians in this country have been working out some pretty choice things to do to the Germans if they get here. So much the better. But for sheer 100 per cent healthy hatred, give me the Poles. They *loathe* the Germans.'

The reality was a good deal less picturesque. The Poles did indeed loathe the Germans, but, like soldiers in every war, their hatred quickly gave way to pity when confronted with the physical reality of the pain they were inflicting. A pilot who, caught by the Russians at fifteen, had been through enough during the two years he spent in the gulags to harden any heart, was thoroughly enjoying himself as he strafed enemy positions during a sweep over northern France. But while he was attacking a personnel carrier he saw a German soldier jump out, straight into the path of his bullets. 'I shall never forget that,' he says; 'I actually knew that I'd killed him.' That evening, back at Northolt, he could not bring himself to eat. The ham on his plate revolted him. Feliks Szyszka was shot down over Warsaw on the first day of the war, and as he hung on his parachute, his face and body badly burned, a German fighter flew back and forth shooting at him. He had seventeen bullet-wounds in his legs alone when he landed, and spent four months in hospital. As soon as he could walk with the aid of two sticks, he contrived to escape from the German military hospital and walked all the way to France, where he arrived in the spring of 1940. In Britain he joined one of the Polish fighter squadrons, and in 1941, over France, bagged his first Messerschmitt. The German baled out, and Szyszka found himself bearing down on the parachuting pilot. 'I really don't know what was happening with me, but my finger was poised on the machine-gun button,' he recalls. 'I only needed to press it. But I had to see his face. So I bore down on him and held my fire. The German grew in my sights, twisting on the cords and waving his arms frantically. In the end I saw his face clearly. It was terrible, but different, oh how different, from the face I had seen over Warsaw. It was crazed with fear. The German dropped his arms and hung there like a rag doll. But I could not shoot. I just couldn't. I banked my Spitfire and passed a few metres from his face. For a while I watched as the parachute drifted groundwards. Then I rejoined the squadron, and when I landed – I suddenly felt deep happiness.' Szyszka was promoted to command the squadron, and a few weeks later perished when one of his fresh pilots collided with him in mid air.

Whether it was a question of hatred or not, it is clear that the Poles' attitude to the war was very different from that of their British colleagues. In a sense, they were fighting a different war, their own war. This was evident wherever Polish units were stationed alongside British ones, even at Northolt, the centre of Polish fighter life.

The base itself was still under British command, but the station commander, Group Captain Theodore MacEvoy, who in spite of having a broken spine still liked to fly and even fight, was a great friend of the Poles and much loved by them, as was his successor, Group Captain Frederick Rosier. The base's Flight Officer was John Kent (Kentowski), formerly of 303. On 25 September 1942 Group Captain Mieczysław Mummler was made station commander, setting a seal on the process of polonization. In addition to the three Polish ones, there was occasionally a British fighter squadron as well as a special communications squadron (which flew Churchill, members of the Royal Family and other VIPs around) stationed at Northolt. But their personnel were greatly outnumbered by the Poles, and while relations tended to be very cordial, they remained, in the words of one RAF officer, 'remote'.

All notices were in both languages, and a large one over the bar in the mess read, condescendingly: 'English Spoken'. There was a chapel, created by the airmen in a disused Nissen hut, in which Mass was celebrated every day, and there was also a Polish library. Poles from other stations were forever dropping in, to visit friends or find out what was going on in the Polish Air Force as a whole. Pilots on leave used it as a convenient springboard for London. 'We came to regard this airfield as our second home,' writes one. Another described it as 'a small corner of Poland'. This feeling was enhanced when, in the autumn of 1942, 2 Polish Wing moved from Exeter to the satellite airfield of Heston.

The dwindling number of British personnel on the base had learned to live with the idiosyncrasies of the Poles, and even the WAAFs spoke pidgin-Polish. Northolt was a favoured posting for them, too, since it guaranteed plenty of male attention and frequent nights out in the capital. One girl, an actress with a white Jaguar of her own (known throughout the base as 'Speedy', and not just for her driving), attached herself to the Polish wing at Northolt as a volunteer driver as her contribution to the war effort.

RAF Northolt itself was one of the most commodious and comfortable stations in the country. Its fine 1920s officers' mess and quarters, with elegant rooms within and a lawn in front that sloped gradually down towards the airfield proper, are almost stately in the way they survey the whole station. The good runways and vast stretch of smooth grass around them meant that whole sections could take off abreast quite comfortably, and there was plenty of room for manoeuvre when forced landings were necessary. It was also an easy airfield to find one's way back to even in poor weather, as it was surrounded by salient landmarks easily visible from the air.

Many of the pilots and other ranks had their own cars – one could buy a perfectly good used car for £25, a month's salary for a pilot officer. But they were hardly needed, with the Metropolitan and the Piccadilly lines within walking distance.

The ground staffs could get to their beloved greyhound racing without difficulty, while the capital beckoned to the pilots in a different way. 'Forty minutes away by Underground there was London – and in London waited lips red as roses,' in the words of one. There were dances every few days at the Royal Overseas League where one might meet nice girls without any trouble. Their favourite nightclubs were the Wellington Club, Studio 1, the Old Windmill Club in Soho and the 400 in Leicester Square. But they soon discovered comforts nearer home. The Alexandra Palace at Ruislip, commandeered for the duration by the War Office, was the venue for dances and ENSA entertainments. There was the Clay Pigeon pub in Ruislip, the Leslie Club in Uxbridge, and, best of all, the Orchard, a large mock-Tudor country-club-style hotel set in a spacious garden.

'The haven of our dreams materialized when we found the Orchard,' writes Zumbach. It was owned and run by a man of Polish–Jewish ancestry, and he took the Polish airmen to his heart straight away. 'Our host never resented having his daily routine and quiet atmosphere disrupted by our riotous lust for life,' continues Zumbach. 'He knew that some of us were running out of time.' The landlord also knew, by bush telegraph, the scores of the day, and he was ready with free champagne when Germans had been shot down. 'Every Pole who was based at Northolt has warm memories of that landlord, who never forgot to send a basket of fruit to the bedside of a wounded comrade.'

'Of course, it was the girls who before anything else kept us coming back to the Orchard Inn,' relates Zumbach. Many were respectable bank clerks' daughters from Ruislip or Pinner, who came to the Orchard with brothers or friends. Others were restless local girls looking for adventure. 'They were pretty, easy going and affectionate. They knew us all by our first names and cried real tears when one of us went missing. Every night they waited for us in the big saloon bar with its miniature dance floor. Every night the party spirit was kept going by a band who made up for their lack of technique with their eagerness to please.' The Orchard was not a night-club, so it closed at 11 p.m., but if the airmen were having a good time the landlord would invite them upstairs, bring out his gramophone and keep them supplied from the bar for as long as they liked.

On account of its proximity to London, Northolt was also used extensively for flying important people in and out of the country.

Churchill, Sikorski and many others passed through on their way to conferences and meetings abroad, and the planes that carried them assured a ready supply of American cigarettes and other luxuries not available elsewhere. With such incomparable amenities, it is hardly surprising that Northolt became a favourite posting for the Poles. The officers' mess held its own dances once a month, and these enjoyed a great reputation. The mess was also the venue for revelry at other times. The pilots of 303 devised a cocktail called a 'Messerschmitt' (containing whisky, gin, port, sherry, cherry brandy, *crème de menthe*, brandy, beer and soda-water) which those who had scored their first air kill had to down. And even without grounds for celebration, there was a great deal of drinking: too much, according to Rolski, who succeeded Mummler as station commander and promptly issued a ban on drinking alcohol before dinner. He was surprised to find everyone sitting around with large glasses of milk in the next weeks, and only after a time did he tumble to the fact that the milk was strongly diluted with whisky.

The stories of wild parties are legion, and certainly the extremes of behaviour could be frightening. In January 1942, for instance, in the Northolt mess, Flight Lieutenant Antoni Daszewski won a bet by shooting a packet of Lucky Strike cigarettes off the head of Captain Ryszard Wiszowaty with his service revolver. Such recklessness was less out of place than it might seem. A few weeks later Daszewski was shot down and killed over Le Touquet.

The pilots themselves learned to live with the presence of death. It was harder for those left on station, who watched them leave, sometimes never to return. The mechanics would be fiddling about nervously in the hangars, and spilled out onto the field the minute they heard the distant drone of engines – long before anyone else could. The squadron might return in formation, sweep over the airfield once and then come in to land in exemplary manner, which usually meant that the operation had been uneventful; but sometimes the planes straggled home singly or in twos, and the anxiety was palpable. A mechanic could tell 'his' plane by the sound of its engine, and while it was a hundred yards off the end of the runway, mechanical diagnoses would already be in progress. The mechanics were the constant element in every squadron. Only they provided the continuity, as only they knew the history of every victory and every loss.

The others who found it harrowing were the WAAFs, who had to watch a procession of young men fly off and never return.

Tadeusz Schiele, who joined 308 at Northolt in 1941, arrived at the station shortly before dinner. He found three empty places at table, and noticed the sorrow of the WAAFs as they finally cleared them away. He himself had to move a dead pilot's belongings out before he could go to bed that night. The following day, he went out with the squadron on a mission, from which two pilots failed to return. Again, two empty places honoured their memory. That evening, as he was leaving the mess, one of the WAAFs, a pretty girl with a cockney accent, called Jean, came up to him in the dark and asked him to show her his plane. They walked over to the Spitfire. She ran her hand over the wing of the war machine, and then turned to him. She was only seventeen, and he was shocked by the emotional intensity with which she kissed him and then clung to him. Later, as they sat side by side on the wing of the Spitfire, listening to the dull thud of bombs raining down on London and watching the searchlights sweeping the sky, he looked up and saw the stars of the Great Bear shining brightly. The next morning he asked his mechanic, Staszek, to paint the seven stars of the constellation on the fuselage of his plane.

Because of the shortage of pilots, tours of duty were extended far beyond their regulation length, but every so often a squadron would be sent away from the front line for what was termed a rest. This was not popular. 'For the second time since starting work in Britain, the squadron has been pulled back for a rest, but it is difficult to find a moment's rest in this new state, as it involves continuous hard work on the ground and in the air,' complained a corporal of 303 in June 1942. The work included intensive training flights and gunnery practice as well as patrol and convoy duties. But this particular 'rest', at Kirton-in-Lindsey, did provide 303 with an unexpected boon. On 3 July four planes were scrambled to intercept a couple of marauding Junkers 88s which were strafing and bombing unsuspecting market towns, and they were able to shoot down both of them, near Horncastle in Lincolnshire. The pilots then drove over to the wrecks in search of souvenirs, and plucked the Iron Crosses from the bodies of one of the crews – marked '1939'. The satisfaction of shooting down men who had bombed Poland was intense.

Even less popular than these 'rests' was the habit of posting experienced fighter pilots to training schools for a spell as instructors. This was deemed important for the education of young pilots, while at the same time supposedly giving the others a chance to rest their 'nerves'. But apart from the fact that they were annoyed at being withdrawn from the front line and parted from their squadrons, teaching inexperienced and often over-enthusiastic novices on old and poorly maintained machines was no holiday. 'I came to the conclusion that being an instructor was more dangerous than meeting the *Luftwaffe*,' wrote one of them.

The high point of 1942 for the Polish fighters was the disastrous Dieppe raid, in which an amphibious landing was attempted by mostly Canadian troops, who suffered terrible casualties before withdrawing. Five Polish squadrons took part in the operation, returning to refuel and then rejoining the battle several times during the course of the day. The German fighters were trying to attack advancing ground troops and bombers, but avoided engaging fighters, so Squadron Leaders Zumbach of 303 and Skalski of 317 devised a trap for them during their second foray across the Channel. Skalski's squadron flew in front, weaving and veering like a bunch of poorly-trained novices, while 303 kept an eye on them from far above and behind. A large formation of Focke-Wulf 190s saw the unsteady progress of 317 and could not resist the easy prize. It dived down on to the Poles, but was immediately set upon from behind by Zumbach's planes. Within ten minutes, fifteen German planes had been shot down, with no own losses. Of the 56 Allied fighter squadrons taking part in the Dieppe operation, only five (less than 10 per cent) were Polish, yet these five accounted for 18 per cent of the German planes downed, and suffered only 4 per cent of the Allied fighter losses.

That summer, even the luckless 309 had its moment of glory. In 1941 the RAF decided that Army Support squadrons no longer had any point, and transformed them all into Fighter-Reconnaissance units attached to the Tactical Air Force. Accordingly, in the spring of 1942, 309 was brought down to Gatwick where it retrained on new Mustang planes, and was then sent back to Dalcross to defend the east coast of Scotland against putative raids from German airfields in Norway. None materialized, and the pilots soon got bored. Flight Lieutenant Janusz Lewkowicz calculated that by flying at certain altitudes the Mustang's range could be extended to permit raids on Norway. He sent a detailed report to Tactical Air Force Command, but this was ignored. So he decided to prove his point. On 27 June 1942, he climbed into his plane and set off. He reached the

Norwegian coast, strafed German positions at Stavanger, and flew back, with fuel to spare. He was severely reprimanded by the commander of Tactical Air Force, and congratulated by him in a personal letter. Lewkowicz's report was studied at staff level, and new instructions were issued. From then on, 309 was allowed to raid the Norwegian coast to its heart's content.

As the third anniversary approached of the first Polish airman setting foot on British soil, on 8 December 1939, the Polish fighters could feel that they had proved their worth beyond doubt, and that their contribution to the war effort was a significant one. And their reputation was as high as ever. In the 11 Fighter Group gunnery competition in April 1942, 303 came top, followed by 316 and 315, all three ahead of the British squadrons, a fact strongly underlined by Air Vice-Marshal Trafford Leigh-Mallory as he presented the cup.

The year ended with a treat that gave more than usual gusto to the New Year's Eve celebrations. As 306 returned to Heston on the afternoon of 31 December after a Rodeo operation over Dunkirk, one of its pilots executed several spectacular victory rolls, and every Pole on the airfield knew exactly what that meant. With his shooting down of a Focke-Wulf 190 over Le Crotoy, the Polish Air Force had notched up its 500th kill since coming to Britain. But 1942 had really been the year of the bombers.

9

Bombing

FOR THE BRITISH public there could hardly be an image more dashing and romantic than that of the daredevil Polish fighters giving their all to defend London from the Hun, even if few realized how decisive their contribution had been. To the Air Ministry, the Polish contribution to the build-up of its bomber force was just as crucial in the critical period before American support came on stream with the deployment of the 8th Air Force. It had been bombers, not fighters, that the RAF had wanted from the Poles in the first place, and the first two Polish bomber squadrons had gone into action while the Battle of Britain was still raging. The first Polish decoration to be bestowed on an airman in Great Britain went not to a fighter ace, but to an armourer of 301 Bomber Squadron. On 18 September 1940 Sergeant S. Nowak was unloading the bomb-rack of a plane that had returned from operations when the fuse of a flare bomb snagged on something and the safety catch blew out, wounding him in the shoulder. Knowing that there were three fitters working inside the plane, which was still fuelled up, he took the bomb in both arms and ran out from under the machine on to the open ground of the airfield. He managed to get fifteen yards between the plane and the bomb when it went off, nearly killing him.

The first, 300 Mazovian Bomber Squadron, was formed at Bramcote on 1 July 1940, the second, 301 Pomeranian Bomber Squadron, on 26 July. Their training presented a slightly different picture from that of the fighter squadrons. Here the Polish officers were in command, and their British counterparts were cast in the role of advisers. The Polish commanders of bombers tended to be older and more mature men than those of fighter squadrons. Wacław Makowski of 300 Squadron, for instance, was forty-three in 1940. He had commanded a squadron against the Bolsheviks in 1920, and then moved into civil aviation, becoming General Manager of LOT and the last pre-war President of the International Air Transport Association (IATA). His British counterpart, Wing-Commander K.P. Lewis, deferred to him in most things, and left the management of the squadron in his hands. The commander of 301 was Roman Rudkowski, also an older man and something of a tough customer, as his British colleague, Squadron Leader C.G. Skinner, and several other top brass were to discover.

It was essential to have a good manager of men in command, since a bomber squadron was much larger than a fighter unit. At full strength it included up to twenty air crews (120 men) and many more ground personnel, bringing the total to anywhere between 400 and 500 men. It was also more diverse in its needs and functions, and required a high degree of co-ordination to ensure efficiency and safety.

The first two bomber squadrons were drawn from men who had reached England in late 1939 or early 1940. They had had plenty of time to learn English and retrain. On 3 August Air Marshal Sir Charles Portal, head of Bomber Command, came down to Bramcote to inspect them, and was highly impressed, particularly by their dive-bombing, noting that the pilots flew their Fairey Battles as though they were fighters. This was hardly surprising, since many of the pilots were frustrated fighter pilots at heart.

On 20 August, the King visited Bramcote (and greatly disappointed some of the less cosmopolitan of the ground crew by not appearing in ermine robes and a crown). A few days later both squadrons transferred to Swinderby in Lincolnshire, a county that was to be their home for the rest of the war. First impressions were not promising. Makowski, who took his squadron to Swinderby on 23 August, was shocked by the rudimentary appointments of the station and the lack of bare essentials. 'There's nothing here,' he complained over the telephone to Rudkowski, whose squadron was to follow five days later. 'There are no chairs, there are no beds, there's no bar, there's no vodka.' However, the Swinderby station commander exerted himself and by the time 301 joined its sister squadron there was an improvised mess with a bar, and a party to greet them. Duly fortified, the squadrons, which were now assigned to 1 Bomber Group, prepared to go into action.

On 14 September the 32 Fairey Battles of the two squadrons took off to bomb the German invasion preparations at Boulogne. They repeated the raids almost nightly for the next five weeks, hitting the ports of Boulogne, Calais, Ostend and Dunkirk. On 25 September they suffered their first casualties, when one of the bombers was shot down by a German night-fighter.

Successive batches of escapees from France and North Africa arrived at Bramcote to make up 304 Silesian Bomber Squadron, formed on 22 August, and 305 Wielkopolska Bomber Squadron, formed on 1 September. They had less time to learn the language, which did not matter so much, as by now OTU Bramcote was entirely staffed by Poles, and their training was done at greater speed. To the great irritation of the men, no sooner were they ready to become operational on their Fairey Battles than they were re-equipped with Wellingtons, and had to start their training all over again. It was not until mid December that 304 and 305, now fully operational, were transferred to their battle station, at Syerston, near Newark in Nottinghamshire.

The first two bomber squadrons, 300 and 301, had also been withdrawn from action in October to retrain on Wellingtons, and on 22 December they were already bombing the oil refineries of Antwerp in their new machines. By the end of the year, the two squadrons had dropped 62 tons of bombs, so far without excessive casualties, but 1 January 1941 brought a reminder of the dangers involved. Returning from a seven-hour flight to bomb the harbour at Bremen, the Wellingtons of 301 ploughed into a thick fog covering Swinderby, and eighteen men perished as three of the planes crashed.

The work had to go on, and whenever weather permitted, the two older squadrons, 300 and 301, and, from April, the younger 304 and 305, set forth at dusk to deliver their bomb loads. The routine was gruelling. Ten hours before an operation, the squadron commander would select the crews that were to take part. At noon, they were summoned to the operations room, where the station commander would explain the day's objectives. The tactical officer would unfurl his maps and give the crews details of the routing, bomb loads, anti-aircraft defences along the route, and the time at which the homing beacon would start operating. The Met. officer would add a report of expected weather conditions along the route and over the target. With the questions that followed, the briefing would take about an hour in all.

The next stage was for the pilot, radio operator and gunners to make a short test flight in their Wellington to check all systems, while the navigators went through the routing once more, in greater detail. After this, the crews would be given a special high-calorie lunch, with such delicacies as bananas, and sent off to their rooms to sleep or rest. Two hours before the flight they were given another meal, after which they went off to dress, something that could not be done in a hurry. They wore long-johns and vests, thick sweaters, and over this a combination-suit and fleece-lined flying boots. Round their knees they wrapped their girl-friends' discarded silk stockings – the knees were particularly vulnerable to the arctic temperatures during long hours in one position. On top of all this came the leather flying helmet with its oxygen mask and microphone, the 'Mae West' life-jacket, and the parachute. This cumbersome outfit made a difficult job harder. The parachute harness was covered in hooks and eyes that caught on the countless pieces of equipment lining the inside of the bomber. The toggle of the Mae West could also snag on something, causing the vest to inflate itself, sometimes jamming the unfortunate crew member in a tight part of the plane.

The crews were taken to their plane by bus or lorry, carrying various additional pieces of equipment, sandwiches, and thermos flasks of hot soup or coffee. A final check of all the systems was made before the pilot signed an 'acceptance form', and then the craft was ready for take-off. This was one of the moments of greatest tension. The Wellingtons, weighed down with bombs and full tanks, were not easy to get off the ground. The slightest mishap was bound to end in an almighty explosion, with no chance of escape for any of the crew. After take-off, all functions would be checked, and the gunners would give short bursts to try out their machine-guns. At 10,000 feet, the crew would put on their oxygen-masks. They would cross the European coast at an altitude of about 18,000 feet, to avoid the anti-aircraft defences, and then there was nothing but the monotony of keeping an eye out for night-fighters.

Things livened up over the target. Hundreds of searchlights raked the sky, trying to get a fix on the planes as they flew through a heavy barrage. The pilot would weave and dodge the searchlights, while the crew held their breath as the shells burst around them, sometimes so close that the whole plane would be rocked violently by the blast, and pieces of shrapnel would tear into its wings or fuselage. Sometimes the blast of a nearby explosion might tear off one of the gunners' turrets, or a piece of shrapnel might start a fire in the plane itself. But however terrifying the barrage, the craft had to carry on towards the target and, if they meant to hit it properly, to descend to a lower altitude. Just before reaching this, the navigator would crawl down into the bomb-sights and take over command of the plane, with the pilot merely responding to his instructions. Nervous tension among the crew would reach a climax, for the plane now had to fly straight, at a constant speed, making it impossible to dodge the searchlights. The navigator would drop the bombs and take photographs, and then the pilot was allowed to take the plane out of danger and head for home. A great sigh of relief went up among the crew, but this soon turned to boredom and weariness – they really began to feel the cold on the long way home. Only the gunners remained alert. Theirs was a lonely job. They could not move, so they got even colder than the others. And although they had nothing to do for most of the flight, they could not afford to let their concentration flag for a second, and had to keep scanning the sky for night-fighters.

As the planes crossed the English coast, pandemonium would break out. The knowledge that they were now safe from German capture and the North Sea combined with permission to break radio silence to produce a veritable shouting match as the crew members compared notes and impressions, swearing at the pilot for having taken them so low over the target, or at some hapless rear gunner who had failed to shoot down a night-fighter. Every member of the crew had his bit to add. Neighbouring planes and WAAFs in control rooms were suddenly assailed with waves of incomprehensible jabber, interspersed with English swear-words, and they would turn down their sets, knowing from experience that there was no way of making oneself heard, let alone of shutting up the Poles. This loquacity was apparently a hallmark of Polish bomber crews.

But if the plane had been damaged by flak, the whole crew remained on tenterhooks, praying that they would not have to jump and end the war in German captivity, or, what was even less immediately alluring, ditch in the North Sea. If either of these occurred, the pilot remained at the controls to the very last together with the wireless operator, in order to give the others a chance to bale out and to give the most accurate possible position to Control. Often these last two failed to make it before the plane fell too low for a parachute jump and sank on hitting the water. Sometimes, a combination of skill, prayer and sheer determination enabled the pilot to reach the English coast and crash-land in the nearest field. The homeward flight was a prolonged nightmare for the wounded. Bronisław Godlewski, a truck driver from Chicago who had volunteered for the Polish Air Force and flew as a rear-gunner in Wellingtons, had both hands severed by shrapnel over Essen. He spent the next hours in agony staring at his lifeless hands still clutching the machine-gun.

After landing back at their base the crews were taken to a debriefing session in the operations room, where solicitous WAAFs served them coffee or cocoa and biscuits, and sometimes a tot of rum. Only then were they allowed to undress, sit down to a meal, and finally go to bed. Little wonder that while fighter-pilots were on the whole desperate to get back up in the air the minute they had returned from a mission, the bomber crews would drift off to sleep with the comforting thought that they had survived one more flight, which meant one less to go in that tour of duty.

Nevertheless, many of those who flew in these operations found them unforgettably exhilarating. The closeness and interdependence of the crew members gave them an extraordinary sense of security as the heavy machines roared through the murderous night sky. 'When a fighter is in the air, one thinks of such-and-such a pilot, but when a bomber takes off, one says that such-and-such a crew has gone,' writes a fitter. 'While a fighter pilot is the brain and the heart of the complicated organism we think of as a plane, in a bomber that brain seems to be divided into several separate cells, fulfilling various functions, but producing a single unified thought.' The same mechanic noticed that the difference between fighter and bomber crews was marked even when they were off duty. 'Amongst the bombers there is a stronger sense of camaraderie – one notices little groups which seem cemented together,' he writes. 'And those same little groups are always together, whether they're drinking or brawling.'

The same sense of community was in evidence among the bomber ground crews. 'I love my aircrew, I love those people with a love that is quite different from the love of a mother for a child, or a man for a woman, or that sung by the poets; it is a special, new kind of love,' wrote one mechanic. 'Our work is rather dull and apparently lacking in glamour,' writes another. 'Who, for instance, is remotely interested by the fact that at 17.00 hours one engine broke down when the plane is supposed to go out on an operation at 22.00 hours, and that a team of mechanics literally besieges the machine, forgetting all about food and rest after a whole day's work, thinking only of getting that engine back into commission on time. Because every one of us knows well that one operational plane less means several thousand pounds of bombs less on the heads of the Germans – and that is something we cannot accept. Evening comes, it grows dark. The planes are drawn up in front of the hangar. The aircrews are standing at the ready around their planes. They chat, they smoke, everything is strangely calm and quiet. The ground crews walk proudly round their "birds", delighted that in a few hours' time their whole day's work will bring its result.' They gave their ungainly bombers girls' names and they felt just as passionately about their machines as any Spitfire pilot. One fitter describes 'his' Wellington 'lifting off the runway with the lightness and grace of a fifteen year old girl'.

If the fighter pilots seemed to steal the show at times, the men of the bomber squadrons derived a deeper sense of satisfaction from the knowledge that they were inflicting a more direct revenge on the Germans. It was not uncommon for Polish crews to breach regulations by breaking radio silence in order to tell the Germans, in their own language, exactly who it was that had just dropped several thousand pounds of bombs on them. And they were not troubled in their minds by the slaughter they inflicted. 'During our flights I often thought about Christianity, which proclaims mercy and forgiveness, while I was full of feelings of revenge and had no scruples about doing as much damage to the Germans as possible in return for the damage they had done in my country,' writes a pilot of 300.

This strong motivation kept morale throughout the Polish squadrons remarkably high. Another contributing factor was that all four squadrons were stationed close to one another, on airfields they came to regard as their own, in a county in which they felt welcome and at home. From 23 August 1940, when 300 Squadron moved to Swinderby, Lincolnshire was home to thousands of Poles. The first operational sortie by Polish bombers was made from Swinderby on 14 September 1940; the last flight made by a Polish aircrew was from Lincolnshire on 26 November 1946. Blyton, Cammeringham, Coleby Grange, Digby, Dunholme Lodge, Faldingworth, Hemswell, Ingham, Kirton-in-Lindsey, Swinderby, Wellingore, and Winthorpe hosted between them not only the bomber squadrons, but also every other Polish squadron at one time or another. Just over the county border, a few miles south-west down the Fosse Way in Nottinghamshire, lay Syerston, for a time home of 301, 304 and 305, and the Polish Air Force cemetery at Newark. Further away, but in the same county, were the Polish training schools at Hucknall and Newton. Lindholme, near Doncaster in south Yorkshire, hosted 304 and 305.

Conditions on these airfields were not always good. Most of them had been improvised or at least expanded recently, so the men lived in wooden or corrugated iron huts with little in the way of heating, and there were no comfortable messes. Everything was devised for the safety of the planes rather than the comfort of the crews, and hangars, barracks, operations room and mess were spaced as far apart as possible. Ingham was like a sprawling village; Digby, stranded in the sodden fenland wastes, was known locally as 'the Polish aircraft-carrier'.

The Poles swamped these stations by their numbers, and, just as at Northolt, it was the British who felt marginalized. 'The place took a lot of getting used to,' relates a British Military Police Sergeant who was posted to Syerston. 'The administrative side was done by pukka RAF, but all the rest were Polish. There were about ten Poles to every one of us, and it was almost like being overseas.'

The British did not always have an easy time of it, as one Polish airman's account demonstrates. 'The belligerent sides were Group Captain Willy, the commander of one of the great bomber bases, armed with four stripes on his sleeve, the thick tomes of King's Regulations, and an arsenal of instructions, detailed rules and other paper weapons, on the one hand, and us, the crews of two Polish bomber squadrons, armed with a great and boundless love of freedom, on the other,' he writes. The opening shots were fired over the unauthorized everyday wearing of sheepskin bomber jackets and flying boots. Lecture and fine them as he might, the station commander could not bring them to order.

It was a confrontation of temperaments. 'At first sight, Willy made a rather positive impression; a middle-aged man of medium height and build, with a red face and blue eyes. When he walked, limping slightly but erect, gleaming with carefully polished buttons, announcing his rank from afar with the gold leaves on the visor of his cap, it has to be admitted that he inspired respect. But in the mess, bereft of the symbols of his rank, he completely vanished into some corner armchair. Invisible, he quietly sipped his whisky, sucked at his pipe, and almost invariably cut himself off from the world with a newspaper, lurking behind it for hours, presumably convinced that this wall of paper he had erected was quite as impenetrable as the wall of a private house.'

Willy decided to show the Polish airmen that he was no stuffed shirt, and announced that he would go on a mission with them. They took him on a relatively safe raid over Ostend, but he insisted that he accompany them on one of the dangerous runs over the Ruhr. As they were approaching the target, he told them they were too high, so they decided to teach him a lesson. They took the plane down to a really dangerous level and, pretending they could not get a good fix, repeated the approach, a nerve-racking business with shells bursting all around them. But his starch held, and they had to admit that he had won the first round of this private war.

'Soon began the second phase of the war with Willy,' continues the chronicler. This revolved around the airmen's illicit use of aviation fuel in their private cars. They were given a petrol allowance of six gallons per month and since they liked to drive into town at night, particularly in winter when there were few operations, this could not suffice – especially as all the road-signs had been removed, the Poles were unfamiliar with the area, and the locals, when asked for directions in a foreign accent, considered it necessary to send the supposed German parachutists on a wild-goose chase. Aviation fuel was specially coloured so as to be instantly recognizable to any military policeman doing a spot check, but the airmen devised a number of methods (such as filtering through gas-masks, charcoal and potato peelings) of removing the treacherous colouring.

One day the station commander called an assembly in the hangar and appeared accompanied by two civilians armed with testing equipment. He demanded the keys to all the garages, and graciously announced that he had insisted that his own car be tested first. One pilot slipped out of the back of the hangar unnoticed and bicycled over to his garage, intending to pour the four-gallon canister of aviation fuel in his boot down the drain. When he got there, he noticed that the station commander's garage was unlocked, so he poured the illicit fuel into the tank of Willy's Jaguar. The upshot was a heavy fine for the station commander and free drinks for a week for the pilot. Willy retaliated by ever more stringent checks on uniforms, and the Poles responded by walking out *en masse* when he entered the hangar for an ENSA show. He acknowledged defeat, and the following day treated everyone to whisky in the mess, with a short speech assuring them how much he admired their fighting skills. 'We, of course, softened, because it is easier to catch a Pole with a nice word than a trout with a dry fly.'

It is hard not to feel for the station commanders who had to keep these masses of self-willed young men in order. They fought a losing battle because, particularly in winter, there was simply not enough work to keep the men occupied. Their only way of killing the boredom and banishing grim thoughts effectively was to pursue some absorbing hobby, one that did not need to lead anywhere. Some chased the WAAFs all the time, others played poker. The mechanics were forever fiddling about making things – model planes, artefacts, jewellery, even some quite ambitious sculptures. But the men could not be confined to the bases.

They acquired old cars or built their own from wrecks. This meant that they could visit neighbouring stations or meet comrades from other squadrons in strategically located pubs. The Caenby Corner Hotel near Hemswell, where visiting wives and girl-friends stayed, was known as the 'Happy Corner'. The Saracen's Head in Lincoln and the Flying Horse in Nottingham were practically kept going through the war by Poles from surrounding stations. And the whole area was full of girls with little to do and happy to be distracted. In general, the slightly old-fashioned and predominantly agricultural county of Lincolnshire, and its inhabitants, suited the Poles well.

Although they lacked the cosmopolitan delights of stations such as Northolt, these rural bases did have compensating features. One was the possibility of procuring choice food. It was not difficult to bribe farmers with aviation fuel or chat up their daughters in order to obtain fresh eggs, for instance. With a little ingenuity it was also possible to procure the raw materials of those ultimate staples of Polish culinary life – ham and sausage. Rationing prevented farmers selling pigs to anyone, but again, Polish charm or black-market operations could obviate this problem, and in any squadron there were always enough men who had been brought up on a peasant small-holding to turn the pig into ham, sausage and black pudding with the minimum of fuss. One bomber squadron actually took to raising its own pigs. The British station commander intervened, maintaining that it was illegal to kill a pig without a butcher's licence, so the men would lead the pigs out into the road and arrange car accidents.

The countryside afforded endless opportunities for the enterprising. One such was poaching. One fighter pilot actually used his Spitfire to drive partridges towards a friend who wanted to shoot. A pilot of 305, a keen shot, used to go rough shooting regularly in Lincolnshire. If caught by a gamekeeper, he would apologise and offer to hand over his booty, but usually the squire would allow him to continue, as long as he did not bring too many friends or scatter the game. After a time, they began inviting him to shoots, and eventually he bought a place in a syndicate and acquired a labrador. Even fried in the nastiest oil or fat on a primitive ring in his bedroom, a breast of partridge or leg of pheasant was a gourmet supplement to the dreary RAF diet.

The same pilot went fishing and laid lines for eels in the fenland drainage ditches. His mechanics smoked his catch in their servicing tent, and even after he had given them half and supplied himself, he still had plenty left over to barter for whisky. There was also the possibility of picking wild mushrooms in the woods, which caused consternation and alarm among the Britons. One station commander stumbled on a group of airmen having a fry-up of *cèpes* in the hangar and assumed that the simpletons were about to poison themselves. He put a stop to the proceedings, and only after a great deal of explanation by their officers did he soften. He nevertheless appointed a commission to look into this alleged health hazard.

Another Polish speciality that caused misunderstandings was the pilots' habit of pinching milk from the mess, starting cultures and letting it sour in their rooms. Over-zealous British batmen would try to pour it away and, when prevented from doing so, wander off muttering about filthy foreign habits. An airman billeted in private quarters was given a dressing-down by his landlady for allowing precious milk to go bad, and when he tried to show her his purpose by eating it, she flew into a panic and called the doctor.

At the root of all the problems lay the very nature of a bomber station and its curiously unreal existence. 'A bomber station was rather a subdued place,' says a pilot of 305, 'because one was always losing people. They came. A week passed. And before you'd had time to get used to them, they'd gone.' There were long periods – sometimes weeks on end – when there were no operations at all, during which life was unimaginably dull. Then, suddenly, an operation was announced, and life took on an entirely different aspect – one of frantic activity, tension and fear. But this was compressed into a few hours, and might be followed again by a week of humdrum aimlessness.

The juxtaposition of these two states of existence was very unsettling. A crew preparing to go on operations that night, and therefore horribly aware of the fact that they might be dead by morning, would sit in the mess next to colleagues who were not flying and whose only preoccupation for the evening was finding a fourth to play bridge. But when they had left on their 'job', the bridge-players were gripped by quiet tension. If the crew failed to return, the bridge-players felt the loss more deeply than they liked to acknowledge.

Unlike most fighter stations, which had been visited by enemy bombers and therefore could 'see' the war, bomber bases existed in a curious limbo, and the great majority of their personnel never saw or heard the enemy. At the same time, everyone on the base, from the station commander to the most junior fitter, felt inextricably bound up with the war that a few they sent out at night waged on their behalf. None were more involved in this proxy than the ground crew, who prepared the planes and saw them off, in much the same spirit as a mother sends a child off to school in the morning. They were incapable of knocking off, and spent the eight hours the plane was in the air waiting for its return. When it did return, they would repair and service it and, as they patched bullet holes or fixed shattered steering gear, vicariously live through the fighting that had caused the damage. If the plane failed to return, they felt bereft and disoriented.

But however ghastly the whole rigmarole might be, they all, aircrew and ground crew alike, preferred action to the long stretches of bad weather which prevented operations. The comparatively uninteresting sorties of early 1941 made the men restive. To begin with, most of the raids were against harbours and dockyards, such as Hamburg, Bremen, Rotterdam and Brest, in a fruitless attempt to sink the German battle cruisers *Gniesenau* and *Scharnhorst.* But they also began to carry out longer operations, against targets inside Germany such as Cologne, Mannheim, Dusseldorf, Frankfurt, Duisburg and Essen. On 23

March whoops of delight went up in the briefing room as the crews of 300 were told that their target was Berlin.

Not only were they now able to take personal revenge for the bombing of Warsaw, they were getting physically closer to Poland. 'My thoughts flew to Poland,' remembers the pilot of a Wellington closing in to bomb Rostock in April 1942. 'We were so near home, and yet so very far. I thought of my mother and father, and memories of my childhood with my brothers and sister brought a smile to my face.' Just then the navigator reported that they would be over the target too early, so the pilot took the plane on and crossed the Polish frontier for a moment. The whole crew gazed out into the night and felt better for it, even though they could see nothing. Many wished they could simply fly on after releasing their bombs and land somewhere in Poland. 'Which of us does not dream of such a flight?' admitted one bomber pilot. 'There are some among us who have already worked out the course and the flying time to the nearest minute.'

Losses mounted steeply with these attacks on the German heartland, and the chances of surviving a tour of duty went down to one in four. In 1941 alone, the four Polish bomber squadrons lost 244 men, representing about two-thirds of their effectives.

Fresh crews came and took their places, keeping the four squadrons at full strength, so that by the second half of 1941 the Poles made up one-sixth of the RAF's effective bomber force. They did not lack recognition. On 27 January 1941 the King and Queen once again visited 300 and 301 at Swinderby, where they were subjected to a snack of herrings and vodka; on 13 June the Duke of Kent visited 304 and 305 at Syerston; and telegrams of congratulation and citations regularly arrived from Bomber Command and the Air Ministry. On 14 July all four squadrons paraded at the cemetery at Newark, where so many of their colleagues were buried, in the presence of President Władysław Raczkiewicz and Prime Minister General Sikorski, who laid wreaths. Two days later, Sikorski ceremonially handed over to 300 the new standard of the Polish Air Force.

The story of this standard is as extraordinary as the story of the Polish Air Force itself. It had been conceived in the head of a fighter pilot, while he was sitting around at Lyon late in 1939. He felt that the Polish Air Force should have a standard made in Poland, and he wrote to a friend in Soviet-occupied Wilno, suggesting the idea. The friend engaged the help of a priest and some nuns, who began collecting money and material for the enterprise with remarkable ingenuity – by a tortuous process silk and gold thread were procured from Berlin. Soon a small group of women were busy embroidering in the secrecy of a convent chapel next to the miraculous shrine of the Virgin of Ostra Brama. The standard figured the likeness of the Virgin and bore the inscription 'Wilno 1940' and a quotation from St Theresa: 'Love demands sacrifice'. When the standard was ready it was smuggled out through Lithuania via Berlin to Sweden in the baggage of an unsuspecting Japanese officer. From Sweden it was brought to London, where it arrived in March 1941. It was decided that the standard would be carried by every squadron in rotation for a period of three months, and 300, the first to be formed in Great Britain, had the honour of keeping it initially.

The legend on the standard, 'Love demands sacrifice', could hardly have been more appropriate, as the coming year was to show. On 23 February 1942 Air Marshal Arthur Harris took over as head of Bomber Command. It was his intention to carry the war into the heart of Germany and paralyse German industry by intensive bombing. This demanded continual raids by large formations of bombers whenever weather conditions permitted.

The four Polish squadrons, mustering up to 76 crews, represented as much as 25 per cent of Harris's total force at this stage, and they were therefore heavily engaged over Germany on most nights, and in mine-laying off Brest, St-Nazaire, Lorient and other ports by day. In addition, 18 OTU at Bramcote could supply up to 24 more crews, and when, on 30 May, Harris launched the first 1,000-plane raid on Cologne, 101 of the bombers were manned by Polish crews.

Since such operations were still in their infancy, the first part of the year was inevitably a period of experimentation and development of bombing techniques, and as a result losses were very heavy. In April alone, the four squadrons made 352 sorties and lost 13 crews, a total of 78 men. The enthusiasm of the men was dented. A groan would go up in the operations room when a target in the Ruhr was announced, and by the summer of 1942 morale was beginning to flag. The temptation to funk the job was enormous. 'It was terribly tempting to just dump the bombs anywhere and turn back,' admits Zbigniew Bobiński, a pilot with 305. 'There was just one problem: you knew you'd have to live with that for the rest of your life.' Nevertheless, there were cases where nerve snapped and bombs were dropped short.

Such intensity of operations demanded not only great courage and physical endurance, but also nerves of steel. The dangers were self-evident: apart from being blown to bits by enemy flak, the men could be killed by the bullets of a night-fighter, roasted alive in a burning plane, killed on impact with the ground, or drowned in the sea, with German captivity as the least of the evils. Even if they did not fall prey to the enemy, they still ran all kinds of risks.

Instruments sometimes failed, and navigators were not beyond mixing up their calculations. A plane could lose its bearings and find itself in a black chasm, not knowing which way to go or where to land. The navigator of one of 305's Wellingtons admitted to being utterly lost on the homeward run of a bombing raid, so the pilot flew on what he believed to be a north-westerly course until, he calculated, he must be approaching England. He took the plane down through the clouds and saw a coastline coming up. Assuming it to be that of England, he crossed it and started looking for airfield beacons. Having spotted one, he fired a green flare. He was answered with a green flare and the runway lights came on, so he came in to land. As the Wellington was finishing its run and taxiing towards the control tower, the navigator suddenly nudged him and said: 'Hello, they're wearing the wrong caps.' The pilot let out a string of curses, slammed the plane around and gave it full throttle. They took off diagonally across the airfield and got airborne, just clearing some low buildings and pursued by a hail of machine-gun fire from the Germans, who had clearly been as taken aback as they were.

Until a plane had actually touched down and stopped on its own airfield, nobody could be sure that the danger was over, for some piece of shrapnel could easily pierce a fuel tank or damage the undercarriage mechanism. Crash-landing a heavy plane was a risky business. The Wellington was an old war-horse that could take an astonishing degree of punishment and still get home. Machines would regularly return to base, 'tattered like the pants of an old tramp who had been attacked by a pack of mongrels', as one airman put it.

Flight Sergeant Pietrach, commander of Wellington B for Baby of 301, was an experienced pilot with a good crew: one night over St-Nazaire they had sustained hits from 30 pieces of shrapnel but still managed to shoot down a night-fighter that dared to attack them. Pietrach did not like taking unnecessary risks, and several times, having suffered minor damage, he had landed on the closest available airfield rather than make the whole journey back to Lincolnshire. This was considered bad form in the squadron, as it denied the crew a good sleep in their own beds, made the operations officer wait for his debriefing, and, perhaps most importantly, appeared to cast aspersions on the ground crew for not maintaining the plane well enough. So Pietrach was teased about his careful landings and his crew complained that they were being made to look silly. The next operation was a raid on Cologne, from which all the planes returned safely to Hemswell, except B for Baby. The station commander was anxious, but the other crews started bandying jokes about Pietrach, assuming that he had landed elsewhere. Then a crackly message came through the radio from Pietrach's Wellington. He announced that he was flying on one engine, that the tip of one of his wings had been blown off, that his petrol tanks were leaking, and that there was a fire raging in the navigator's cabin. He was ordered to land at the nearest airfield, which happened to be Spalding. As he was acknowledging, his radio gave out. Fifteen minutes later the station commander at Spalding telephoned Hemswell to say that a Wellington flying on one engine, with a piece of wing and strips of fuselage hanging off it, its bomb-bay doors open and flapping, had just overflown the airfield. Some minutes later Grantham rang with much the same story. The whole station at Hemswell then spilled out onto the airfield, and watched in amazement as B for Baby approached, its one engine misfiring and bits of aluminium and canvas flapping about it. As the plane came in to land, the entire tail fin came away and dragged behind it on a few wires. Pietrach landed his machine safely on its belly, and the crew emerged unhurt. There were no more jokes.

It was just as bad *not* being hit: waiting for the unexpected was an even greater strain than facing a murderous reality. 'Each flight exacted enormous nervous tension, as a result of which we were often dripping with sweat, even though the temperature in the cabin might be minus 30 degrees,' a bomber pilot remembers. It did not help to tell oneself that the plane was in good condition, or that the pilot was an experienced flier. The best, the most experienced, the fittest and the steadiest were wiped out just as easily as anyone else. On their return from the second 1,000-bomber raid, on Bremen, on 26 June 1941, one crew of 305 came down in the Channel. All were saved except for the second pilot, Group Captain Stanisław Skarzyński. Yet Skarzyński had flown the Atlantic solo in 1933.

There seemed to be no more to it than simple luck, or fate. And as a result, all forms of superstition flourished. Certain pubs, where too many crews had had their last drink on earth, were shunned. The Poles quickly adopted the British belief in Gremlins, enthusiastically adding varieties such as the 'Mess Gremlin' (which chalked up more drinks than one thought one had had) to the standard 'Fuel Gremlin' (which guzzled badly on the home run) and the 'Rubber Gremlin' (which feasted on the Wellington's tyres). The Wellingtons were cluttered with holy pictures, photographs of loved ones, rag dolls, teddy bears and a bewildering variety of lucky charms.

There was also 'mascot-fever', which developed when squadrons, flights, crews and even individual airmen began to vie with one another for the most distinctive creature. The most common mascots were dogs, either strays that had wandered on to the base or gifts from girl-friends. These creatures would hang about the dispersal huts or the hangars with the men, defying death a hundred times a day as they pottered about between starting planes and whirring propellers. A number of them were taken along on operations. There were also cats, at least one of which flew regularly, equipped with its own miniature parachute, and various birds such as sparrows and pigeons.

There were some decidedly odd mascots. One pilot of 303 had a pet monkey, and another had a grass-snake which lived up his sleeve. At one stage the Northolt mess began to resemble a menagerie, and all pets were barred. One Polish airman's quest for a distinctive mascot led him into the dock of a magistrate's court, as the *News Chronicle* reported on 4 June 1941. The man had chanced upon a large white duck, and promptly taken it back to the station, where he built a small pool for it. As it happened, the duck belonged to the local policeman, who recognized it as he was cycling by one day. The airman, a rear gunner with 301, was fined five shillings, but on hearing that he had shot down a German plane the previous week, the magistrate paid the fine on his behalf, and the policeman donated the duck to the squadron.

The psychology behind collecting mascots in this extraordinary way may not be entirely clear, but it was directly linked with the uncertainties of life, and therefore was much more prevalent among the bombers. It was not just that death was always present, it was also the very strangeness of death in a bomber squadron. In the army, people can usually see the death of a colleague, and as often as not they recover the body and bury it. In the air force, and particularly in bombers, the men rarely saw the death of their comrades. One minute they were drinking with them, and a few hours later they were reported 'missing'. On hearing such news, it was natural to start wondering what had happened to them and how they had died – if indeed they were dead. It was comparatively rare to see a plane actually blown up in front of one's eyes. It was therefore difficult to believe that those who had gone had actually died, and the haunting doubt only added to the strangeness of fate.

No quirk of fate could be stranger than that which saved one of 305's mascots, a little black mongrel called Ciapek (Spot). He had wandered on to the base one day and been adopted by the mechanics, who built a grandiose kennel for him just outside one of the hangars. He also hit it off with the crews, who took him along on bombing raids. From his collar hung carved miniature bombs, one for each raid he had been on. One night, the Wellington on which Ciapek was flying failed to return, and the crew, and Ciapek, were posted missing. A couple of months later, a policeman walking his beat along the waterfront at Cromer in Norfolk noticed something black washed up on the beach. On going to investigate, he found it to be a small dog with a collar ringed with little bombs and bearing the inscription '305 Polish Squadron, Syerston'. The animal seemed more dead than alive, and the local vet advised putting it down, but the policeman telephoned Syerston. The squadron had in the meantime moved to Lindholme, but as one of the Military Police corporals was going on two days' leave to Norfolk, he was instructed to fetch the dog and bring it back to Syerston.

'It was him all right,' recalled the Military Police sergeant, 'but the poor little tyke was just about on his last legs . . . the first day he didn't move off the blanket we'd put him on, and was sick after he ate anything. The second night he got up and wandered down to "B" hangar with one of our patrols but came back very depressed and miserable. His kennel had gone and I suppose he couldn't find anyone who spoke his language, either.' The sergeant called Lindholme, whence a Wellington was promptly despatched to collect Ciapek. When three Polish officers walked into the guardhouse at Syerston, the mongrel immediately got up and wagged its tail. They proceeded to attach another bomb to his collar before bearing him back to the squadron. Ciapek recovered fully, but nobody ever discovered what had happened to the six members of the crew.

The loss of a crew was often made all the more depressing by the quality of the men involved. On 1 November 1942 one of 304's Wellingtons went down in the sea and the whole crew were lost. The pilot, Stanisław Krawczyk, had been hit badly over Germany once, and had ordered his crew to bale out. The rear gunner had forgotten to take his parachute, so Krawczyk gave him his own, and remained at the controls of the plane, which he miraculously managed to nurse back over the coast and crash-land. The co-pilot, Ignacy Skorobohaty, was a veteran flier who had seen combat in 1920. The navigator, Aloizy Szkuta, had been shot down over Belgium once, had reached Spain on foot, been captured, escaped, and walked to Gibraltar. The radio operator had escaped from German-occupied Poland and reached England after many trying adventures. The loss of people such as these was tragic. It was also irreparable: the RAF could endlessly replenish its forces, the Polish Air Force could not. And it was bound to affect morale.

'A British plane fails to return. Who knows about it? Only the immediate circle of one Allied squadron out of a thousand,' writes one airman. 'A Polish plane is posted missing. Who knows about it? Everyone! Every one of our squadrons, every unit, every Polish base!' Most of the Polish airmen, fighters and bombers alike, had been through the same schools in Poland, they had subsequently been moved around between the six air regiments, and they were anyway a far smaller force than the RAF. The long trek from Poland, the chance encounters at Beirut, Marseille or Casablanca, and finally their meeting up in Britain, had strengthened this familiarity, and by 1942 the Polish Air Force did behave more and more like some huge family. And it felt with much the same intensity as a family, so the blood-letting affected it particularly deeply.

A Growing Family

THE POLISH RANK-AND-FILE regarded General Sikorski as more than just their commander. For this wandering people he was also something of a father-figure. And he was certainly very sensitive to their needs and their moods. He was, perhaps, most concerned for his air force, which, on account of its high degree of specialization, was his least expendable asset, and the most severely exposed to attrition. In 1942 alone the Polish bomber force had lost 89 planes, with 291 men killed, 16 missing and 91 captured. A further 39 died in the course of training, bringing the total up to 437 men, or 72 crews, virtually 100 per cent of the effective strength of the four squadrons. One man in five survived.

The Polish Air Force could not sustain such haemorrhage. In Britain it was cut off from its natural pool of manpower and could only make losses good from existing reserves. As early as July 1940 Sikorski had set up a recruiting office in Canada, and he later did likewise in the United States and Argentina. Over 500 Americans of Polish descent volunteered for the air force in the first two years of the war. But many of them later transferred to the USAAF – a flight sergeant in the USAAF was paid more than a wing-commander in the Polish Air Force, and no agreement had been reached with the British government on pensions for Polish airmen. Another 485 volunteers came forward from other countries around the world. In 1942 a further 1,500 Polish Air Force personnel, interned in Russia in 1939 and freed under the Polish–Soviet treaty of 1941, arrived via the Middle East. As many as 525 prisoners-of-war, Poles pressed into German ranks, joined the air force, in spite of British opposition. There was also a steady trickle of volunteers from the Polish land forces. But although the air force gained some 7,900 men to its ranks between October 1940 and May 1945, it lost about 3,300 of its best cadres killed, missing or seconded to other arms. The dwindling human resources had to be husbanded carefully. This went hand-in-hand with Sikorski's plans to build up the comprehensive experience and all the ancillary services needed to provide Poland with a functional air force by the end of the war.

In May 1942, 304, which had lost six of its crews in the space of a couple of weeks, was transferred to Coastal Command in order to save it from annihilation and to allow it to acquire new skills. Their first posting was to the island of Tiree, beyond Mull on the west coast of Scotland. This came as something of a shock to the men. Apart from the makeshift airfield there was nothing on the island except a few bothies. What English they had mastered was useless with the natives. Gale force winds whistled through the tin huts in which they were housed and between the fingers of the mechanics who had to service the planes out in the open, and occasionally flipped over a Wellington as it taxied along the ground. An additional hazard came from sheep straying on to the runway. The task was an entirely novel one, requiring a whole range of hitherto unknown skills, but the men went to work with a will. Only a couple of weeks after their arrival they sighted what they took to be a U-boat, and bombed the guts out of an unsuspecting shark. The work was monotonous and dangerous – the squadron lost a crew over the North Atlantic in the first month – and they were relieved to be moved to Dale in South Wales in June.

The squadron remained with Coastal Command for the rest of the war, operating mostly from Predannack and St Eval in Cornwall, with occasional stints at other bases, all of them hangar-less and uncomfortable. Most of their time was spent sweeping the Bay of Biscay hunting for submarines setting out from the French ports. Such sorties lasted between eight and twelve hours, testing endurance and alertness, and were both extremely monotonous and highly demanding on navigators and pilots, as it was comparatively easy to stray from a course and lose one's bearings, and by no means easy to find them again. Sightings of U-boats were rare, and successful attacks rarer still. However fast his reactions, a pilot could not change course, dive and attack in under two minutes from spotting an enemy craft. A submarine could dive in less than that, and usually sighted the approaching plane before being spotted itself. It was therefore very unusual to be able to attack before the U-boat dived. Even when depth-charges were dropped on the diving U-boat, it was usually impossible to tell whether it had been sunk or damaged, or how badly. In 1943 the squadron was given Wellington XIVs, specially designed for sub-hunting and equipped with anti-surface-vessel radar, Leigh lights and other aids which permitted them to hunt at night, but this did not improve chances greatly. In the three years the squadron spent with Coastal Command, it made 2,451 sorties, but only attacked 31 German submarines.

To add to the strain of these operations, ditching in the sea was not much of an option. The huge Leigh lights halfway down the bellies of the Wellington XIVs made it virtually impossible to put the plane down on the water – the protrusion had the effect of breaking up the plane when this was tried – while even a success-ful ditching in the Bay of Biscay was most unlikely to end in rescue. And the lone Wellingtons were frequently attacked by German fighters, usually on the homeward run as they were passing the Breton peninsula, on their last reserves of energy and alertness. The Wellingtons were easy prey for small groups of fighters, and many were shot down. But there were some miracu-lous escapes, won by sheer determination.

On 16 September 1942 Wellington 'Ela' was set upon by no fewer than six German fighters near the Spanish coast, but managed to shoot down one, damage a second, and shake off the remaining four. The pilot, Stanisław Targowski, was recom-mended for the DFC, and the signal that he had been awarded it came through two weeks later, while he was again out on patrol. His comrades prepared a surprise party – which was to be a double celebration, as news had also come through that his wife, whom he had heard nothing of since 1939, was safe and would soon be arriving in England. But Wellington 'Ela' did not return from patrol.

On 9 February 1943 Flight Lieutenant Eugeniusz Ladro's Wellington was jumped by four fighters. They came at him again and again, but he dodged and swerved so cannily that, although they knocked out his front gunner and caused minor damage, they did not hit his plane in any vital place. After 58 minutes of fighting the Germans had run out of ammunition, and they came up alongside in formation and dipped their wings in salute before flying back to base.

The results of the squadron's three years of sub-hunting look paltry: of the 31 submarines attacked, only two were destroyed, two badly damaged and three slightly damaged for certain, while the results of the other attacks could not be verified. This was achieved at a cost of 106 dead and 14 planes. Yet it has to be remembered that, since every U-boat could sink hundreds of thousands of tons of shipping and wipe out thousands of lives, even such a seemingly disappointing result was a valuable addition to the war effort. Perhaps more important was the fact that the continual patrols prevented the U-boats from spending much time on the surface, which they needed to do in order to recharge their batteries. As a result of being kept submerged so much of the time, their effectiveness was greatly reduced. And from the point of view of the Polish Air Force, the great advantage was that the squadron was no longer bleeding to death, like its sister squadrons still engaged in bombing Germany.

On 31 March 1943, 301 Bomber Squadron was dissolved. Seven of its crews were seconded to 138 Special Duties Squadron based at Tempsford. This unit, in which three Polish crews had been flying since the autumn of 1941, was run by the Special Operations Executive (SOE) and specialized in transporting people, cash and arms in and out of occupied Europe. By swelling the Polish presence in the squadron, and making 301's forceful commander Roman Rudkowski liaison officer, Sikorski was hoping to engage SOE more actively in the Polish cause. Rudkowski had already flown a Halifax on the 2,000-mile round-trip to Poland in November 1941, in order to show that it could be done.

The trip took up to fourteen hours, and could only be undertaken on moonlit nights with perfect atmospheric conditions along the whole route. All too often the planes had to turn back half-way because of worsening weather, and then wait for another promising night. This had the effect of magnifying all the tensions and frustrations, as well as the unsettling division of life into alternating spells of fear and boredom that characterized bomber work, producing a greater sense of desperation in these crews. 'The normal trip meant leaving Tempsford in daylight to arrive at the Skagerrak just after dark,' writes Frank Griffiths, who commanded a flight in 138, 'then they quickly nipped across the tip of Sweden, got a fix on Bornholm, and when Poland was reached it was a question again of navigation by moonlight and water, though the illuminated POW camps did help. Because of fuel shortage the route back had to be shorter, so a dash across Denmark between Kiel and Flensburg was the ordained route. Not with the Polish crews, however. They would streak across Germany at nought feet, shooting up trains and generally causing mayhem. They were always out of ammunition on their return and they generally arrived back somewhat early because a longer, safer route did not appeal to them.' He found them self-willed and trying, and could not grasp why they were so 'difficult'. And he was never quite sure whether they were being pig-headed or whether they had simply misunderstood his orders.

'The crews were to carry out some drops in France and I was to follow them across the Channel from Brighton to the estuary near Le Crotoy, then inland to the great forest of Crécy. We knew that there was light flak on the French coast and the briefing was to cross the Channel at wave height and to climb quickly to 7,000 feet just before the coast, then drop down to 250 feet as soon as we got to the Forest of Crécy. I knew that the light flak wouldn't touch us as 7,000 feet. We took off one after the other and I had the exhaust flames of the two Polish aircraft in sight ahead of me when crossing the Channel. When the time came to "jump" the flak the Poles made no attempt to gain height. I climbed and soon lost sight of them. Then we could see ahead of us and below a stream of tracer and suddenly an enormous fire. Both Poles had gone in at deck level with guns blazing. The first was shot down and all the crew killed, but the second aircraft was lucky.'

The squadron operated as a whole, and non-Polish crews flew to Poland while Polish crews made drops in France, Norway, Austria and Czechoslovakia. During the whole of 1942, only 21 flights (one-fifth of the total number made by the squadron) were to Poland. In 1943 this went up to 55 flights, but Poland remained a low priority for SOE. This annoyed the Poles, who made up more than a third of the unit's fliers. 'Integrated in every respect into a British unit, we are undervalued and our enthusiasm is misunderstood,' wrote one of them in a report to the Polish Inspectorate on 2 February 1942. 'We are treated as a necessary evil, some quirk of the Anglo-Polish agreement. From the way the British behave towards us and the way in which they service the planes allocated to us, it is difficult to reach any conclusion other than that we are viewed as intruders.'

The reinforcement of the Polish element in the squadron in March 1943 did little to ease the friction, and in November the Polish crews were withdrawn from 138, formed up into 1586 Polish Special Duties Flight and posted first to Tunis and later to Brindisi in Italy, where they were better placed to carry assistance to Poland. In spite of the restrictions imposed by meteorological conditions, they flew a total of 423 missions to Poland and 912 to other countries, delivering 1,577 tons of equipment and 693 people. Most of the deliveries were made by parachute, but on occasion their planes would land on improvised airstrips lit up with stable-lamps by reception squads of the Polish underground army. These landings were always risky, as the plane had to get airborne again and the reception detachments had to melt away with the supplies and personnel before the Germans located them. And it was not uncommon for the overloaded Dakotas used for this type of operation to get bogged down in soft turf. These sorties were carried out in close collaboration with the air force units of the Polish underground. These consisted of airmen who had failed to get out in 1939, supplemented with a few escaped POWs and, later, with air force officers sent in from Britain. These units regularly reported on *Luftwaffe* movements. They also included aeronautical engineers, who monitored German secret weapons testing from 1941 onwards and eventually retrieved a whole flying bomb, which was transported to London.

The dissolution of 301 Squadron and the transfer of 304 to Coastal Command left only two Polish squadrons on Bomber Command's strength: 300 and 305, both stationed at Ingham. Improvements in bombing techniques and equipment perfected over the previous year had the desired effect of saving lives. In 1943 the Polish bombers flew 1,306 missions, well over half as many again as in 1942, and lost 132 aircrew, less than half the 398 lost in 1942. Sikorski had achieved his aim of reducing the death-toll while at the same time widening the participation of his men in the RAF's war effort, and he continued to pursue this aim.

With the fall-off in German raids over Britain, 307 Night-fighter Squadron was redeployed to other duties. It was equipped with the all-wood De Havilland Mosquito fighter-bomber, the fastest plane in the air, with a range of 1,500 miles, boasting such luxuries as radar and a heated cockpit. The squadron now flew Intruder missions, night-time raids on enemy targets, and Ranger daytime sweeps. Then, from Predannack in Cornwall, it joined in the Battle of the Atlantic, patrolling the Bay of Biscay to protect Allied shipping and sub-hunters from German fighters.

Similarly, 309 Fighter-Reconnaissance Squadron was redeployed to carry out operations over France and Holland, and another, 318 Fighter-Reconnaissance, was formed at Detling in 1943. It was intended for co-operation with General Anders's forces in the Middle East, and was sent to Palestine, whence it followed the Polish Second Corps to Egypt and then throughout the Italian campaign. It was during this campaign, in September 1944, that the last Polish unit in the RAF, 663 Artillery Observation Squadron, was formed.

In the interests of broadening the experience of his fighters, Sikorski also persuaded the Air Ministry to allow a group of them to be sent to join the Western Desert Fighter Wing in Egypt, which was operating against the German and Italian forces under General Erwin Rommel. The 15 pilots chosen were led by Stanisław Skalski, twenty-eight years old, an impulsive, determined and often quarrelsome man, but a good fighter. On arrival in North Africa in February 1943 the Polish Fighting Team, or 'Skalski's Circus', as it quickly became known, was attached to RAF 145 Squadron, a curious assemblage of volunteers from Ireland, Canada, New Zealand, Argentina, South Africa, Rhodesia and Trinidad. It was commanded by Squadron Leader Lance Wade, known as 'the Arizona wildcat', an American who had volunteered for the RAF in 1940. They were a battle-hardened unit not likely to be impressed by the new arrivals.

The airfield at Bu Grara, where a transport plane disgorged Skalski and his men, was no more than a strip of flattened land, surrounded by tents. There were no hangars, and the station command, operations room, mess and living quarters were all accommodated in tents, which provided little shelter from the burning sun during the day, and no comfort against the intense cold of the desert night. The camp-beds with which they had been issued were made of poor quality wood, and the struts regularly snapped in the middle of the night, spilling the occupant on to the hard desert sand. There was hardly any water, and washing had to be done in the sea. Rations consisted of bully-beef and dry biscuits, and only occasionally was it possible to buy fresh eggs or a scrawny chicken from the locals, in return for some piece of equipment. There was no whisky in the 'mess'. Above all, there were sand and flies everywhere, in their food, their water, their clothes, their eyes and their mouths.

Skalski's team were issued with the new Spitfire IXs and became operational on 13 March 1943, when six of them went up on patrol for the first time. The early days passed without any contact with the enemy, but matters picked up after a couple of weeks, and there was plenty of action during the Allied offensive against the Mareth Line. The Polish pilots quickly won the recognition of their colleagues. On 2 April, while supporting the advance of the New Zealanders, they shot down three Messerschmitts, and bagged two more on 4 April. On 20 April a flight of six planes shot down six German fighters, and repeated the score two days later. By 12 May when the Axis forces in North Africa surrendered, Skalski's men had in a period of just under two months destroyed 25 enemy planes, with 3 probables and 9 damaged, at the cost of one of their own planes shot down (the pilot survived).

Western Desert Air Force Command decided to dissolve the Polish Fighting Team, as they considered such a concentration of talent and experience wasteful, and proposed that the Polish pilots be given command of British squadrons. Only three of the Poles took up the offer: Skalski, who took over 601, Horbaczewski, who took command of 43 Squadron, and Władysław Drecki, who took over a flight in 152 Squadron. The rest preferred to go back to Polish units, even if it meant forfeiting a command.

Polish fighter pilots also acquired a range of experience with the Americans. Four of them were seconded to Hub Zemke's 56 Fighter 'Crack Group', but here they passed on more than they picked up. 'I might say that if each and every one of my officers possessed the determination these Polish officers displayed, a much greater material value and gain could be attained by my Group,' Zemke wrote in his valedictory letter. Witold Urbanowicz was asked by the USAAF to tour America and lecture to trainee pilots. In the spring of 1943 he met General Claire Chennault, commander of 14 Air Force in China, known as 'The Flying Tigers'. The two aces hit it off and Urbanowicz wangled a posting to southern China in August 1943. He flew with several units, and commanded a section of the prestigious 75th Squadron. 'We were an élite outfit in China and we knew it,' writes Myron Levy, the squadron's adjutant. 'To be in the 75th was something special. We accepted Group Captain Urbanowicz with a degree of reservation. We had seen some of these European heroes fall flat on their butts. Not Urbanowicz. He measured up fast and we were proud that he was one of us.' He brought his Battle of Britain experience to bear against the Japanese Zero fighters, and taught his men the Polish practice of continual looking, or 'rubber-necking' as they called it. By the time he came back to Britain in early 1944, he had added 2 Japanese planes to his score.

The high-profile exploits of these units and individuals can only give a faint idea of the importance of the Polish Air Force's contribution. By 1943 the RAF had an impressive collection of European squadrons fighting alongside it. The Free French supplied 5, the Czechs 4, the Greeks 2, the Norwegians 2, the Dutch 2, and the Belgians 1 – a total of 16. The Polish Air Force mustered 15 squadrons, all with their full complement of ground staff, unlike most of the other Allied units. But even this only accounted for a fraction of its war effort.

Pilots, however old, were loath to sit behind desks and did everything to get airborne again after regulation tours of duty. 'I felt like a drug addict whose opium-pipe had been snatched from his lips,' wrote one when he was grounded after 111 operations. And almost a quarter of the entire Polish Air Force personnel were pilots. The area that inevitably benefited from this was Air Transport Auxiliary, a civilian pilot pool, and Transport Command. If a pilot could not, for reasons of age, injury or fulfilled tours of duty, get a posting to a front-line squadron, he would avoid a desk job by joining one of the Polish units within these. The first had been founded in the autumn of 1940 within the RAF's ferry system. It consisted of some 300 older flying personnel and LOT pilots, who delivered new planes from factories to airfields and moved around planes needed on other stations. They might fly a Tiger Moth, a Wellington, a Spitfire and a Blenheim one after the other in the course of a single day, and one pilot calculated that he had flown twenty different types of plane and landed on fifty different airfields within two months.

Another Polish Transport group was sent to Takoradi on the Gold Coast to keep Middle East Command supplied with aircraft. The only reliable supply route between Britain and Egypt was by sea round the Cape of Good Hope and then up the eastern coast of Africa and through the Suez Canal. But this was a long journey, and ships were vulnerable to U-boat attack at every stage of it. Instead, planes were sent by sea from Britain as far as West Africa, whence they were flown to Cairo, a distance of 6,000 miles over jungle and desert, with refuelling stops at small airfields along the way. From Cairo the pilots would return along the same route to Takoradi by passenger plane or converted bomber.

It was a dull job for the pilots, as they would set off in flotillas of planes of all kinds, and they had nothing to do except follow the leader and keep on course. The monotony induced drowsiness, and the journey was not free of danger. The planes were new, so teething troubles could easily develop in the engine or equipment. The Saharan wind, the *Hamsin,* blew up such clouds of sand that even at a high altitude the flotilla might suddenly find itself in a thick brown fog. They occasionally lost their bearings or crash-landed in jungle or desert. Survivors of a crash were unlikely to be picked up before they died of thirst, or snakebite. The usual dangers of Africa were ever-present whenever they touched down. They found scorpions in their shoes and their beds, snakes curled inside cockpits, and leopards prowling the airfield. In spite of taking regular doses of quinine, the pilots often went down with malaria or yellow fever in the unhealthy climate of the Gold Coast.

Life at Takoradi was not without its pleasures. Instead of WAAFs, and orderlies bringing morning tea, black boys served them pineapple juice. The pilots kept pet monkeys or even lion cubs, and some bought themselves 'wives' for the duration. One Polish airman purchased his, a fourteen year old girl, for £4 10s. and grew extremely fond of her. At Kano, the first refuelling stop, black girls would line up on the edge of the runway and sell themselves for two shillings. At Fort Adi, a small airfield in French Equatorial Africa, the black policemen would as a matter of course bring girls from the village to pilots spending a night there. One airman remembers that when he complained that the girl he had been brought was dirty, the French station commander obligingly lent him one of his own three, who were freshly scrubbed every night for him.

Sometimes they would have to wait for days in the baking heat of Khartoum airfield, but at others they might find themselves relaxing in the elegant ambience of the luxurious hotel at Wadi Halfa. And at the end of the journey lay the amusements and fleshpots of Cairo. In 1941 the Takoradi unit was renamed Polish Air Force Detachment Middle East, and based in Cairo. The headquarters, mess and accommodation was a cruise-ship moored on the Nile, and this was the venue for many a party. The city was the social as well as the military nexus at the mid-point between Britain and India, and it was also swamped by refugees, combatant and non-combatant, from Eastern Europe, the Balkans and the Middle East. This 'café society in khaki', as someone dubbed it, was strangely unaffected by the war which ebbed and flowed in the desert nearby, and although the night-clubs were reputed to be dens of spies and the red-light district was officially out of bounds, everyone contrived to have a good time.

A major attraction of the Takoradi run was its mercantile potential, as Cairo was also a vast emporium for luxury goods. Snakeskins which could be bought in Kano for five shillings fetched three or four pounds in Cairo. Diamonds, trickling illegally out of southern Africa, were easy to buy in Takoradi or at one of the stops along the way, where local traders and black-marketeers would materialize out of the desert or the jungle as if by magic whenever the planes landed. The same diamonds fetched several times their purchase price in Cairo. The trade worked the other way, too. Workers in the gold mines of the Gold Coast regularly stole ore but lacked the mercury with which to separate the gold from it. Pilots would buy mercury in Cairo, sell it to the locals in Takoradi, and then buy the resulting gold, which they would resell at enormous profit in Cairo.

On reaching Khartoum, one batch of pilots was instructed to leave the planes, which were to be picked up and taken on to Cairo by other pilots. The angry Polish pilots were crammed into a Hudson transport plane which was supposed to take them back to Takoradi, but it crashed on take-off, killing all passengers. As they retrieved the bodies, the Khartoum station officers found pockets bulging with diamonds and gold nuggets, and the secret was out. All pilots bringing planes into Cairo were henceforth searched on landing at Heliopolis; this was inconvenient, but the Poles then found ways of developing 'engine trouble' as an excuse to land at some other airfield, where there were no checks.

These less-than-glorious distractions could not obscure the fact that the Takoradi run was a trying, dangerous job, requiring real flying skills. 'In pre-war days such a flight would have excited the admiration of the world, but every week for two years Allied pilots have braved the perilous journey,' *The Times* reported on 26 October 1943. 'So well have the Poles carried out their job that to date they have flown more than 1,000 aircraft over this

West African route with only 2 per cent loss, a striking tribute to their skill and endurance, for it is one of the most testing flights ever made.'

Most of the pilots, desperate for combat postings, were disqualified by age or some disability. They included General Rayski, the pre-war commander of the Polish Air Force, determined to remain in active service, but far too old for any other job. One group was briefly allowed to make up a flight in 112 Fighter Squadron RAF in Libya, but their fighting skills were as nothing to their piloting experience and this was at a premium over the jungles and deserts, which were quite as testing and potentially dangerous as air combat. Of the 115 pilots and 5 navigators who served on the Takoradi run over the three years, 20 were killed. And death could be agonizingly drawn-out, as the note found on the body of Flight Sergeant Mikołajczak, lying in the shade of the wing of his crashed plane in the desert, illustrates:

I doubt if I shall live till morning, I am getting weaker and weaker every minute. I have only three more gulps of water and I have such a terrible thirst. I should go somewhere, but where? I am completely lost. Good-bye, we shall meet where we all have to go one day. Please see that the little money I have is handed to my parents. I am dying thinking of them and Poland. I give myself up to God. Time, 20.00 hours, 9 May [. . .]

Time 12.00 hrs, 10 May. It is terribly hot. I drink, or rather lick my scanty sweat. I am suffering terribly.

13.45 hrs – I hear an aircraft flying to the south, to my right, my last hope; I cannot get up to have a look. My last minutes . . . God have mercy on me.

There were also Polish flights operating in 45 Transport Group in Canada, delivering new planes from North America to Britain, North Africa and the Middle East, the so-called 'Atlantic Bridge', and another within 229 Transport Group which delivered planes to India and Burma. In addition, there were Poles in 216 Group in the Middle East, 511 Squadron at Lyneham, which transported personnel and equipment to the Far East, in 84 Spare Pilots Group, as well as six pilots, three navigators and three radio operators flying for BOAC. In all, Polish pilots in various branches of transport had made 23,202 flights, ferried 12,634 planes and carried 25,187 people by the end of the war.

Among the first volunteers for transport duties in the summer of 1940 were three women: Anna Łęska, Barbara Wojtulanis, and Jadwiga Piłsudska, daughter of Marshal Piłsudski. Anna Łęska carried out several liaison missions in the September 1939 campaign, and had flown out to Rumania at its close. There, she and Barbara Wojtulanis had worked as couriers smuggling papers and money into camps, and both of them later worked in the Polish Air Force administration in Paris. When she reached Britain, she volunteered as a ferry pilot and flew hundreds of planes around the country in all weathers over the next four years, a job requiring reserves of endurance and courage as well as skill.

It is less easy to summarize the contribution, and to evaluate the skill, endurance and courage, of the men involved in training of one sort or another. In addition to the fighter OTUs, there was 18 Bomber OTU at Bramcote, with a staff of 84 officers and 580 other ranks by January 1942. As the volume of men coming forward for training declined, 18 OTU was reduced, and incorporated into the RAF training centre at Finningley in March 1943. In May 1945 it was closed down, having trained a total of 2,186 bomber crew. In 1942 a technical school was set up at Halton, and a Coastal Command school at Silloth. In 1943 a staff college was established at Peebles (moved to Weston-super-Mare in the spring of 1944). These Polish centres trained a total of 4,434 aircrew, including 1,665 pilots. Polish pilots withdrawn after long tours of combat duty or waiting for postings to front-line units also served in British training units of one sort or another – some were even engaged in towing sleeves for the Royal Artillery to practise their anti-aircraft gunnery.

Flying was only a small part of the Polish Air Force's activity. Each squadron had its own full complement of ground crew, and behind them stood thousands of others who remained earthbound. There was a Polish barrage balloon unit, formed in December 1940, consisting of 155 officers and men, which took part in the defence of Glasgow and later of London. But most of the Polish Air Force's personnel did not even have this tenuous link with the air. Blackpool, still the recruitment centre and concentration point for the Polish Air Force in Britain, also had a ground crew training centre. In 1942 four Mobile Maintenance

Units were set up, and 1944 saw the creation of a Vehicle Maintenance Unit, eight Communications Units and one Meteorological Unit. In 1945 a Polish airfield construction squadron was formed.

Where it was not possible to build up independent Polish units, Sikorski placed small groups or individual men in British units in order to train up cadres in every field. So Poles served as instructors on a variety of specialized courses, in operations rooms and flight-control centres, and some 300 Polish engineers and experts were assigned to British aircraft factories. After its initial reticence, the RAF learned to pick out and make use of qualified Poles in any position. Sometimes, this could give rise to curious situations.

Jerzy Kaliniecki, a technical officer with the Warsaw Fighter Brigade in 1939 and from 1941 with 305 Squadron, was in 1942 appointed Station Maintenance Officer for two airfields in Lincolnshire. He then went on to work for Bomber Command at High Wycombe, and was given the job of inspecting airfields throughout the country and reporting on their condition and management. He was much younger than most of the station commanders and technical officers whose stations he was called upon to inspect, and his English was elementary. 'At first, I could see that the Englishmen were not pleased to find a Pole in such a senior position, but in a relatively short space of time, by dint of diplomacy and holding my ground on practical matters, relations became very good,' he recalls.

Towards the end of 1942, partly in order to boost the number of men available for combat and other strenuous duties, and partly in order to emulate the singularly successful WAAF, the Polish Air Force Inspectorate decided to create a women's service. In March 1943 the Air Ministry gave its assent, and in April the first 36 volunteers were accepted and underwent training at Wilmslow near Manchester at the hands of the WAAF. They came from places as distant as America, China and Africa, with the largest influx from the Middle East. These were women who had been deported to Russian gulags in 1939 and released at the end of 1941 as a result of the Polish–Soviet pact.

A total of 1,436 women had joined the Polish Women's Auxiliary Air Service by the end of the war. Many of those who had been through the gulags were in terrible condition. Two years of near-starvation and hard labour had undermined their constitution, diseases such as tuberculosis and cholera had left permanent damage, and frost-bite had ravaged hands and feet. Some had also suffered nervous and psychological damage as a result of seeing their whole families killed by either the Soviets or starvation. These were of limited use to the Polish Air Force, and the service acted as something of a refuge for them, but the majority did prove their worth.

After learning English and basic military jargon, they were trained in a variety of specialities. As well as cooks, waitresses and cleaners, the Polish Women's Service supplied telephonists, radio operators, drivers, aircraft fitters, parachute packers, typists, operations room personnel, nurses and quartermasters. The idea was that they should replace men wherever possible, freeing them for active service. Alicja Kaliniecka, one of the original 36, worked in intelligence and operations rooms. 'I think, on balance, that we proved our usefulness,' she says.

The women were mostly used to replace WAAFs at Polish airfields, such as Ingham and Faldingworth, but their arrival did not meet with enthusiasm on the part of the Polish airmen, who had grown used to the pretty and flirtatious WAAFs, with whom they would carry on undemanding relationships based on the minimal conversation allowed by language difficulties. The arrival of the Polish women proved something of a shock. Their attitude was not quite so easygoing. Years of suffering in Russia weighed heavily on them. Their desire to join the service was dictated not, as so often in the case of the WAAFs, by a sense of adventure, but by ardent patriotism. 'I wanted to return to Poland in uniform,' explains one. The Polish girls were so keen to prove their military prowess that they overdid the strictness. 'There were no locks tumbling onto collars, no dishevelled hairdos and there was no coquettish slanting of caps,' one of their officers writes proudly. Worst of all for the airmen, they had to watch their language, and could no longer treat the women on the base as dumb girls provided for their pleasure. But after some initial readjustment they began to appreciate the possibility of having a real conversation with someone of the opposite sex, and kindred feelings reasserted themselves, particularly when the girls learned to relax a little.

As well as women there were many children among the Poles released from the gulags under the Polish–Soviet Treaty of 1941 and subsequently brought to the Middle East by General Anders. These were taken under the wing of the Polish forces, and some 200 joined the Air Training School set up at Heliopolis in

February 1943. Here, as well as receiving a general education, they were put through the RAF 'Flight Mechanic' and 'Fitter' courses, so that they would be fully qualified by the time they reached school-leaving age. A second such school was opened a few months later at RAF Halton, and trained some 1,500 pupils aged between fifteen and seventeen. A third, specializing in radio and wireless, was opened at Cranwell in January 1944.

By the end of 1942, Sikorski had the makings of the comprehensive air force he craved – there was even a Polish Air Force ENSA troupe, a soccer team, an ice-hockey team and a boxing team, one of whose members won the Allied Services title in 1941. But he could not carry through the ultimate stage of his plan – to prise it away from the RAF while the war was still in progress, so as to be in a position to throw it into the Polish theatre of operations at a strategic moment. His Achilles' heel was a shortage of staff officers. He kept sending senior officers off to do stints with RAF staffs, and even seconded a total of 38 officers to various staff posts with the 9th USAAF, while a further 22 attended the American staff course at Fort Leavenworth. But the minute they could, the men would wangle a transfer to an active service unit. If they were too old to fly in combat, they would obtain a desk job at a front-line airfield, knowing that often they would be able to go on operations with the unit by squaring it with the commanding officer. So in spite of all his efforts, Sikorski never succeeded in creating the administrative backbone that would have permitted him to detach the Polish Air Force from the RAF.

In every other respect, by the end of 1942 it was a self-contained service increasingly independent of the RAF. Men starting their training after 1941 no longer bothered to learn any English beyond the few words needed on operations, as their entire training was done by Poles; and on a station such as Faldingworth, where every single man and woman of the 854-strong personnel was Polish, the need for any other language was minimal – though it has to be admitted that the Polish they used had been enriched with curious words such as *flajt* (flight), *sekszen* (section), *redynes* (readiness), *Haryken* (Hurricane) and *majtenans* (maintenance). Even in matters of command and discipline the Polish units were gradually adopting Polish practices, and this drift was formalized in April 1944, when a clause added to the Anglo-Polish Agreement brought the whole Polish Air Force under Polish military law rather than King's Regulations. Not surprisingly, this increasing self-containment and self-sufficiency had the effect of cutting the airmen off from their British colleagues, and from British life in general.

A whole Polish topography was gradually superimposed on the country, beginning with London. The seat of the Polish government was at Stratton House in Stratton Street off Piccadilly, the President's residence and chancellery were at Park Street in Mayfair, the Prime Minister's office was in a house rented from the Rothschilds in Palace Gardens Terrace – Millionaires' Row – in Kensington, the Polish General Staff had taken over the Rubens Hotel opposite the Royal Mews in Buckingham Palace Road, with the Polish Air Force Inspectorate just around the back in Prince's Row; the Polish Red Cross was in Belgrave Square, and a plethora of ministries and offices were housed mainly near the Polish Embassy in Portland Place and in the Queen's Gate area of Kensington. The busiest of these addresses was the military headquarters, and the London press reported that there was more hugging, kissing and waving of arms to be seen around the Rubens Hotel than in the whole of the rest of the British Isles.

On top of this, there were a number of social and cultural centres, as well as two large Polish clubs, the White Eagle opposite the French Embassy in Albert Gate and the Polish Hearth in Exhibition Road. A special club was opened for Polish airmen in August 1942 – financed, intriguingly, through a charity ball given by British butlers in New York. A number of restaurants, bars and coffee-houses with Polish connections were favoured by different sets. Zdzisław Radomski, a 306 pilot who lost his arm in a sweep over France, married and opened a bar off Baker Street much favoured by his colleagues.

Wherever there were large concentrations of Polish servicemen, there were similar landmarks. There was a Polish Hearth on the Promenade at Blackpool, a Polish Air Force Club in Nottingham, located in the basement of the Cathedral Hall and founded by the Red Cross and the Union of Catholic Mothers, and a special air force rest home in the spectacularly situated Rattray Castle at Craighall.

Blackpool remained the base-camp of the Polish Air Force, and that was where people waited for postings and returned after completed tours of duty. It therefore continued to bulge with Polish airmen, most of them with nothing to do. Richard Cobb remembers an unnatural society of men without women, without

children, with only a few creased photographs as evidence of a
broken past lived in another place. The older ones suffered both
because they could not forget families left in Poland and because
they found it more difficult to get postings. They would sit
around in gloomy formality trying to ignore the vulgarity and the
noisy exuberance that Blackpool managed to generate even in
wartime. Various schemes were thought up to distract them and
at the same time to promote Anglo-Polish relations, such as
sending them off in twos and threes to help with the harvest on
nearby farms. But most of the time they were to be found
hanging about, the older ones in hotel bars, the younger in pubs
or dance-halls, at the Tower and the Winter Garden.

There was much drinking, which led to brawls and fights with
comrades or British soldiers and sometimes with the police.
Gambling was also a disease in Blackpool, and the Trafalgar
Hotel on the Esplanade was a den 'in which cards rule from
morning till late at night'. There was also a good deal of sexual
promiscuity, with which some of the men filled the emptiness of
their lives. One airman referred to Blackpool as 'the centre of
moral degradation and sexual depravity'. Polish airmen were frequently cited as co-respondents in the Blackpool divorce courts.
Much of this stemmed from intermittent depression, usually as a
result of having to wait idly for a posting, or being passed over for
a job in a squadron or a promotion. Matters improved in late
1941, when all the new squadrons had been formed, but the
heavy losses of 1942 depressed many, and there was grumbling.
'Let the English fight – why should we be their coolies?' was an
opinion picked up by the intelligence unit in October 1941.
There was also grousing about the 'high life' supposedly being
led by the senior officers and political leadership in London.

Blackpool was also where those who had been thrown out of
the squadrons were sent, so it was where the least desirable elements in the force naturally ended up. There was a hard core of
difficult cases, whose motto was 'For King, Bed and Breakfast'.
Some of the men, finding their experiences too much for them,
had cracked under the strain or given way to depression. The
Polish Air Force intelligence unit kept an eye on the situation,
and its reports often quote from letters written by demoralized
airmen to illustrate points. 'I don't bother thinking about things
any more, Joe, because I'm sure that we won't get back to Poland
anyway, and that's our fucking, shitty fate,' one was writing to a
colleague in May 1941. 'I just drink, fuck and enjoy myself.'

In the circumstances, it is remarkable that there was so little of this kind of thing. A Mass Observation report on RAF morale in March 1941 states that 43 per cent were 'fed up with their job', while only 18 per cent could be described as 'content'. By June, the picture was even bleaker. 'Among the ranks of the Royal Air Force today nothing is so noticeable as the great, staring wastes of apathy,' runs the report, stressing that morale was 'lamentably low'. 'The will to win is weak,' it concludes. The situation in the Polish Air Force never came near to this at any time.

And the Poles did have an excuse. Every one of them was emotionally scarred by what he had been through, none more so than the later arrivals. The 1,500 or so airmen who arrived from the Soviet Union in late 1942 and early 1943 had spent two years in unspeakable conditions and survived torture in the gulags; many of them were marked for life by their experiences. 'At that stage none of us was quite sure he had a right to be alive,' writes Stefan Knapp after arriving in Britain in 1943. 'We were still inclined to feel we had no right to all this: being fed and clothed and taught seemed largely an act of charity.' Another always kept a small suitcase tucked under his bed, even after he had joined his squadron. When he was shot down his room-mate, who had always been intrigued by this, discovered that it contained a supply of woollen underwear and dry biscuits – the man had spent two years in the freezing camps of Kolyma.

Only slightly less disoriented were those who had been pressed into the German army or labour battalions and subsequently taken prisoner by the Allies. The British authorities took a great deal of persuading to release them, but the Poles, who were both anxious for their well-being and desperate for manpower, managed to get their way. And they were vindicated, according to the Polish Air Force internal security office, which noted that these men were shaping up well in training. 'This new intake into our air force is proving itself quite valuable,' ran a report.

A significant group of airmen had failed to get to Britain after the fall of France and had mainly been interned in North Africa or Spain. Such was Captain Eugeniusz Prusiecki, a bomber who had flown in 1939. When France capitulated he tried to fly to Africa, but his plane was blown off course by a storm, and he landed in Spain, whence he was deported back to France and thrown into gaol. He escaped with a group of Polish and Dutch airmen and stowed away on a freighter bound for Gibraltar. They were discovered by the Vichy French when the ship called at

Oran and placed in a POW camp, where there were some 300 Poles. They escaped again, made their way to the coast, and made contact with the Royal Navy, which regularly evacuated personnel from there. But they were again discovered while waiting for the British ship, and this time sent to a camp on the edge of the Sahara. They were only liberated by the American invasion.

Mieczysław Pruszyński, who had come out of the Soviet Union through the Middle East and reached Blackpool in March 1943, worked out that the 18 Poles with whom he went on a training course in Torquay had between them been in 65 different camps, received a dozen death-sentences and been condemned to a total of more than 350 years' hard labour.

These late arrivals did not benefit from the British enthusiasm and euphoria of 1940. They were plunged into the dreary and none too salubrious life of Blackpool and then sent on for training. Some of them were not even Poles, but Ukrainians, Estonians, Lithuanians or Russian Jews who had been clever enough to claim Polish nationality when the Soviets started releasing the Poles in 1941. They were on the whole delighted to serve in the Polish forces and some of them were good airmen, but they represented an unstable element. Recruits from the United States and South America, often cock-sure and independent-minded, were also sometimes difficult to control.

That this mass of men was kept in any sort of shape, let alone turned into a first-rate fighting force, is something of a miracle. One thing that undoubtedly counted for much was their faith. 'They were all deeply religious: heroic boys but deeply pious,' recalled Harold Acton. 'If you went to Mass in Blackpool it was all Poles at that time. They sang beautifully, and in their voices you could hear their faith ringing out. It was quite splendid, an inspiration.'

The word that recurs most frequently when British officers write or talk about the Polish airmen is 'determination', and this seems to have been their saving virtue, distinguishing them from their RAF colleagues. 'I lived for flying, and only for flying, I learned everything it was possible to learn about it,' writes Tadeusz Schiele, who was then towing targets for gunnery practice but desperately wanted to become a fighter pilot. At every opportunity he would take his ungainly Fairey Battle up in the air and try out manoeuvres and aerobatics. 'Mad Pole!' his British colleagues would remark with a shrug. 'There is work to be done – glorious long dreamed-of work – and it absorbs my whole being; I have more or less stopped drinking, for I have no need of it any more,' Tadeusz Szumowski wrote in his diary when, after months of being sent from pillar to post, he was finally assigned to 317. 'For the English, flying into action was just duty, for us it was something quite different,' writes a pilot of 305 Bomber Squadron.

The Home Front

THE FOURTH YEAR of the war was a difficult period for the Poles. They had fought extremely hard, giving all they could to the cause, yet this had had no effect on what was most important to them – the situation in their own country. Worse and worse news filtered out of Poland. Through the Red Cross or other sources they learned of wives, mothers and sisters killed, sent to slave-labour in Germany or to concentration camps. The sense of powerlessness was debilitating. British society had not begun to take in the full horror of Nazi rule, so the sympathy of British friends, however well-intentioned, was hollow. This added to the sense of isolation of the Poles, and it gave a powerful edge to their homesickness.

The Polish airmen were not for the most part sophisticated cosmopolitans, but people with a strong sense of country and family. They felt their exile in almost physical ways. 'I'd give my life to land on Polish soil and see my parents just once more,' one twenty-two year old fighter pilot told an American journalist in 1941. 'That's all I want.' A pilot of 138 Special Duties Flight, making a drop for the underground army near Częstochowa, found himself wishing his Halifax would break down, so that he could land in Poland and stay there. During one of the missions when the squadron's Dakotas touched down in occupied Poland in order to pick up men and documents as well as deliver supplies, the underground army officer in charge of the secret landing-strip noticed some of the crew jump out and start filling sacks with earth while the plane was being unloaded. He assumed that they needed ballast, and offered to help, but it transpired that they were collecting Polish earth to sprinkle on their dead colleagues' graves in England.

This deep attachment to their country was never more evident than at times such as Christmas Eve. The whole unit would assemble in one of the hangars. There would be a roll-call of all their dead and missing colleagues, followed by a prayer. Then the youngest mechanic would step forward, share a traditional wafer with the commanding officer and embrace him. Everyone else followed suit, after which they would sing carols before going to dinner. As they did so, they knew that wherever they might be, their families would also be gathered together and thinking of them.

'Our fourth Christmas Eve abroad,' noted the commander of 303 at Northolt on 24 December 1942. 'Unconsciously, everyone is asking himself – How many more such Christmases will he have to spend far from his family? We repeat the same wishes to each other – that the next one should be free, celebrated in Poland, that next year it should be not only thoughts but also hands that go out to our dearest ones, that no more Polish blood should flow, that Polish children should not have to wander lost and abandoned in the taiga of Siberia or the wastes of Russia.'

The squadrons based at Northolt or one of the Polish stations in Lincolnshire were fortunate at such times. They were at home and among friends, they had sympathetic British personnel around them, and their well-worn scrounging networks could ensure that tearful embraces were followed by a feast of sausage, *bigos* and other native specialities, not to mention delicacies such as home-distilled vodka. It was different for those stationed on some distant airfield in Scotland, Northern Ireland or Wales, where primitive conditions and an often uncomprehending station staff combined with cold and mist to plunge them into fits of depression. The description of a Christmas spent by a dozen Polish and British officers in the draughty, whistling mess of RAF Wick at the northernmost tip of Scotland makes harrowing reading.

The old-fashioned, traditional and self-centred Britain of the 1940s was not a natural home-from-home for the Poles. Everything from the climate to the food was totally different from what they were accustomed to. Every aspect of British culture, manners and customs was utterly foreign to them. Both the climate and the food depressed them – not so much by their quality, but because they were not those of home. But they could be got used to. In the event, neither raised more than the occasional gripe; they were accepted as part and parcel of the hardships of war.

The perceived oddities of British life took more getting used to. Many, such as ritual queuing, observing silence at breakfast or talking pointlessly about the weather, were regarded as quaint but harmless. They were often ridiculed, but not resented. Greater difficulties were encountered in mastering correct procedures and forms of address. Many a bank manager received, in reply to a formal letter asking for an overdraft to be paid off, a cheque to cover it drawn on the same account, accompanied by an equally formal letter beginning 'My Obedient Servant', and signing off with 'Your Dear Sir'.

The British sense of humour encompassed great expanses in which the Poles wandered resourceless. A pilot with 305 used to pore over *The Field* and *Country Life* and study the plays of Oscar Wilde on foggy days at Ingham in an attempt to penetrate British wit, and spent months assiduously contemplating the cartoons in *Punch*, asking himself: 'Why is this funny?' His face still lights up as he describes the moment when he first got the joke. But some British comic traditions remained inscrutable. At Hutton Cranswick in Yorkshire, a Polish squadron and a Naval Air Arm unit sharing the base held a joint party with the station WAAFs and some local girls one night. When the girls had all left, a Naval Commander came on in drag and did a suggestive turn, which had the Poles astonished and utterly scandalized.

'I shall never understand you English,' one airman told a reporter. 'When you want to express that a man is no good, you say "he runs after women".' The British scale of values often appeared quite skewed to the Poles. Minor misdemeanours, such as getting drunk in a Lincoln hotel and having a fight with the policeman who had been summoned, ended not, as in Poland, with six days of guardroom arrest, but with appearances in a magistrates' court. And British reactions sometimes seemed out of all proportion. In August 1942 Aircraftman Katryniak was hauled before Exeter magistrates on a charge of cruelty to animals: while returning to base drunk one night, he had kicked a cat off a bridge into the river. 'Exeter plenty bombing dead,' he observed in his own defence '– why worry about cat?' To his astonishment, he was fined the very substantial sum of £2, a week's pay.

Polish sentimentality was channelled in different directions. On 20 February 1942 *Horse and Hound* carried a letter from an embarrassed farmer, who had had three airmen billeted with him over a period of several months. When the time came for them to leave, they had apparently scoured the shops of the local market town for a suitably dignified gift, and presented him with a funerary urn inscribed: 'In Memory of Three Polish Officers'.

Solemn at the best of times, the Poles are never so solemn as when they go in for international gestures, and their pocket dictionaries were of little assistance in selecting the correct English words. One British bomber crew setting off on a dangerous mission was nonplussed when one of their Polish colleagues drew himself up and sent them on their way with a valedictory 'May God pickle you, gentlemen!' The solemnity of manner and exaggerated politeness of the Poles astonished and amused the British. The Poles were always saluting, bowing and shaking hands. 'It is quite impossible to get one of them to precede you through a door,' commented one British airman. But Polish stiffness and 'strutting' could be irritating, and was sometimes taken as arrogance or self-importance. And the Poles were quick to take offence at an over-casual response. Two entirely different concepts of good behaviour confronted each other in the messes. One Pole was appalled at the manners of British officers, who lounged in armchairs with their feet on the table. Those same officers found the foreign jabber and the raised voices of the Poles a rude infraction of club-room etiquette. The Poles' lack of deference and respect for personal space must have jarred, too.

'Some of the English regarded themselves as a superior race,' recalls a Polish pilot. Within the air force, British assumptions of superiority do not appear to have bothered the Poles very much, and they were professionally self-confident enough to laugh them off. RAF officers were frequently annoyed by the cockiness of the Poles, but on the whole they were too well-bred to show their feelings. There were lapses, but they were rare.

Those who had to work closely with the Poles tended to be better disposed to them than those who did not, either because they succumbed to their charm or because their resistance was worn down by daily contact. 'Despite the fact that the Polish crews were always in trouble or saluting, you couldn't help but like them, writes Frank Griffiths of 138 Squadron, adding that 'they were a magnificent headache'. The image is a recurring one. 'You have given me many headaches during the time we have been together, but I would willingly have them all again,' wrote the British adjutant of 303 when he was leaving the squadron in January 1941, signing himself 'Uptonski'. 'They were absolutely terrific chaps,' explains one of 302's British flight lieutenants; 'they were utterly lovable.' This quality often seems to have drawn out generosity in the Britons serving alongside the Poles. On Christmas Eve 1940, the British station officers organized a surprise dinner for 302. They got it all wrong, marinading kippers instead of herrings, but the goodwill was there. When 304 returned from their first bombing raid over Germany, they found a huge sign in the mess put up by their British comrades which read, in Polish, 'Long Live Poland!'

Other ranks and ground personnel tended to be less well disposed to 'the Polskis'. They were often fed up, and indifferent to the war. A survey by Mass Observation among RAF rank-and-file revealed that in June 1941 only some 15 to 20 per cent considered the independence and integrity of Poland a worthwhile war-aim, and the report added that this figure was probably declining. Given such attitudes, it was hardly surprising that they were irritated by the febrile commitment of their Polish colleagues. 'There is only one fault to be found with Polish mechanics,' a British officer told a reporter of the *Glasgow Herald*, 'they cannot be persuaded to stop working even when they are long past their normal hours of duty.'

The difference in temperament was the greatest stumbling-block. Polish memoirs and recollections abound in descriptions of 'cold', 'stuck-up' and 'stupid' RAF officers, who were generally referred to as 'ostriches', 'islanders' or 'jam-eaters', while British accounts throw up images of 'quarrelsome', 'undisciplined' and 'tiresome' Poles. It is not hard to see why. Air force personnel divided into two categories – those who were coping with unimaginable terror on a daily basis, and those whose principal struggle was with boredom. Generally speaking, Britons waging war against boredom responded in one of two ways: either by imposing rigid routines and regulations with obsessive punctiliousness, or by giving way to apathy, and shirking. Bored Poles either worked extremely hard, or channelled their energies into having a good time. The two sets of recipes were clearly incompatible.

The British way of dealing with fear and loss was based on the stiff upper lip and forced jollity, supported by a stream of silly jokes. The Polish way of dealing with them was to talk about them and to cry over dead comrades. 'For the habitually reserved Englishman, for whom the concealment of his emotions is the first and cardinal rule of gentlemanliness and social grace, this Polish openness and emotionality was quite incomprehensible, perhaps even shocking,' noted one commander of 303. Worse, it undermined the efforts of the British to banish unpleasant thoughts. It cannot have been easy to joke and behave as if nothing was happening if there were a couple of Poles weeping at the bar.

Ultimately, and in spite of the existence of some cordial and occasionally very deep friendships, both sides sought refuge in national stereotypes. It was less of an effort than exploring foreign territory, and it allowed anything alarming to be put down to the otherness of the others. People see what they expect and to some extent what they want to see. So the Poles were classed as drunk and reckless, the British as stuffy and unfeeling, however much experience might undermine these views. And if it was so within the air force, it was even more so in the outside world.

Troops are not popular with civilians for very long in any situation. Soldiers, particularly foreign soldiers, represent an invasion and a threat. Even where civilian communities have reason to welcome their arrival, this fundamental truth does not take long to reassert itself: liberating armies and peace-keeping forces quickly lose their popularity and become a focus for all the discontents of those they have come to assist. In this respect, the Poles in Britain were no exception. They did, after all, represent a huge influx of foreigners, the greatest for several centuries, and, in the case of the airmen, they penetrated into the most secluded areas of provincial Britain. There was no ignoring their presence. And if their foreignness was amusingly exotic to the inhabitants of a metropolis such as London, it was disturbing to those of the Lincolnshire fens.

It is unwise to generalize too broadly, but British reactions to the Polish presence did fall into a number of patterns and evolved in various ways. From the summer of 1940 to mid 1941 was what might be described as the honeymoon period. The novelty began to wear thin by the middle of 1941, and closer acquaintance had, as it must, transformed the Poles, in the British mind, from an abstraction into a more prosaic reality. People got used to their presence and treated them more like normal human beings – to be liked, disliked, welcomed or

resented, according to their individual merits and behaviour. By
the second half of 1941 there was a marked falling-off in the
number of press stories about Polish acts of derring-do, and proportionally more references to court appearances by Poles on
charges of drunkenness, disorderly conduct, motoring offences,
criminal damage and even, occasionally, theft. Lady Jersey soon
tired of playing 'Mama' to them and started holding parties for
American officers instead (although, after the Americans went
home, she did marry one of her 'Polish boys').

The political developments of 1941 – the entry of the Soviet
Union and then the United States into the war – had an enormous impact. Vast numbers of American soldiers and airmen
flooded Britain, causing a new sensation and eclipsing the Poles
in glamour. They had smarter uniforms than the other Allied
troops, and every GI looked like an officer. He also washed,
changed his clothes every day and used deodorant and after-
shave. Aside from a vague aura of Hollywood, he also had at his
disposal a seemingly limitless supply of cash, nylons, chocolate,
cigarettes, chewing-gum and transport. He was also bursting with
childlike vitality, brazenly accosted every female on the street,
and was ready to jitterbug all night.

Curiously enough, these English-speaking invaders found it
far harder to acclimatize than the Poles; it turned out that the
cultural chasm of the Atlantic was greater than that separating
Poland from Britain. A huge programme of information book-
lets for the troops on the one hand and the British population
on the other, of meet-the-people events and 'Welcome Clubs',
had to be put in hand to bridge it. The arrival of the Americans
contributed to the process of de-exoticizing the Poles, who suddenly appeared quite familiar to the British by contrast. The
Poles of 304 stationed at Chivenor near Barnstaple in Devon had
been treated as thoroughly alien by the natives, but this changed
overnight when the first American detachment arrived in the
locality. 'Suddenly we were treated as old friends,' notes one of
the pilots.

The other great event of 1941 was to have far more serious
consequences for them. The German invasion turned the
Russian people into the next recipients of British compassion,
and their increasingly heroic struggle against the onslaught, well
publicized by a flood of patriotic propaganda, stole the show. But
there was, as far as the Poles were concerned, a more sinister
dimension to this. Ever since the Ribbentrop–Molotov pact and

the joint Russo-German invasion of Poland in 1939, British Communists and fellow-travellers sympathetic to Russia had been embarrassed and cowed by their ideal country's collaboration with the Fascist enemy. Now they could revert to the pre-war socialist world-view, in which Fascist Germany could only be defeated by an ideologically correct Communist power such as the Soviet Union, not by bourgeois democracies such as Britain. In this world-view, Poland ranked as a 'Fascist' state, only a few degrees less damnable than Spain or Italy, and it was certainly in the wrong ideological camp as far as the Soviet Union was concerned.

Allied propaganda glorifying the Soviet struggle against Nazi Germany, conducted through books, articles, talks and films, had the secondary effect of marginalizing the Polish cause. And very soon it began to undermine it. Press indifference soon gave way to press hostility, led by the *Guardian* and the *New Statesman*, which had consistently questioned the credibility of the Polish government since its arrival in Britain. Lord Beaverbrook's Express Group of newspapers supported a vigorously pro-Soviet line and its star cartoonist Low regularly represented the Poles as ridiculous and bigoted. The *News Chronicle* and the *Star* were also adopting an unpleasantly anti-Polish tone. 'It is as well that the Poles should know that besides good friends, they also have some ill-wishers in this country,' warned Richard Cobb in the Polish Air Force's fortnightly magazine in October 1941.

For the most part, the Polish airmen were blissfully unaware of any unkind feelings on the part of the British population. 'Relations with British people were fantastic,' recalls Stanisław Wandzilak. 'Wherever a Polish squadron was posted, the local community, even the aristocracy, did everything to make life pleasant for us.' This was certainly true of airfields in rural areas, where people knew little of international politics and where the contacts between the Poles and the local population were more direct. At Church Fenton, where 306 was stationed during its first winter in Britain, a delegation of local ladies knitted warm scarves and presented them to the sentries, whom they had seen shivering in the cold. People met in country or market-town pubs were welcoming and cordial, local tradesmen were obliging. Farmers were prepared to sell eggs and other produce, and invited the officers pheasant-shooting. The local gentry tended to see it as their duty to look after the Polish officers, and would ask them to tea, to dinner or to stay. One Polish pilot remembers staying in a castle in Monmouthshire and riding to hounds with his host. But even at suburban stations such as Heston the local population showed remarkable concern, telephoning or turning up at the gate to enquire whether all the pilots were safe if they noticed the squadrons returning short of a few planes.

At some airfields there was a shortage of living quarters, so a few of the men were billeted with families in nearby houses. Such families often took a personal interest in their lodgers, and tried to entertain them by holding tea parties and inviting friends. This was not always welcome, since 'the atmosphere in such a home is sometimes a little too stiff and strait-laced for a young man full of life and verve', as one airman put it. But sometimes the warmth of such a home could be extremely welcome and touching. Anna Lęska remembers that her landlords treated her like a daughter, while a Polish fitter billeted with a family whose son, a rear gunner in an RAF bomber, had been killed, was adopted wholeheartedly.

While 302 Squadron was stationed at Westhampnett, the people of nearby Chichester showered the men with attentions and held dances for them every Saturday night. They were asked to every party given in the neighbourhood, often by a carload of girls turning up at the airfield. The pilots began to suffer from surfeit and often baulked at going out after a hard day's flying, and there were occasions when the squadron commander felt obliged to select a delegation and order them to go. One of the pilots had an affair with the Mayor of Chichester's daughter, and when the squadron was posted elsewhere, the farewell party given by the town lasted well into the next day.

Even Blackpool, which had reason enough to tire of the Polish airmen, treated them exceptionally well. The population remained well-disposed and actively supported the Polish Assistance Fund set up by the Lord Mayor. They held concerts, jumble sales and dances. Many shops and bars had notices in Polish welcoming the airmen, and local firms were generous with their sponsorship. John White Ltd, makers of 'Impregnable Boots', collected enough money to pay for a Spitfire, and insisted it be given to a Polish squadron.

But attitudes were changing. A Mass Observation survey in January 1941 indicated that the Poles were a good deal more popular than the Free French, who were regarded with universal scorn and suspicion, but decidedly less popular than the Czechs. A similar survey carried out in April 1943 revealed that the Free

French had gone up in British estimation and popularity, with the Czechs topping the charts, while the popularity of the Poles had declined. One of the surveys notes, with surprising astonishment, that 'the most striking thing about the Poles is that they are nearly twice as popular with the women as with the men'.

The sexual prowess of the Polish airmen entered British wartime folklore very early on. In an end-of-year speech in 1941 the headmistress of a girls' school admonished those who were leaving about the pitfalls of life in the outside world, ending with the words: 'And remember, keep away from gin and Polish airmen.' They were reputed to be irresistible. They were also, apparently, credited with exotic powers. One airman who started an affair with a beautiful divorcée was unexpectedly dropped, and he asked a colleague to find out why. The friend took her out for a drink and steered her round to the subject. 'I'd been told that the Poles are wonderful, and do it quite differently,' she answered. 'But now I see it's just the same, and the truth is I've never liked sex.'

This reputation actually owed as much to British women as to Polish men. 'We were supposed to be "fast workers", but I believe that this was the result of a misunderstanding, the clash of two cultures,' reflects Zbigniew Groszek. Most of the airmen were normal young European males with a no more than average sexual drive. They were not a bunch of Don Juans, and many of them had sweethearts back in Poland whom they still hoped to marry. But, being Poles, they were peacocks, and highly flirtatious. They made a fuss of women, clicked heels, kissed hands, paid exaggerated compliments and sought to impress by every available means, including sometimes bragging of non-existent titles and country houses back home. This did not mean that they were desperately trying to jump into bed with every girl they talked to; they principally wanted to flirt.

On their arrival at Blackpool in 1940, the airmen evacuated from France were lectured by a British officer who told them that England was not France, and that the only way into a nice girl's bed was via the altar. They had no particular reason to doubt this, until they began to meet English girls. 'These English girls are quite different from Polish girls,' Wacław Król noted in his diary after a date. '"Do you love me?" she asked, just like that. She's very sweet, but that's no way for a girl to win a man!' He was shocked, and a little put out, as he had a girl in Poland he intended to marry as soon as the war was over. Equally shocked was Zumbach, who felt pleased with himself at having bedded a pretty girl called Ann on their second date, only to discover from a diary which he found lying around that he was the thirtieth Polish pilot she had had in the space of a couple of months.

'When I was a young man and started going out with young girls, it might take two weeks before I managed to get a kiss out of a girl,' explains Groszek. 'Even to get to the point of holding hands with her took a certain amount of time. But in England, you'd invite a girl out to the cinema, then escort her home, and then she'd start kissing you – and very intimately, at that. Well, that was for us a kind of signal, and this is where the misunderstanding arose – they were so taken aback that they just didn't defend themselves.' This is borne out by the words of a WAAF stationed at Beachy Head near Eastbourne in 1944.

'We met them, of course, in town at dances or in the pubs; they were remote, courteous and rather shy, more "foreign" than any of the Allied troops who had passed through,' she writes. 'They were homeless, saddened, made bitter by their own war, and – Anton Walbrook and *Dangerous Moonlight* fresh in our minds – we took them to our hearts with naïve concern. We were rudely awakened when we discovered that the charming mid-European heel-clicking and hand-kissing went by the board once night fell; we could not exchange more than a dozen words, but this proved no barrier to their more primitive urges, unleashed by that same fatalism that made them such good fighters in the air.' But she soon discovered that their 'more primitive urges' were of secondary importance to them. 'Several of them began calling – not to see me, the young, unmarried daughter of the house, but to gather at [my grandmother's] feet, to tell her about home and family in Cracow and Warsaw,' she writes. 'Sitting upright in her upright chair, she held court, for they found in her a warmth and a sympathy that was lacking in mere girl-friends.'

One nineteen year old girl working for the Civil Service who had never been away from home in Kensington was relocated with her office to Blackpool. She had never had the opportunity to meet young men in large numbers, and being a middle-class English Catholic compounded the problem. 'It was fantastic to suddenly find all these Catholic young men about,' she recalls. 'And if they realized one wasn't going in for that sort of thing, they were very respectful and didn't push.' She eventually married a 303 pilot. It seems there was something for every taste in the Polish Air Force.

Another nineteen year old, a nice, somewhat nervous middle-class girl from Pinner, met a pilot from 302 at the Orchard, where she had gone with her brother and one of his friends. She asked him to her semi-detached home for tea. 'Trying to make conversation with somebody who really does not understand half one is saying is a little difficult,' she writes. 'I was sure that he did not understand me most of the time because he would smile and say "Yes!" to almost everything I said. I think he appreciated my effort. He took my hand and stroked my arm, said something in Polish that sounded very romantic to me, even though I did not know what he meant. Then he leant forward and kissed me gently on the lips.' They were married within four months.

Wartime conditions made it somehow acceptable for a girl to approach a man, particularly a man in uniform, and the blacked-out streets were a great help in breaking down embarrassment. At weekends, thousands of single girls from the Midlands descended on Blackpool, where they knew they could find any number of Polish airmen wandering about. 'Since the war started, many girls in the North West have been eager to learn foreign languages – or shall I say *a* foreign language,' reported the *West Lancashire Evening Gazette* in August 1942. 'Waitresses and factory girls are learning foreign languages with a speed that is astonishing their teachers. "Love works wonders," one of them says.' All this linguistic activity did raise some eyebrows. The Polish and British intelligence services actually investigated one lady who seemed suspicious, as she had moved to Blackpool from another part of the country, and picked up Polish airmen in bars with astonishing frequency, always paying for the drinks and dinner. But they concluded that, far from being a spy, she was merely a rich young widow 'with a somewhat exaggerated erotic sense'.

The same kind of thing occurred around airfields where Polish squadrons were stationed. Some of the girls virtually became Polish Air Force groupies, wending their amorous way through whole squadrons. They were often given the decorative silver stooping eagle, the Polish 'wings', which made a pretty brooch. This constituted a signal for the men of the next squadron on the station. Not that the Poles ever found them-selves short of choice. 'You were torn to pieces and passed from hand to hand, girls pounced on you and dragged you into the dance,' is how Stefan Knapp, who was training at Hucknall, describes the dances in Nottingham, where the factory girls outnumbered the airmen by as many as a hundred to one. 'They all insisted that your watch was too fast and that your last bus would not leave for another hour. The idea was to make you miss the bus and take you home.'

The success of the Poles with the girls came as a nasty shock to their British comrades-in-arms. 'We are worried because we can't get a woman to even look at us,' ran a letter from 'six Romeos of the RAF' to the *Daily Sketch* agony aunt. 'Why? Because this drome is overrun by Polish airmen, and they are commandeering anything that's prim and pretty. We wouldn't moan if we weren't handsome, but we are, very much so. We are all dark, the gypsy type, nice wavy hair, bubbling over with love. What can you suggest for us to do?' The agony aunt had no time for them at all, merely observing that 'Your sex-appeal needs a bit of de-coking,' and wishing 'good luck to the Polish boys!' The situation prompted some resourceful British airmen to sew borrowed 'Poland' flashes on their sleeves when they went to dances, and to put on accents and kiss hands when they met girls, which apparently worked. 'Ah can't get me crumpet otherwise,' argued one of them when caught out by an officer. And even the Americans found that their direct charm, their glamour and their back-up of material enticements were hard put to it to dislodge the Polish monopoly. 'It usually took a Pole about ten seconds to tell a girl he wanted her,' commented one GI ruefully.

The popularity of the Poles is hardly surprising. A seventeen year old working-class WAAF could hardly fail to be bowled over when a Spitfire pilot sent her a month's pay's worth of red roses after their first date. A woman journalist sent to interview some Polish pilots in their dispersal hut was already enchanted by the 'blue eyes, dashing manner and fascinating charm' of one of them by the time they were scrambled. 'Before he went off on his job he asked me if he could borrow my soul to take up into the clouds for luck, so of course I gave it to him,' she writes. As Doris, the barmaid who marries a Polish bomber pilot, 'Count Johnny', in Terence Rattigan's *The Flare Path*, puts it: 'First time I met him, he kissed my hand. Of course, I had to fall for him after that, didn't I, Johnny ducks?'

Even the ground crews, who did not have the advantage of 'wings' or aristocratic pretensions, had a head start on their British counterparts. RAF fitters tended to be class-bound in their mentality, very much the products of mill-town fish-and-chip culture, more interested in football than female company.

The Poles were mostly from rural areas, and therefore much healthier-looking, more self-assured, more subversive, and far more interested in women. 'They had a certain conceit; they knew they could get away with it,' according to a girl who saw a great deal of them.

The Poles were often described as 'dangerous'. Before a date, Joan Wyndham was warned that 'he's one of those Poles who can kiss your hand and throw you onto a bed in one consecutive movement'. The man did take her up in his plane and take his hands off the controls to embrace her when she was too terrified to resist. And there were plenty of other tricks they resorted to with shy girls. Tadeusz Schiele wanted to get a look at the legs of Jean, a WAAF he was dating, but she was very proper and kept her skirt pulled well down at all times. One day when they were alone in the dispersal hut he suggested she try on a parachute she was examining (they were always fascinated by flying equipment). She sat down and he carefully fastened all the straps, so that when she stood up those that fitted between the legs pulled tight, jacking her skirt up to her waist. Consternation was followed by embarrassment, and feverish struggling with the release catch by a more amorous tussle on the bed.

But it was not so much the Polish pilots who were 'dangerous' as the reactions they provoked. Their attraction went far deeper than looks, manner and romance, as many girls were not looking for husbands, or even boy-friends. 'British officers had no idea how to treat a girl; when they took you out you felt that they'd be far happier with their chums at the club or in the mess,' one English lady explains. 'The Poles had that look in their eye – you knew that the fellow saw you as a woman and wanted you. That was an extraordinarily sexy feeling, quite new for us. It drove us wild.' This may seem a little sweeping, but there is some truth in it. Interviewed by a women's magazine, a Polish pilot said that he was astonished by the low expectations of English women when it came to men. 'A few little attentions, some appreciation of what they look like and what they wear – and then they are happy,' he said, 'and when an English girl is happy she is irresistible.' This is confirmed by a Briton interviewed on the subject. 'They notice what the women are wearing. Seems they know about clothes as well as fighting. Odd, isn't it? But it seems the girls like it.'

They certainly did. British women had had enough of their prescribed role in society, and by 1940 they were ready to break out. They wanted to be treated as human beings, but also as women. 'We carried our virtue around like albatrosses, longing to shift the burden,' one WAAF complains. 'English girls were seriously under-loved, so we had to do something about it,' in Groszek's words. 'We must have come as a welcome change, at a time when change was in the air,' adds Zumbach.

They came as a welcome change not only for those in search of romance or sexual liberation, but also for many who simply felt hemmed in by the stuffiness of middle-class British life. The Poles represented other values, and their willingness to show emotion and talk about their deepest feelings helped to unlock some tightly shut emotional and psychological compartments in the psyche of many Britons.

They elicited an extraordinary degree of devotion in some quarters. 'How it all began I can scarcely remember,' Mrs Hopley related to a *Blackpool Gazette* reporter. 'We've never been to Poland. We'd never even spoken to a Pole before the war. All I know is that as soon as I heard of the invasion of their country I felt an unutterable compassion for these people.' She had started by offering stray Polish airmen wandering about Blackpool tea and sympathy in her little house, 'Ravenswood', in South Shore. As the reporter observed, the house might more appropriately have been called 'Little Poland', as it had become a home from home to hundreds of Poles. The front room was full of framed photographs of them, and every so often a black silk ribbon would be stuck across the corner of one when she heard of his death. 'Now, when you think of them, homeless, oppressed, yet still so proud, so brave, what else can you do but be as kind to them as you know how?' she explained. 'It is an honour to do it, and it is little enough.'

Some of the most heartfelt friendship and hospitality towards the Poles was to be found in such humble places. Tadeusz Schiele proposed to his seventeen year old WAAF and set off to the East End of London to obtain her father's consent. Charlie, who was a docker, readily gave it, and took 'Ted' off on a pub crawl. It would not be their last. Schiele loved the eel shops and pubs of the East End and revelled in the warmth of the people he encountered in them. When, a year later, he was posted to the training station at Penrhos in North Wales as an instructor, he was the only Pole on the base, and the British officers cold-shouldered him, probably on account of his cockney wife. But he made friends with the local fishermen instead, and they welcomed him into their houses and sympathized with his plight.

The whole issue of marriages between Polish servicemen and British girls was a vexed question. At first, the men were too busy training and fighting, they were moved about a great deal, they spoke too little English to form any deeper relationships – and most of them did not wish to, assuming still that they would be fighting their way back to Poland soon. And although hours were spent in discussing the relative merits of Polish and English girls, the general verdict seemed clear. 'Most of the men maintain that while the English girl is a charming companion in the dance-hall, the bar or on an outing, she is not suited to be a wife to a Pole, who is brought up with different attitudes to the role of the woman in domestic life,' noted the commanding officer of one of the fighter squadrons at the beginning of 1942. But time and closer acquaintance were beginning to take effect, and by the middle of 1942 a couple of hundred Polish airmen had tied the knot. Their superior officers tended to discourage them, using a whole range of reasoning, including the line that 'just because you want a glass of milk, you don't need to buy a cow'.

Soon, British voices were beginning to be raised in concern. The Revd Dr Cox, Principal Clerk to the Assembly of the Church of Scotland, voiced his misgivings in the press. He warned Scots girls against marrying Polish servicemen, adding that 'in many foreign countries living conditions are anything but desirable from our point of view, and the women might find life unbearable'. Such warnings had little effect, and by February 1943 the 303 diary noted that 'marriage-fever is spreading through the squadron, among the young and the old alike'.

As the problem grew, it elicited more intelligent comment. 'It is felt that official action is needed to safeguard the welfare of the young wives after the war,' ran the *Daily Herald.* 'They may not fully realize what life in Poland may be like. When many of these boys return to Poland they will have absolutely nothing. Probably homes will have been destroyed. Food will be scarce and life, for a time at least, will be hard.' By the beginning of 1944, the Polish military authorities were getting worried, as by then more than 2,000 mixed marriages had been contracted, most of them in the land forces, and applications for permission to marry were flooding in.

The Polish Air Force periodical carried articles in English for airmen who wished to marry to show their fiancées. 'How many know what kind of life awaits them in a strange land?' one asked.

'Detached or semi-detached houses are as rare in Polish cities as are bananas in England at present,' it went on. 'About 95 per cent of all living accommodation is in flats, so the dream of a front garden with roses over the door must be discarded.' Another went into even greater detail. 'Bathrooms, water supply, plumbing, electricity or gas for cooking and lighting, cinemas within easy reach, are but a few of the minor luxuries of life which are infinitely rarer in the Polish than in the English countryside,' it ran, adding that girls should not always believe the rosy descriptions of their fiancés. It then got down to the serious arguments.

'Apart from the material surroundings, a summer heat which she may find extremely trying and a lack of lawns which may make her pine for the vacillations of the English climate, she has to consider the new personal relationships. The glamour of Janek's uniform, the excitements of youthful love, the fascination of his delightful accent and foreign turn of phrase, which made his every trite remark into a witticism, may not long outlast the return to Poland. There, he will speak Polish, to his parents, to his friends, to their children. . . . Will she not feel shut off from those around her by this barrier? Relations-in-law are proverbially, and even with the best intentions, a trial – are they likely to welcome as the wife of their son one whose language, upbringing, tastes and standards of behaviour are so foreign, so quite unintelligible? Probably for a long time she will have to share a home. Whose ideas on child-rearing, housekeeping, or cooking are going to prevail? How can Janek's wife hope to compete with Janek's mother in providing dishes that he most likes from recipes and even ingredients with which only the elder is familiar?' A thousand other good reasons for not marrying were adduced, with the final advice – 'Don't!'

No Victory

THE WAR IN the air carried on relentlessly, taking its daily toll in human lives. The fact that by 1943 the Allies were on the offensive in no way removed ever-present danger from the lives of the airmen. Nor did it lighten their workload. All the Polish squadrons were heavily engaged, bombing Germany, attacking ground targets in France, carrying out fighter sweeps or patrolling the Atlantic. The busiest were the fighters: 1 Polish Fighter Wing at Northolt was principally engaged in escorting daylight raids by British and American bombers over targets in France and Belgium; 2 Polish Wing, stationed at Kirton-in-Lindsey, performed the same task over Holland and Germany. When there were no bombers to escort they swept the skies over France and Belgium in search of German fighters. In June 1943 a third Polish fighter wing was formed, bringing the number of fighter squadrons engaged in the front line to nine.

These operations were very demanding, as the wings were often sent out three or even four times a day, and their sorties were much longer than before: the 200-mile range of the Hurricane had limited the amount of time a fighter could spend in the air, but now the Polish units were equipped with the Spitfire IX, with a range of up to 1,000 miles, or the American Mustang, which had an even longer reach. Escorting the daylight bombing raids required long periods of high-altitude flying, which meant hours of intense cold for the pilots. They often had to spend the night at some coastal airfield, so they could not even have a good night's sleep in their own beds.

These long-distance missions were fraught with danger. Engine trouble was always a possibility, and, so far from home, not to be taken lightly. No amount of experience could save a pilot if he had to bale out over enemy territory or face the perils of the Channel. Just how unpleasant these could be is reflected in the story of Pilot Officer Lew Kuryłowicz of 316, who had the far from enviable distinction of spending longer 'in the drink' – 85 hours – than any other.

On a sweep over northern France in the autumn of 1943, he attacked three Focke-Wulfs, shooting down one at close range and managing to evade the other two by flying into the sun where they could not see him. The enemy plane had disintegrated before his eyes, and he was tremendously proud of the pictures he would be able to show the intelligence officer back at base. 'What a photo! Never seen a picture of a Jerry falling to bits at such short range!' he said to himself. He recrossed the French coast between Le Havre and Cherbourg, and confidently made for home. 'Nothing, it seems, divides me from the happy moment of getting home and talking of my adventures,' he recorded. Just as he was over the coast, the engine cut out. He tried all the possible trouble-shooting drills, but it was no good. A hundred miles separated him from the English coast, and for a brief moment he thought of turning back and landing in France. But that would mean captivity. After crossing into Rumania in 1939 he had gone back for his wife, which had resulted in his capture by the Soviets and two years in a labour camp.

'The thought of turning back was rejected as soon as it came. No Oflag for me! Not after all I'd gone through to join the air force. I contacted my controller, gave him the gen. and told him I intended to make for England and walk out if necessary. "Ops" gave my position. I had been at 25,000 feet and, gliding along, was now about half-way across the Channel. "Ops" fixed my bearings and advised me to bale out when at grade five. That moment came all too soon; I told them I was walking out; they told me I wasn't far from England and that the wait wouldn't be long.'

He took off his flying helmet, opened the cockpit, undid his straps and turned the plane on its back. He had a struggle to kick free of the plane, with the centrifugal force pressing him down into the seat, but at last he was out.

'The chute opened up and I looked round: no land in sight. I looked down: the toe-caps of my new boots had got scraped – I was furious. As I descended I tried to inflate my Mae West, but only half-succeeded, because the gas-cylinder was nearly u/s; I hit the drink and was dragged under before I released the harness but after a few moments I emerged. The chute cupola was swaying about limply on the surface and before I could get away a huge wave threw it over me. I struggled desperately to get out of the clinging stuff as the waves dashed over me; just as I reached the open my foot caught in the lines and the now sinking chute began to drag me under. But at last I got away.

'My under-inflated Mae West was nearly useless and I could keep afloat only by striking out with my arms. The waves kept on swamping me and slapping my face and I swallowed loads of salt water. I hunted for the dinghy-cylinder [which inflated the dinghy] but time after time had to interrupt the search whenever I sank: finally I found it, but before I could find the valve, had to let go because I was sinking again. I swam on, choking and coughing, so tired out that every moment was an enormous, heart-breaking effort.

'Dusk began to fall. Around me ten-foot walls of water. Then I saw two Typhoons pass low overhead. They were perhaps looking for me but of course could not see my head in the rough water – and it was dark. Despondency came over me and for a moment I thought of giving in. I shook it off, however, and again tried to inflate the dinghy but again couldn't turn the gas on. I went under and had quite a job getting back to the surface. Stifling, coughing, vomiting, I was on my beam-ends when I saw a seagull hovering over me; she inclined her head, looked at me askance, screeched and flew off; probably she had seen more than one tragedy of this kind. That thought was the last straw; this is the end – this is how World War No 2 ends for me – the papers will report tomorrow: "One fighter pilot did not return." A very curt, cold epitaph. I prayed: ". . . and forgive us our trespasses, as we . . ." but I could not think of anyone who had trespassed against me and broke off. I thought of Lydia and said: "Well, little girl, this is where you become a widow!"

'That livened me up and I decided to carry on. I floated on my back and coughed up some water. The dinghy was dragging me down; I thought of jettisoning it but decided once more to try and inflate it. To my delight the gas cylinder valve worked this time and the dinghy assumed its proper shape. I laid my head on it, rested and gathered strength to clamber in it. This was done by slow stages; half in, half in the water; lying on my chest with my legs sticking out; then I turned over and finally sat up. Although I rested a long time between each operation, my head was swimming and I felt very ill. Sea-sickness racked me time after time. I trembled with cold and my teeth chattered away like castanets.

'I again began to feel optimistic, however. Getting into the dinghy was an enormous step forward. I fastened the apron, drew on the hood, and tried to warm my hands. "All I have to do," I told myself, "is to wait until morning. They'll come along then and rescue me – they know where I am." True, a regular gale was blowing me away from England, and this was mildly disturbing. But they'd be sure to find me if they took the trouble.

'This more cheerful mood did not last long. The sea got rougher and stormier. The waves reared up even higher, until an especially big one crashed down upon me. The dinghy was upset and there I was, under the surface, held upside down by the aprons, frantically struggling to get out and raging against the irony of fate which placed me in this undignified position. After all I had gone through, with rescue certain the next morning! In the end, with my lungs bursting, I forced the apron back, slewed around and stuck my head out of the water. A few deep breaths and I got under again to free my legs. Finally I succeeded. After a long rest I righted the dinghy and again pulled myself in little by little.

'No more apron for me! I decided, and fastened myself to the dinghy with a long line. There was far less trouble thereafter during the seven successive times I turned turtle that night, although I was getting weaker and weaker. The torch wouldn't work – a great shock, as I had counted on its light being spotted in the dark, better than the dinghy by day. I dozed off when morning came, still confidently expecting rescue. It didn't come that morning nor that day, nor, of course, the next night. It was galling to see aircraft passing over me and not spotting me. I took off my collar and wrote my last message – wanted to leave some trace, as I had very little hope of surviving.'

Pilot Officer Kuryłowicz was eventually picked up by an MTB that was actually looking for someone else, as he had, after three days, been given up for lost. It was not for nothing that the airmen hated the sea. And it was the sea which was to deal them the cruellest of blows that year.

On 5 July 1943 the plane carrying General Sikorski from the Middle East back to London crashed into the sea shortly after take-off from Gibraltar, killing all the passengers. His death was a tragedy for the Polish cause. It exposed the widening gap between Poland's reason of State and that of the Allies.

In September 1939 Poland had been invaded by the Soviet Union as well as Germany. The Soviets proceeded to behave towards the Polish population in a manner no more benign than the Nazis, and the Poles could not regard them as anything but an enemy. But in 1941, when Hitler attacked it, the Soviet Union became one of the Allies. Churchill managed to persuade a hard-pressed Stalin to make peace with Poland, and a treaty was duly signed. But as Stalin grew stronger, it became clear that he had no intention of allowing an independent Poland to emerge after the war, and in 1943 he broke off diplomatic relations with the Polish government. Poland was now an ally of Britain and America, but not of their principal ally, Russia. This was the beginning of the political nightmare that was to end in the tragedy of Yalta, but in the immediate term it was a headache for the military planners.

Sikorski had always envisaged building up his forces in Britain and throwing them into the Polish theatre at a critical moment, when Germany was in retreat. He also had a huge underground force – the Home Army – organized in regiments and divisions ready to join them. Two elements were crucial to this plan. One was to drop enough small-arms into Poland to enable the Home Army to take the field effectively when the time came. The other was to build up the Polish Air Force in such a way that it could spearhead the liberation of Poland. In January 1943 Wing Commander Roman Rudkowski and a team of air force officers were dropped into Poland to work out the logistics of the transfer of airborne units to Polish territory.

It had become clear to the British that Stalin would be sweeping the Germans out of Poland, and that any Polish intrusion there would provoke, at best, hostility. They had no intention of jeopardizing their alliance with Stalin by supporting the Poles against him, and they were not keen to waste arms on the Polish Home Army, or to devote to their delivery planes that could be more usefully engaged in bombing German industry or looking for U-boats in the Atlantic.

Although the Polish forces in the west were larger than those of the Czechs, Dutch, Free French, Norwegians and Belgians put together, their importance to the Allied cause was radically diminished when America and the Soviet Union joined Britain in the fight against Germany. The Polish government's influence shrank proportionally, but Sikorski's personal stature and authority guaranteed its survival. After he had been laid in his grave at Newark (he had expressed the wish to be buried beside the bomber crews), the Polish cause began to look weak. And, as often happens at such moments, all the existing internal problems and dissensions came to the surface.

The Polish forces after 1939 were an entirely volunteer army, and a volunteer army has a tendency to be politicized, since every soldier feels a right to debate what he is fighting for – a tendency magnified in the case of the Poles, many of whom had gone to extraordinary lengths and run terrible risks in order to join this army. A high proportion of those who had managed to escape to France and then England were officers, and as a result the Polish forces were somewhat top-heavy.

The pre-war military establishment and staff had been discredited by its failure to provide the air force with adequate planes and supplies, and the air command's failure to put together a coherent strategy. But they had got out of Poland and over to France early in the proceedings, and had largely hung on to the higher posts, giving rise to indignation and resentment among junior officers. This resentment took the shape of a 'conspiracy' which included a couple of hundred air force officers. It was not much of a movement, and its only achievement was to get the inspector of the Polish Air Force, Air Vice-Marshal Ujejski, replaced on 1 September 1944 by Air Commodore Mateusz Izycki.

This made very little difference to the majority of the airmen, whose work and daily struggle with death absorbed them fully. They tended to leave politics to the politicians, and in spite of the unpromising international situation, they believed that things would sort themselves out at the end of the war.

In the second half of 1943 the Allied command began to prepare for the invasion of the Continent which they intended to launch in the following year, and this entailed extensive reorganization. The existing division between Fighter Command and Bomber Command was broken up into Air Defence of Great Britain (ADGB) and Tactical Air Force (2 TAF). The latter was a force of about 1,000 fighters and light bombers with its own support services. Its aims were to maintain Allied supremacy in the air, carry out reconnaissance, prevent supplies from reaching the enemy's front line, and give support to Allied ground forces in action when the invasion started.

The Poles were entrusted with running a sizeable element of 2 TAF: 18 Sector was commanded by Wing Commander Tadeusz Rolski and included five Polish, one New Zealand, one Belgian and two RAF fighter squadrons. In addition, 305 Bomber Squadron was assigned to 2 TAF, and no fewer than 45 staff officers were attached to various levels of its command, bringing the total Polish contribution to 230 officers and 2,143 men.

Since units would be changing airfields all the time as they kept up with the advancing land forces, the old system of each squadron having its own servicing, repair and supply set-up was no longer practicable. The squadrons were stripped of all their ground staffs, bar one adjutant and one intelligence officer, and all maintenance personnel were pooled into larger units. These would function on an echelon system, sending the necessary crews to any airfield in the battle zone where planes were going to land, and then moving them on to another, regardless of which squadron was where. This dismayed the mechanics, who would be separated from 'their' planes. It also broke up the closely-knit squadron 'families', which had been so effective in replacing the comfort and moral support the men lacked as a result of being cut off from home. But as the Polish ground crews were transferred into the echelon units of 18 Sector, they stayed together. These units included 408 Polish Air Stores Park, 411 Polish Air Salvage Unit, 72 Polish Light Repair Unit and a Polish Mobile Vehicle Park.

During the last three months of 1943 their Spitfires and Mustangs were adapted to carry additional fuel tanks and bombs, and the pilots had to acquire new skills. They had to learn precision dive-bombing and strafing, low-level navigation using map and compass, and to operate from improvised mobile airfields. The squadrons continued to raid ground targets in northern France throughout the spring of 1944, and then, on 1 April, 1 Polish Wing, renumbered 131, left Northolt for good, moving to Deanland, an improvised airfield near Lewes. The men lived in tents and did their own cooking. Along with their comrades from 3 Polish Wing, now 133, which had moved to nearby Brenzett, they went to Brighton in the evenings to pick up girls and dance in the Norfolk Hotel.

It was from these airfields that the Polish fighter force, commanded by Group Captain Gabszewicz, took off at dawn on 6 June, D-Day, in support of the Allied landings on the Normandy

beaches. The two wings flew three times over the landing
beaches, and in the first two days of the operation clocked up the
top score of 30 German planes shot down, as well as bombing
and strafing German positions and columns in the enemy rear.
On 11 June three of the squadrons landed on an improvised airfield at Plumetôt in France. Anxious lest the Germans should
have drunk France dry, one of the pilots took the precaution of
filling his 90-gallon spare fuel tank with beer for their makeshift
mess.

The next weeks were highly enjoyable for the pilots, who ram-
paged around northern France preying on the enemy's ground
forces. A new source of pride and pleasure was that as they
hedge-hopped over the Normandy countryside they occasionally
saw tanks with the markings of the 1st Polish Armoured Division
advancing on Caen. They flew up to five sorties a day, often
helping the ground crews refuel and re-arm the machines so they
could get back to their hunting. They were given specific objectives to hit, but once they had dealt with these, they could go and
look for their own. There was no lack of targets, and part of the
fun was that they could see clearly the damage inflicted, as they
were attacking from low altitudes. During the battle of Falaise,
131 Wing destroyed 600 enemy vehicles and field-guns, while
133 Wing under Skalski scored the Allied record for the first
month after the invasion, with 38 enemy planes shot down.

Although German resistance was stiff, at least one hazard
could be ignored. Having to bale out was no longer an alarming
prospect. The Germans were in no position to organize great
man-hunts, and the French were now more likely to give shelter
and food. The long trek to Gibraltar was no longer the only way
back: the Allied lines were close by and advancing. When one
pilot of 315 baled out behind the German lines, he hardly had
to wait at all. His commander, Eugeniusz Horbaczewski, saw him
go down and himself landed in a field just behind the Allied
lines. He borrowed a jeep from some Americans and, running
through an enfilade of German fire, picked up and brought back
his pilot. After returning the jeep to its owners, he loaded the
wounded pilot into the cockpit of his Mustang. Even after casting
off his parachute, there was so little room in the cockpit that
Horbaczewski had to sit on his passenger's knees in order to pilot
the plane back to base.

Deliverance took a little longer for another pilot, who was shot
down not far behind the German lines on his first sortie. Having

concealed his parachute, he started looking for somewhere to hide until the Allied ground forces arrived, which would only be a matter of days, and knocked at the gate of a convent. The nuns did not want to let him take refuge there for fear of reprisals, but finally relented, on condition that he keep to a cell and dress up as a nun, just in case the Germans decided to search the premises. He submitted to this indignity, but after a few days of boredom he decided to try to get back to the Allied lines. The mother superior would not hear of this, as he might be spotted leaving the place, so he began to plan his escape. He needed an ally among the nuns, and his natural instinct told him to try the only youngish-looking one. He approached her in the kitchen garden and turned on all the charm at his disposal. 'Cut it out, you bloody fool!' snapped the nun, who turned out to be a British pilot who had been languishing there since the Dieppe raid.

The bombers were also having a field-day. The men of 305 Light Bomber Squadron carried out intruder operations with their Mosquitoes by day and by night on specified targets. Those of 300, now equipped with Lancasters, flew back and forth across the Channel to bomb deep in the enemy rear. Their successful attack on German motor torpedo-boats in Le Havre harbour won them praise from the Air Ministry, while their crippling of German ground forces in the Caen area earned them a personal 'thank you very much' from Field-Marshal Montgomery. The bombers could operate in relative safety, since the *Luftwaffe* were keeping out of the way, but there were always risks from ground fire – and narrow escapes.

While it was bombing targets near Caen on 18 July, one of 300's Lancasters was caught in heavy flak. The rear gunner's turret was knocked askew by the blast, which sucked him from his seat, and he fell out. But his left foot jammed in the turret mounting, and he hung upside-down below the plane. The upper gunner and the flight engineer went to his rescue, but could not haul him up by the boot, the only bit of him they could reach, for fear of pulling it off and sending him plunging to his death. The flight engineer, Sergeant Jan Pialucha, climbed out with a length of rope. Clinging to the underside of the plane by one arm, he tied the rope round the rear gunner's waist with the other, and then, climbing back in, made the other end fast. The Lancaster flew back across the Channel with the unfortunate rear gunner hanging upside-down from its tail, causing some consternation as it came in to land. The pilot managed to touch down delicately, so the gunner's head missed being shattered on the runway. He was bleeding from his nose and ears, and his skin was a little raw, but he was otherwise unhurt, and flying again a few days later.

Occasionally German fighters did appear, usually *en masse* in order to make up for the fact that most of the pilots were young and inexperienced. On 18 August, for instance, the 12 planes of 315 Squadron encountered a swarm of 60 Focke-Wulfs over Beauvais. They destroyed 16 of them, but lost their much-loved commander, Squadron Leader Horbaczewski, who was shot down and killed after himself downing 3 German planes.

The pilots of 2 Polish Wing, which had been assigned to Air Defence of Great Britain, were disappointed at having been left out of the invasion and envious of their comrades in France. But they were unexpectedly faced with a new challenge. Only ten days after D-Day, on the night of 15 June, strange-sounding planes were heard approaching London. When they were over the city, their engines cut out, and huge explosions followed: the first V1 flying bombs had arrived. Regular anti-aircraft defences were unable to bring them down in any significant numbers, and at first the fighters of ADGB could not get at them either. American Thunderbolts and Tempests, with which some RAF squadrons were equipped, could give chase, but Mustangs had to be modified in order to have a chance of catching up with them. As it happened, one of the first of the bombs to be shot down by a fighter was notched up to a Polish pilot serving with 219 Squadron.

Two Polish squadrons, 306 and 315, were withdrawn from France and joined 316, which was already in ADGB, in order to counter this new threat. The challenge brought out the best in the pilots. Bohdan Arct, now commander of 316 Squadron, was moved to West Malling, which lay directly in the path of the flying bombs as they made their way towards London. The first encounters were experimental in nature. The planes would be sent up singly to patrol a specified area, and then informed by radio when a bomb was flying through it. They were given its position and height, but it was no easy matter to spot it, as the V1s were less than half the size of a plane. There was also the question of how to come at them. The best attack position was from behind, but then the target was small, while the slip-stream of the bomb made it difficult for the attacker to keep his own craft steady.

There was another problem, as one of 316's pilots, Jan Pietrzak, discovered. He approached a bomb from behind and, in Polish fashion, waited until he was close – 100 metres – before opening up. As he hit the bomb, it exploded. The blast tore off his propeller, bent both wings, shattered the steering-gear, and he had to bale out. After that, pilots were instructed not to open fire at less than 200 metres.

Another hazard was ground fire from London's anti-aircraft defences. The gunners ignored the chasing planes as they opened up on the flying bombs, and as they were often behind their target, the plane tended to take the flak. As a result, pilots were sent out further into the Channel, right up to the Belgian coast, so as to have time to attack the bombs away from the anti-aircraft defences.

In spite of having to patrol for up to seven hours a day, the pilots delighted in this work. It was partly the old spirit of 1940, the knowledge that every bomb that got through would bring death and devastation to the city. But it was also something to do with the vey nature of the exercise. 'The squadron fell into a sort of trance, a strange zeal, as though infected with a "flying-bomb bacillus",' writes Arct. 'The pilots were desperate to go to work, the mechanics sacrificed their nights.' At one stage he stopped all leave, but nobody noticed. Once up in the air, they would patrol for as long as fuel permitted. If they expended their ammunition before they ran out of fuel, they went on patrolling, and, if they spotted a flying bomb, or a 'witch' as they called them, they went for it with the means at their disposal.

Tadeusz Szymański had shot down two bombs, using up all his ammunition, when he saw a third coming his way. He gave chase and came alongside the flying bomb. He edged closer and closer, moving the tip of his wing into position just beneath that of the bomb. When it was right underneath, he jerked his steering-gear, tipping the wing of the bomb so violently that it swerved off course and spiralled down into the sea. This became standard practice, and pilots enjoyed doing it even if they did have ammunition left. But it was not always foolproof. Once, Szymański had to repeat the exercise twelve times, as the bomb kept swinging back and righting itself. In trying to tip over a bomb one day, Tadeusz Karnkowski, also of 316, jolted it so violently that when it swung back, equally violently, its wing shattered the tip of his own; he had to dash back to West Malling in his careering Mustang while the bomb flew on towards London.

The three Polish squadrons acquitted themselves honourably, accounting for 190 (nearly 10 per cent of all the bombs brought down), even though one squadron was withdrawn to other duties after six weeks. The top score went to 316, which was officially credited with 74. Indeed, Polish fighter units did well on every front, as they managed to shoot down a total of 100 enemy planes as well during the course of 1944.

But 1944 was an increasingly unhappy year for the Poles. As the war drew towards its conclusion, the problem of the post-war settlement loomed larger and the Polish government's influence over events dwindled. Stalin was grooming a Communist government for Poland and had fielded a Polish army made up of those unfortunates who had not been released from the gulags under the 1941 agreement. In 1943 he had even started a rival air force, which included two pilots, one navigator and twenty-two ground staff of the pre-war Polish Air Force. (It went into action in mid 1944 and had shot down 16 German planes by the end of the war.)

The future of Poland was up for discussion, and the tenor of that discussion in the British press was increasingly high-handed and hostile. The Polish government was regularly described as 'Fascist'. Its soldiers were surprised to find themselves being referred to as a 'White Army' and a threat to world peace. The hostility of the British press to the Polish cause brought resentment and latent doubts to the surface. The unsatisfactory nature of the explanations of the accident in which Sikorski had died spawned unpleasant rumours of sabotage, bringing into question Britain's good faith and commitment to her Polish ally. It was increasingly difficult for the Poles to maintain their absolute trust in Britain. Communist propaganda was circulating in the form of pamphlets distributed by young British activists, mainly women, and its tenor was vehemently anti-Polish. And while the majority of the British public remained cordial, they were bored with the war, and utterly 'fed up with the wretched Polish question'.

The airmen noted that their successes were now reported in the press merely as RAF victories, while in the cinemas they had to watch newsreels extolling the heroic struggle of the Russians against the Nazi invader. They felt increasingly isolated. Even the Czech airmen, with whom the Poles had until now entertained such cordial relations, began to keep their distance, their government having taken a pro-Soviet stance. They behaved 'correctly, politely, but with reserve' towards Poles stationed on the same bases, according to an intelligence report.

In March 1944 four mechanics of 307 Squadron on a visit to the De Havilland works were forced to leave when the workers, many wearing red stars, downed tools and began booing them. In Blackpool, a Polish pilot riding on the Fleetwood tram with his wife was beset by a group of trawlermen and their wives, shouting 'Go home, you dirty Pole!' There were even reports of Polish Air Force officers being spat at in the street by young women with Communist sympathies.

More significantly, such sentiments had even begun to surface within the RAF. Junior administrative officers were showing increasing hostility to Polish colleagues, often using red tape or regulations to make their lives difficult. At Cranwell, where a group of Poles were training, someone scrawled 'Poles Go Home!' on the main notice-board. At Sealand, the British station commander did not attempt to disguise his dislike of the Poles, and actually kicked one of them at a party in the mess. Such unpleasantness remained the exception, and an editorial in the Polish Air Force magazine made the point that, bearing in mind all that had been said, written and done by British soldiers, politicians and civilians over the past four years, 'probably no people has ever been the recipient of such moving expressions of friendship on this island as the Poles'. And, in the final analysis, what was said and written in Britain was far less important than what was happening in Poland.

In January 1944 the Red Army had advanced into Poland in pursuit of the retreating *Wehrmacht,* and by July it was closing in on Warsaw. On 1 August the Polish Home Army rose against the Germans in Warsaw. The Red Army reached the opposite bank of the Vistula and halted, in order to allow the German forces to liquidate the Polish Home Army. There followed 63 days of street-fighting, with poorly armed Polish soldiers defending every square metre of the city against an overwhelming onslaught by SS troops supported by tanks, artillery and dive-bombers, until the whole city was reduced to rubble.

The soldiers in Warsaw needed arms and medical supplies. Britain and the United States were prepared to help, but Stalin refused to allow British or American planes to land and refuel on Soviet-held airfields in eastern Poland, which meant that the planes would have to make a round trip there and back. This ruled out the use of most bombers and precluded the possibility of fighter cover.

The only force that could help in the circumstances was 1586 Polish Special Duties Squadron, based at Brindisi. This had been carrying out supply drops to the partisans in Yugoslavia and, less frequently, to the Home Army in Poland. It had only been able to carry out 205 drops to Poland in the year that it had been stationed at Brindisi, delivering 145 parachutists, 286 tons of supplies, 16 million dollars, 6.5 million marks and 40 million zloty, and losing 16 planes in the process. They had also carried out three landing operations, bringing out couriers, political leaders and, on 25 July 1944, a V1 flying bomb the Home Army had managed to capture.

Three days after the outbreak of the Warsaw uprising, on 4 August, four planes of 1586 flew to Warsaw and dropped arms. They repeated the exercise as often as atmospheric conditions permitted. Air Commodore Rayski, now aged 54 and titular commander of the Polish Air Force in Italy, personally piloted a Halifax three times over the blazing capital. It was a difficult ten-hour flight over German-held territory, with mountains and heavy concentrations of anti-aircraft defences, made all the more dangerous by the poor condition of the old Halifaxes and Dakotas the squadron was equipped with. The planes were overloaded because the airmen filled every nook and cranny with supply canisters, knowing that every rifle was like manna from heaven to the soldiers of the beleaguered Home Army.

The crews could see the glow of the fires in Warsaw up to a hundred kilometres away, and they could smell the smoke fifteen kilometres away. As they approached the city, they had to fly as low as they could along the Vistula, shaving the tops of the bridges so as to avoid flak, and then veer across the burning city at rooftop level. A thick pall of smoke blotted out the night sky and filled the cockpit and cabin with an acrid stench. 'The barrage of enemy fire, the blazing city and the flight at an altitude of a couple of hundred metres through clouds of smoke made an extraordinary impression,' notes Jan Cholewa, who piloted four flights over Warsaw.

In the first weeks of the uprising 1586 made 83 sorties, losing 16 of its 18 crews. The other Polish bomber squadrons were stripped of crews to replace them, and a number of British and South African crews stationed in northern Italy volunteered to make the perilous flight. The results were pitiful. Of the 196 sorties (91 by Polish, 55 by South African and 50 by British crews), only 42 managed to reach Warsaw and drop their loads, of which only 25 fell into Polish hands. Thirty-nine planes were lost.

For the British air staffs, the Poles' desperate attempts to succour their beleaguered capital were an organizational nightmare, made all the more irksome by their evident futility. But they assisted their Polish colleagues loyally, realizing how important the issue was for them. When the rising was virtually over, Stalin relented, and 110 bombers of the USAAF escorted by 70 fighters carried out a drop over Warsaw and landed on Soviet fields. Only two planes were lost. But by then the area held by the defenders was so small that most of the supplies fell into German hands.

Those were the two worst months of the war for the Poles in the west, and particularly for the airmen, who felt they should have been in a position to bring help to their brothers-in-arms. Never before had they felt their powerlessness so intensely. They badgered their superiors to allow them to go and assist in any way they could, and the pilots of 303 wrote a letter to the King, begging him to allow them to go. With extra fuel tanks fitted the Mustang might get to Warsaw, though not back again, and some pilots wanted to go on kamikaze missions. A group of officers of 305 begged their commander to defy orders and take the Mosquitoes to dive-bomb German positions around Warsaw. But there were no acts of indiscipline.

'As we sat around the radio, we died a little during each of those 63 days of the rising,' one pilot of 316 said. 'I'm a Warsaw man, born and bred, and my wife and children were there.' The gradual withdrawal of Allied support from the Polish cause was incomprehensible to people like him who had thrown themselves into the common cause without reserve, giving freely of themselves to defend London and support Allied operations in different theatres.

Unit commanders began to bombard the air force inspectorate with requests for lectures and more information on the political situation, which was baffling to the rank-and-file in particular. 'Every member of the air force is gnawed by deep anxiety over the future of Poland,' confirmed an internal security report. Morale fell markedly as black clouds gathered over the future of Poland, and political discussions and mutinous sentiments began to invade the messes. This was particularly true of isolated units such as the unfortunate 309, which was at last given Mustangs and turned into a full fighter squadron, only to be

posted to Drem and told to defend Scotland against a non-existent threat. Spirits were not much lighter in 304, transferred to
the Hebridean island of Benbecula, 'a moonscape of craters and
mounds' which made Tiree seem like Paris.

For front-line units there was a cure in action, and the airmen
threw themselves into the fight with grim determination. The
Lancasters of 300 were bombing Germany from their
Lincolnshire bases at Ingham and later Faldingworth. The
Mosquitoes of 307 Night-fighter Squadron took part in the
Arnhem operation. The three squadrons of 131 Fighter Wing
were following the front in France, changing airfields frequently.
After the battle of Falaise they moved to an airfield at Rouen,
then to another south of Lille. To their surprise, they met with
little cordiality from the local French, who were strongly affected
by Communist propaganda, and an intelligence report noted
that 'the French population is generally ill-disposed to the Poles'.
But they were warmly greeted by thousands of Polish emigrants
who had come to work in the French coal-mines before the war,
and who showered them with gifts and hospitality. On 20
October the wing moved to Antwerp, where they were almost
'embarrassed' by the cordiality of the population. They spent
Christmas in Ghent, whose burghers received them with open
arms. The ladies of the town opened a club for them, and smoth-
ered them in attentions. At Christmas itself, the Polish wing
joined forces with the ladies and organized a party for 500 local
orphans.

The squadron that really made its mark during the invasion of
France and the offensive into Germany was 305, originally a
Wellington squadron, but since 1943 a light-bomber unit flying
Mosquitoes. It was known as 'the flying grandads', on account of
the age of its crews. Its commander, Orliński, was a veteran who
had flown from Warsaw to Tokyo in 1926 and left the air force to
become a LOT pilot before the war. Most of the other pilots and
navigators were in their forties and fifties, and the youngest was
thirty-five. It had an atmosphere all its own.

'I had the pleasant feeling that I had been assigned not to a
front-line military unit, but rather accepted into a comfortable
club,' writes Mieczysław Pruszyński, who had transferred to the
air force from the Carpathian Lancers and, after a period of
training in Canada, been posted to 305 in 1943. And it was no
ordinary club: 'night-club first, aero-club second'. He walked
into its mess on an airfield in Hampshire to find a relaxed group

of men in blue sitting around talking. 'What'll you drink?' a man leaning on the bar asked him, without introducing himself. Drinks were followed by lunch and yet more drinks. When Pruszyński asked whom he should report to and what time morning parade would be, there was a snigger. His commanding officer was the one who had bought him the drink, and there were no parades in 305.

But the squadron was by no means idle. They slept by day and went raiding virtually every night in their Mosquitoes. The planes were fast and well-armed, but as they were dive-bombing heavily defended targets, they were very vulnerable to ground fire and losses were high. 'When the plane lifts off from the airfield on a dark night, I can feel fear climbing into the cockpit of my Mosquito and taking its place beside me,' Pruszyński wrote. 'It settles threateningly on my parachute or the dinghy, and does not leave me throughout the four hours of the flight.'

As the Polish Air Force began to run short of aircrew, particularly navigators, it filled gaps with RAF personnel; since 305 did not seem to attract many young Poles it gradually acquired more and more foreigners, until in early 1945 it had more non-Poles than Poles among its aircrew. Moreover, it seemed to attract a curiously un-RAF kind of person.

Pruszyński, an intellectual from a literary family, was delighted to find himself sharing a room with the bookish Simon Sitwell, one of 305's British acquisitions. Another in the same vein was Lord Charles Ossulston, a music enthusiast who took the opportunity of the squadron's frequent changes of airfield in France to try out every church organ in the area. Nor were those drawn to 305 predominantly British. There were representatives of ten nations, including a Belorussian, a Bahamian, an Estonian and an Indian. They all learned to speak pidgin-Polish, and, in a curious reversal of the practice elsewhere in the air force, they all acquired Polish names such as 'Kuba' and 'Jasio'.

'Christmas 1944 will always be associated in my memory with dirt, fatigue, hunger and rivers of champagne,' writes Pruszyński. The squadron was stationed in north-eastern France, and scrounging in the locality had produced some sausage and pickled cucumbers made by Polish emigrants settled in the area, as well as a trove of 500 bottles of champagne. They all drank too much, which was unfortunate, as they were roused from their celebrations by orders to get airborne at once. The Germans had launched their offensive in the Ardennes.

The ferocity of the offensive caught the Allies off-guard, and they had to fly round the clock in appalling weather conditions to try to pin down the German advance. On 1 January the *Luftwaffe* launched a massive attack on the airfields round Ghent, and succeeded in destroying dozens of Allied planes on the ground. The Polish wing had 24 planes destroyed, but two of its squadrons were on their way back from an operation and managed to catch the Germans at it. The Polish pilots were delighted to be able to up their scores: those of 308 shot down 12 German planes, those of 317 another 8, and they damaged another 7 between them, for the loss of two of their own pilots.

Being in the thick of the fighting was what kept them going. By the end of 1944 most of the Poles realized that their country's future was under threat, and did not by this stage have much faith in the Allies. An internal intelligence report of January 1945 notes that the majority of the airmen had lost their respect for Churchill. But the same source reports that, while there was little cheer to be felt, 'the level of morale amongst the men is really high and worthy of admiration'. They would soon need all the morale they could muster.

On 13 February 1945 the decisions of the Yalta conference were announced, confirming that Poland was to lose a vast chunk of her territory to the Soviet Union, and that what was left of the country would remain under Soviet domination. One British station commander took the precaution of confiscating the side-arms of all the Poles on his base a couple of hours before the announcement, under pretence of issuing them with new ones, fearing a mutiny. His anxiety, natural enough in the circumstances, was ill-founded.

At Faldingworth, the aircrews of 300 assembled for their operational briefing just after the news had been broadcast on the Home Service. They were in gloomy mood, and there were audible murmurs of discontent. Then the operations officer announced their target: they were to bomb German communications centres in support of the Red Army's advance. 'Why should we go, since we've been betrayed?' one of the pilots shouted, and his comrades backed him up with similar outbursts. The squadron commander calmed them down and reminded them of their military duty. That night they bombed Dresden, and two days later again bombed targets in support of the Soviet advance. 'If the Germans get me now, I won't even know what I'm dying for,' a pilot of 300 wrote in a letter to a friend that day. 'For Poland, for Britain, or for Russia?' He was killed over Pforzheim ten days later, still unsure of what he was fighting for. It had certainly not been for his native city, Lwów, which had been incorporated into the Soviet Union.

The Yalta decisions had 'driven a deep wedge' between the Poles and their RAF colleagues, in the words of an intelligence report. The British officers were visibly embarrassed and subconsciously avoided the Poles, while the other ranks could not understand what their Polish comrades were making a fuss about. After hearing the news of Yalta, one of the pilots of 305 announced that after the war he would keep an English servant, so that he could call him a traitor to his face every day. A certain cynicism could also be detected as the pilots of units based on the Continent began trafficking on a large scale. It all started innocently enough, with pilots swapping British cigarettes in France for French scent to bring back to their girl-friends in Britain. They soon began selling the scent, and then they moved on to smuggling dollars and gold in their cockpits as they hopped back and forth across the Channel. But on the whole morale and discipline remained astoundingly high.

The Polish fighter wing continued to move forward behind the advancing ground forces, through Belgium and Holland, and, on 10 April 1945, it landed at Nordhorn airfield in Germany, the first Polish unit to set foot on German soil. There was elation among the airmen as they finally achieved their military goal and landed their planes in a prostrate Germany. This sense of having won through was enhanced by emotional reunions. As POW camps were liberated, some of their colleagues who had been shot down and taken prisoner turned up at the airfield and there were boisterous celebrations.

They also came across Polish soldiers and civilians released from concentration camps and labour battalions, who greeted them as conquering heroes. Among them were family, friends and acquaintances who communicated snippets of news about other loved ones, not all of it welcome. One squadron leader stopped a little girl who was wandering among the planes. He told her in German that it was too dangerous a place to play, but she replied in Polish that her mother had been killed and that she was looking for her father, who was an airman. He asked what his name might be, and heard his own in reply. He had last seen his daughter in Poland, aged two.

On 9 April 303 and 316, operating from Andrews Field in Essex, had their first encounter with the new German jets, the Messerschmitt 262s, and shot down one of them. This was the last air kill of the Polish Air Force. On 25 April, 131 Polish Wing gave air cover to the great raid on Berchtesgaden, in which sixteen Lancasters of 300 also took part. This was to be the last major operation of the Polish Air Force.

The German surrender brought them up sharp. '"Victory!" every radio-set shouts, "Victory!" every Anglo-Saxon says in greeting instead of the traditional "Hello!",' someone wrote in 305 Squadron diary. 'The word "Victory!" is devoid of meaning, power and any sense today only for the Poles.' Their isolation had become total.

On 8 May, VE Day, Group Captain Robert Beill assembled the officers and men of 300 Squadron at Faldingworth. 'We must not only understand the joy of our hosts today; we must likewise respect it,' he told them. He reminded them that the squadron had won 106 British gallantry awards and 15 commendations (what he did not know was that it had also suffered more deaths than any other bomber squadron in the RAF). He ordered them not to make any comments in front of British people that might upset them, and not to refuse to join in their celebrations if invited to do so. It did not come easily. 'All was gladness and jollification, crowds were lighting fires and burning the benches and huts in riotous good humour,' writes Stefan Knapp, a pilot with 318 in Italy. 'It almost made me cry.'

On the next day, Air Vice-Marshal Iżycki, commander of the Polish Air Force, received a message from Sir Archibald Sinclair, Chairman of the Air Council, which ran:

> In this hour of victory over a resolute, vindictive and barbarous enemy the Air Council send their greetings and congratulations to all ranks of the Polish Air Force. They do not forget that you were the first to resist the aggressor, neither do they forget that you came after manifold trials to our aid when we most needed your help. Your valiant squadrons fighting alongside our own were in the forefront of the Battle of Britain and so helped to restore the fortunes of the Allies throughout the years of struggle.
>
> In good times and bad you have stood by us and shared with the Royal Air Force their losses and their victories. The Council would ask you to convey to the Officers and Other

Ranks of the Polish Air Force their admiration for their indomitable courage in the air and for their industry and skill on the ground. They trust that the comradeship which has grown up between the Air Forces of Poland and Great Britain will prove a lasting bond and that their exploits may have laid the foundations of an enduring peace.

These fine words sounded remarkably hollow to Iżycki as he sat gloomily briefing staff in his office at the back of the Rubens Hotel, trying to ignore the sounds of jubilation drifting in through the open window.

Some found it difficult not to get carried away by the joy of peace and joined in the dancing in the streets. But most could not bring themselves to rejoice. 'Our war is lost, the war which we fought so hard and so long to win,' wrote Tadeusz Szumowski in his diary. 'So many million lives have been laid down. In Poland itself. On foreign soil. In alien seas and skies. And for what?' Pruszyński celebrated the coming of peace in the British Officers' Club (now the US Embassy) in Paris, but he felt left out. He longed to get into his Mosquito and fly to Kraków. 'This was not how we had imagined the end of this bloody war,' he writes.

13

Redundancy

'AFTER SO MANY years of anticipation, the end of the war, when it came, took us by surprise,' writes one of the airmen. Another, stationed with 308 on an airfield in Germany, also found the peace strangely unreal. 'We had thought that the combat squadrons would suddenly become idle, that we would get bored, but in fact we are kept busy and flying – maybe on purpose,' he wrote. 'In reality, nothing has changed. Flying has become our daily work. Every day I greet the mechanics, who are as overworked as ever.' Rumours circulated to the effect that they might be sent to help fight the Japanese.

In the meantime the fighters patrolled German airspace and carried out the other duties of an occupation force. Their life in Germany was enlivened by the large numbers of released Polish concentration-camp inmates, POWs and refugees, also awaiting developments. There were many young women among them, and a number of marriages took place, but six years of separation had left their mark, and the airmen were teased about how 'English' they had become.

The bombers, still based in Lincolnshire, were employed in 'wastage' operations, which involved dropping surplus live ammunition into the sea, in flying food supplies into Holland, and in ferrying elements of the British 8th Army back from Italy. Life on these large stations continued as normal, for there was a great deal of work involved in simply keeping them running.

This apparent normality concealed a highly abnormal situation. On 5 July 1945, less than two months after VE Day, Britain and the United States announced that they no longer recognized the Polish government in London as the lawful government of Poland. This turned the Polish forces overnight into what one British judge called 'the largest illegal private army ever known in this country'. From being a useful ally in the war against Germany, the Polish soldiers, sailors and airmen had become an object of acute embarrassment to the British government, and what to do with them a major headache.

There could be no question of transferring them to the command of the Communist Warsaw regime, as it had requested. But they could not be treated the same as British or Empire troops; they had no homes or jobs to go back to, they would get no pensions and no war gratuity, and, most crucially, they were stateless. Back in February, Churchill had told the House of Commons that 'In any event, His Majesty's Government will never forget the debt they owe to the Polish troops who have served them so valiantly, and for all those who have fought under our command, I earnestly hope that it may be possible to offer the citizenship and freedom of the British Empire, if they so desire.' This was going to be a difficult pledge to honour.

Great Britain was in very poor condition by 1945, physically exhausted and materially ruined by the effort sustained in the war. Her people wanted a return to normality and hoped for full employment, which they felt was threatened by the presence of large numbers of foreigners. Her government urgently needed to curb military expenditure, and the economist Lord Keynes calculated that the Polish forces under British command were costing the country £2.5 million a month. (This seems excessive, since the cost of the entire Polish Air Force in Britain, including that of the planes they flew and the bombs they dropped, only totalled £8,269,873 11s. 11d. from the beginning of 1940 up to 30 June 1945.) Churchill suggested using them as an army of occupation in Germany and, later, turning them into 'a British Foreign Legion', but both of these ideas were quickly dismissed as unrealistic.

The new Labour government of Clement Attlee felt little sympathy for what many of its supporters called the Polish 'Fascists', and it craved harmonious relations with the Soviet Union. That was why the Poles were excluded from the Victory Parade held in London on 6 June 1946. Distinguished political and military figures wrote letters of protest to the press at this insult. 'Have we lost all sense of decency and gratitude?' thundered Air Marshal

Sir Philip Joubert. But they were in the minority. The Polish contribution to the Allied war effort was being consistently ignored or belittled in the press, and even the achievements of the Polish Air Force were being called into question. The view was gaining ground that they had been very brave but not much use. A Gallup poll held in June 1946 revealed that while only 30 per cent of those interviewed favoured allowing Poles to remain in Britain, nearly twice as many, 56 per cent, were for deporting them. The government was of the same mind. Its Cabinet Polish Forces Committee felt that 'everything should be done to ensure that as few Poles as possible remained in this country'.

Every Pole fighting alongside the Allies since 1939 had entertained only one dream – to return to a free homeland. But few of them contemplated the idea of returning to a Soviet-dominated one, and the British government had a problem on its hands. The Polish government in London protested vigorously at the betrayal of Yalta and its stand was endorsed by the 400,000 troops and dependents scattered throughout British dominions. This unwanted legion was not going to melt away. The Foreign Office feared they might start deserting *en masse*. The Home Office actually consulted the War Office about measures to be taken in the event of a wholesale mutiny. But there was no trouble.

The Poles made it a point of honour to behave with dignity and discipline, and the British military were tactful. British officers were instructed to show consideration to the Polish servicemen with whom they came into contact. Senior RAF commanders held a banquet for the Polish Air Force top brass at the Dorchester Hotel. Sir Archibald Sinclair gave them lunch at Claridge's. The RAF organized an exhibition of the Polish Air Force's exploits under British command and Sholto Douglas opened it in Warsaw.

The air force was the most tractable part of the problem. By the end of the war it numbered about 14,900 men and women. They were highly professional and disciplined, and it was relatively easy to keep them busy. Apart from normal flying duties, they were given courses of lectures and instruction. It was all very much business as usual as the Polish command struggled to fill the terrible vacuum. It was no easy task. The end of the war had brought a sense of relief, but pilots, who loved the flying and the fighting, were suffering from withdrawal, and everyone had something of an adrenalin hangover. The events of the past two years had undermined the men's confidence in authority, and a thick layer of cynicism spread to cover the wounded feelings and the shattered illusions.

The British government proceeded with caution, having to take into account the feelings of the Poles, of the British population and of the Warsaw regime. An Interim Treasury Committee for Polish Affairs was set up. This was to dismantle the Polish government and liquidate its assets, in effect dissolving a whole embryonic state, complete with ministries of justice, health, education and all the other functions which not only the armed forces but the 180,000-odd civilian dependants had required. What to do with the military remained the key question, and this was the subject of lengthy discussions between the Home Office, the Foreign Office and the War Office, which dragged on throughout the remainder of 1945 and the first months of 1946.

In March 1946 the government announced that the Polish forces would be disbanded. A statement from the Warsaw regime inviting all Poles to return to Poland was circulated to all servicemen, with a covering letter from Ernest Bevin, the Foreign Secretary, politely urging them to go. Some of the British officers who had to issue the documents baulked at the distasteful task, and the commander of the WAAF training camp said that she would not have blamed the Polish girls if they had set fire to the mess. But the servicemen took it calmly. Nevertheless, very few of them showed any willingness to comply. A large proportion of them had spent two years in Soviet gulags and had no intention of laying themselves open to another stint. So the British government had to think of alternative arrangements.

On 20 May 1946 Ernest Bevin announced the formation of a Polish Resettlement Corps. This would be a British military unit which the Polish servicemen would be invited to join. On doing so they would cease to be members of the Polish armed forces, but they would not find themselves on the street. As nominal members of the British forces, they would receive pay and full medical care. They would be employed in a number of tasks such as bomb-clearing and helping with the harvest while civilian jobs were found for them. They would be released from the ranks of the Resettlement Corps as and when they found employment. If they did not like the work or were fired, they could return to the Corps until a new job was found. There was to be a special Polish Air Force Resettlement Corps, which would remain on air stations and only carry out work connected with the air force.

The men could not legally be forced to join the Corps, and for a time it was doubtful whether the scheme would work at all. The men were loath to leave the Polish ranks and pass into a foreign service. Their trust in the British had fallen so low that many were highly suspicious of the scheme, and from time to time wild rumours would circulate concerning the consequences of signing on. And while the British government was promising one thing, the British trades unions seemed to be saying another.

The TUC had been consulted when plans for the Resettlement Corps were being drawn up. There was an acute shortage of labour, particularly in mining, agriculture and building. Far from being a burden, the Poles, many of whom had experience in these very trades, could help rebuild the country. The TUC accepted the government's arguments, but it had little control over its members. Although the mining industry was in urgent need of some 100,000 men, the National Union of Mineworkers was adamant that the Poles should be kept out. The same went for the National Union of Agricultural Workers. In October 1946, a couple of weeks after the Polish Resettlement Corps started enrolment, the TUC Conference met at Brighton, and the issue of the Poles was extensively aired in the acrimonious debates, with many harsh words.

Various ministers and friends of Poland intervened in the debate, which had spread to Parliament and the national press. The *Sunday Times* was stalwart in its defence of the Poles, as was the *Daily Telegraph*, whose owner, Lord Camrose, launched an appeal to erect a memorial to the Polish Air Force (unveiled at Northolt on All Souls' Day 1948). But the unions could not control the xenophobia at grass-roots level. There was much tub-thumping at pitheads and on factory floors, and increasingly overt expressions of hostility. Walls near Polish Air Force stations were daubed with 'Poles go Home' and 'England for the English'. Airmen were regularly jeered in the street. There were confrontations and even fist-fights, and occasionally things turned nasty. On the evening of 26 October 1946, twelve airmen returning to their base at Hucknall were surrounded by a gang of armed men and beaten up. All twelve had to be hospitalized. Similar incidents occurred at Nottingham and Chesterfield. On 5 November a Polish Air Force intelligence report warned that 'unless there is a change of attitude towards the Poles among the British population, it is to be expected that our men will be driven by exasperation to acts of active self-defence'.

The job of keeping the men in shape was not getting any easier. By the beginning of 1946 Polish Air Force intelligence was reporting that although the officers continued to carry out their duties conscientiously, they did so without enthusiasm. They had too much time on their hands, as a result of which alcohol consumption and gambling were on the increase. This had an effect on the other ranks, with predictable lapses in discipline and reliability. By the spring, offences such as petty theft were also on the increase, and in June a group of airmen at Cammeringham actually tried to hold up the paymaster. Demoralization was setting in, and there were even a few suicides.

The airmen began to remove their 'Poland' flashes, once the source of such pride, whenever they left their bases – not from fear of violence, but out of a desire to avoid the expressions of ill-will they invariably aroused. 'I was choking with the bitterness of it,' writes Stefan Knapp. 'Not so long ago I had enjoyed the exaggerated prestige of a fighter pilot and the hysterical adulation that surrounded him. Suddenly I turned into the slag everybody wanted to be rid of, a thing useless, burdensome, even noxious. It was very hard to bear.' Many who had not even considered doing so to begin with, now decided to opt for repatriation to Poland. Some were also swayed by the Warsaw regime's threat that anyone joining the Resettlement Corps would automatically forfeit forever all rights to Polish citizenship.

Those who were afraid of returning to Poland clung desperately to the only stable thing in their lives – their unit. Many of them had been adolescents when they joined up, and their regiments and squadrons had come to replace the families and communities they had lost. Leaving these surrogate families in a foreign land represented a traumatic leap into the unknown. They were cruelly torn. They wandered about their bases arguing the pros and cons among themselves, which often led to heated arguments, political discussions and accusations of treason. They agonized over the dilemma, and the feeling of being caught between a number of unpleasant choices made them increasingly paranoid, emotional and quarrelsome. The suicides increased.

The ground started slipping from under their feet in the autumn of 1946, when the dissolution of the squadrons began and they lost their planes. On 18 September four fighter squadrons staged a farewell parade and fly-past before Air Marshal Sir James Robb at Coltishall. On 11 October it was the turn of 300, the first unit formed in Great Britain – also the longest in action of any Allied bomber squadron, and the one that suffered the highest losses. There was not a dry eye on the station at Faldingworth as the squadron's twenty Lancasters roared over-head in tight formation. On 19 November, at Chedburgh, 301 and 304 bade their farewell. Parting from their machines was an emotional moment for many of the airmen. Tadeusz Schiele of 308 savoured every minute of his last flight and dragged out the actions of leaving the cockpit of his Spitfire. 'I stood before the machine looking at its proudly jutting nose and beautiful slim wings,' he writes. 'The seven stars had faded, but in spite of being spattered with oil were still distinctly visible. I walked up to the propeller and, clutching the cold metal very hard, I kissed it with a love that welled from the depths of my soul.'

Over the next few weeks and months the airmen made their decisions, often on an emotional whim, sometimes because one more muttered 'Filthy Poles!' overheard on a bus made the cup of bitterness overflow. Nearly 3,000 eventually opted to return to Poland. By the beginning of 1947 some 11,000 had joined the Air Resettlement Corps, which was housed at Hucknall, Cammeringham, Castle Combe, East Wretham, Framlingham, Portreath, Skipton-on-Swale, Melton Mowbray and Dunholme Lodge. They were more fortunate than their comrades from the ground forces, who were scattered in 265 camps all over the country, some of them only recently vacated by German POWs.

The 'free elections' in Poland pledged by Stalin at Yalta took place in January 1947 amid massive vote-rigging, intimidation, arrests and wholesale murder. The British authorities could no longer press the servicemen to go home, and a Polish Resettlement Act was passed in February, giving them all the right to remain in Britain. This was not a popular move, for the xenophobia had not let up. Hardly a week passed without some Labour MP griping about the costs of resettling the Poles, and one was wont to shout 'We don't want the Poles here' in the Chamber. The press echoed these sentiments, particularly *The Times*, the *Daily Mirror*, the *News Chronicle*, the *Star* and the *Evening Standard*, which all fanned groundless fears of unem-ployment and regaled their readers with often spurious stories of black-marketeering by Poles.

In January 1947 the NUM agreed to admit Poles into the mines in return for the government concession of a five-day week. Individual pits still opposed the measure, but by the summer some 2,000 Poles were already working down the mines, and more were taken on there, and elsewhere. But the problems did not end with getting a job.

A sociologist who was observing the Poles' integration into British life noted that the Polish worker took his work more seriously, had a more emotional tie to his machinery, greater respect for his employers, and a deeper sense of duty and commitment than his English counterpart. Polish-language newspapers advised the men to avoid showing zeal and to take the pace from their British workmates. 'Heaven forbid that you should work with excessive speed or enthusiasm, for you would be well on the way to creating enemies for yourself,' warned one. 'Workers in this country conserve their strength.' But the Poles were materially destitute and eager to start a new life, so they threw themselves into their work with determination. The consequences were predictable. In a factory producing pins for carburettors, where one worker's average daily production was 500, two demobilized Poles managed to produce an average of 1,500 pins a day each and after a mass walk-out by the other workers the management had to fire them. In July 1947 the Amalgamated Union of Engineering Workers (AUEW) was demanding that all Poles be expelled from the engineering and shipbuilding industries and sent back to Poland. The following year the conference of the Union of Agricultural Workers at Scarborough called for all foreign agricultural workers to be sacked. The Amalgamated Union of Building Trades Workers' conference at Eastbourne voiced similar demands.

Much of this was the result, not of strong feelings on the part of the workers, but of agitprop by left-wing union activists. Underlying it was a chasm of ignorance and stupidity. George Orwell, who felt affronted by it, recorded a conversation he had overheard between two small businessmen in a Scottish hotel. They were sitting in front of a peat fire because there was a shortage of coal, yet they were adamant that allowing Poles into the mines would create unemployment. They then turned to the housing shortage, which was also apparently being caused by the Poles, and rounded it off with some indignation over the alleged take-over of the whole medical profession by Polish doctors.

The younger man remarked that he belonged to several business and civic associations, and that on all of them he made a point of putting forward resolutions that the Poles should be sent back to their own country. The older one added that the

Poles were 'very degraded in their morals'. They were respon-
sible for much of the immorality that was prevalent nowadays.
'Their ways are not our ways,' he concluded piously. It was not
mentioned that the Poles pushed their way to the head of
queues, wore bright-coloured clothes and displayed cowardice
during air raids, but if I had put forward a suggestion to this
effect I am sure it would have been accepted.

One cannot of course, do very much about this kind of
thing. It is the contemporary equivalent of anti-semitism.

The airmen suffered less from discrimination and were more
fortunate in every respect than their comrades of the ground
forces. Their vital contribution in the Battle of Britain was harder
to forget than the army's heroics at Tobruk, Monte Casino,
Arnhem or Falaise. Having been based in Britain, working alongside British airmen for the past five years, they had a far better
knowledge of the language than the members of the ground
forces, the majority of whom had spent the war in the Middle
East and Italy. Many had made friends in the RAF who were prepared to help them start a new life. All, from the most experienced pilot to the lowliest fitter, had some technical skill.

The airmen were also more cohesive, more of a family than
their colleagues of the ground forces. On 24 June 1945 they had
started a Polish Air Force Association, and in November this
spawned a self-help organization. The Association immediately
set about collecting money, through subscriptions and fund-
raising ventures. It collected £1,000 before the end of 1945 and
a further £17,000 in the following year. It husbanded its
resources well, and by 1948 its income was £45,000. This permitted it to spend £12,000 on buying and restoring a house in
Earl's Court as a headquarters and hostel for its members. It gave
out £14,000 in loans to members wishing to start up their own
businesses, set up a flying club for its members, and even
financed a book about the Polish Air Force during the war.

More important was the vigorous part the Association played
in helping its members start a new life. It was flooded with
requests from eager employers, to the extent that during 1946
and 1947, while the men were joining the Resettlement Corps or
still making up their minds whether to return to Poland or not,
it received three times as many job offers as applications for
employment from its members. The RAF was keen to take on
large numbers of the Poles, and some 500 joined its ranks. The

Dutch Air Force wanted ground crews, the Argentine Air Force wanted up to 900 pilots, navigators, radio operators and ground staff, and the Pakistan Air Force wanted 450 men. Commercial airlines the world over, starting with BOAC, were also very keen to avail themselves of this concentration of talent and skill.

The Polish Air Force Association processed offers and matched them to applicants, keeping an eye on the suitability of both and warning the men on the possible disadvantages of emigrating to other continents. It also gave advice on visas and work permits, and on living conditions, levels of pay and health care in countries they were considering emigrating to. It received help from the WVS, and the WI, the British Legion, and various Anglo-Polish and Catholic charities. It also received generous assistance from a large number of solicitors, accountants, bank managers and other professional people, particularly in the provinces, who offered their services free or at very low rates. It was therefore able, through the pages of its magazine, to illuminate for its members the mysteries of mortgages, conveyancing, leasehold, taxation, and a thousand other arcana. It instructed its members on how to take part in British social life, and even told them which works of English literature and newspapers they should read. Here it was perhaps least successful, as the airmen on the whole only bought papers for the football pools and tips for greyhound racing.

The Polish Air Force Association urged its members to avoid confrontation with trades unions by eschewing employment in British industry and starting up their own businesses. Most of the airmen were eminently suited for this, as they had engineering skills and their experiences over the past few years had forced them to use their imagination and improvise. The association helped them with loans and advice, and hundreds of small workshops, mostly light engineering or motor repair, but also watch making, leather-working and photography, sprang up all over the country.

The Polish forces were officially disbanded in July 1948, and the Air Resettlement Corps was wound up in October of the same year, having served its purpose of translating the men into civilian life. Some 2,500 had emigrated, to South America (850), Australia and New Zealand (400), Canada (300), the United States (150), South Africa (100) and western Europe (600), while the remainder had been found employment or had started up businesses in Britain.

Those who returned to Poland were not so fortunate. For most of them, any sadness they might feel at seeing the country devastated or misgivings they might have about the new regime were initially outweighed by the joy of homecoming. Tadeusz Schiele wept with emotion when he saw the Polish coastline, while his three year old son, Kazik, jumped up and down on the deck at his side shouting 'Hello, Poland!' His English wife, however, must have been shocked at their reception.

The returning airmen were not fêted. 'I was made to feel like some sort of criminal, a bandit,' recalls Stefan Witorzeńc, a Battle of Britain veteran. Nor was it easy for them to find accommodation or work. Some, including Marian Wędzik, who had flown in 302 during the Battle of Britain, and Wyszkowski of Skalski's Circus, found work as pilots for the national airline LOT. Kazimierz Wunsche, one of 303's Battle of Britain aces, got a job piloting a flying ambulance. Wacław Król, who had found and married his childhood sweetheart in Germany in 1945, had trouble finding any work at all. He was sacked from a succession of manual jobs and was often taken in for interrogation by the security services. Karol Pniak, another Battle of Britain veteran, found himself working on a building site as a labourer. Mieczysław Pruszyński of 305 had to swallow his literary pride and take a lowly job in the mining industry. He was also under surveillance, and had to avoid meeting the British Air Attaché, an old friend, for fear of being arrested for espionage.

It was worse for those, like Skalski, who volunteered for the Polish Air Force. He had turned down jobs with the RAF and the USAAF in order to offer his services and his experience to his own country, and he was duly accepted, with the rank of major. On 4 June 1948 he was arrested, along with Tadeusz Nowierski, who had flown with 609 Squadron during the Battle of Britain. They were locked up in tiny underground cells and interrogated under torture. In April 1950 Skalski was condemned to death for espionage, but the charge was commuted to life imprisonment. Nowierski was later released, and worked as a taxi-driver in Warsaw. Radomski, the fighter who had lost an arm and opened a bar in London, also returned, with his wife Judy. He too was arrested, on charges of black-market currency dealing. But he was eventually released and in 1958 managed to escape to the west, ending up in the Bahamas, where he opened a hotel.

Many were less fortunate. Władysław Śliwiński was shot, and his English wife Myra was thrown into jail. Eight other pilots were shot with him. Zygmunt Sokołowski, a navigator, was given a job in the Polish Air Force pilots' training school, but he was arrested at the same time as Skalski. He was shot in 1953, along with thirty others. In 1956 Skalski and the other survivors were released under a general amnesty, but they were forced to rejoin the air force. These 'English' officers, as they were sneeringly referred to by their Communist colleagues, remained under constant suspicion and were given the worst jobs. On retirement, they retreated into a frugal way of life, supplementing their wretched pensions and the financial support they received covertly from the Polish Air Force Association by writing books about their experiences. In the 1960s those who were still alive began to visit their former comrades in the west.

These had survived remarkably well, and some had prospered. Those that had joined the RAF remained in active service for some time. Some continued to fly, mostly in transport command on account of their age, and, ironically, a large number took part in the Berlin airlift. When Jerzy Kmiecik retired in 1981, he was the oldest flying pilot in the RAF. Others went into training or staff work, and attained high rank. Others still found jobs as test pilots and technical experts for such aircraft manufacturers as Gloster, Avro, Boeing, Cessna and Victa. Wacław Makowski, the first commander of 300, went back to work for the International Civil Aviation Organization, advising on the setting up of commercial aviation in a dozen developing countries, from Iran to Upper Volta.

Even straightforward mechanics were well placed to prosper. Skalski's fitter refused enticing and insistent offers to transfer to the RAF, went to work in an aeronautical factory, where he earned £18 per week, about three times the average worker's wage, and within six months had bought himself a house. The pattern of getting a job and saving up the first months' pay-packets for the down-payment on a mortgage lay at the root of the airmen's future well-being, if not their prosperity. The ground staffs in particular had had ample opportunity to acquaint themselves with the localities in which they were stationed. Many married local girls, but even those who did not had a good idea of what kind of small business to start and where to find cheap housing. They found it easier to put down roots near their favourite stations than in large towns. The same was true of some of the pilots. One fighter pilot married a girl from the Northolt area, got a job, and bought a house with a view of the airfield, in which he brought up three sons to be good Poles.

For all their skill and ingenuity, most of the airmen remained hopelessly naïve, and many allowed themselves to be cheated royally, both by Britons and fellow-Poles. But as long as they were prepared to start again and work hard, they could hardly go wrong. At a time when there were no Asians running corner shops or small service businesses, the Polish airmen who managed newsagents, grocery stores or garages did extremely well for themselves. Some of those who started small manufacturing workshops did even better. Karol Czajka, who changed his name to Charles Dugan-Chapman, and two other fighter pilots pooled £1,000 to start a plastics factory and made a killing.

They were outdone by Squadron Leader Włodzimierz Miksa of 317. At the end of the war Miksa married into the Pilkington glass dynasty, and his father-in-law wanted him to take a job in the family firm, but he had his own ideas. He had noticed that all leather substitutes dried out and cracked, and a relative who was a chemist put him on to a new paste which appeared to have possibilities. Miksa got together with his fitter from the squadron and began boiling the stuff up in his garage. As they needed to obtain extremely high temperatures, they had to build their own oven, but for this they required various unobtainable materials. The mechanic figured out that some of them went into the making of domestic irons, so Miksa donned old clothes and did the rounds of electrical repair shops collecting discarded irons. While loading a batch into his sack in an Uxbridge shop, he overheard the electrician whisper to another customer: 'That fellow over there was a brilliant fighter pilot, Battle of Britain and all that; he's gone a bit funny in the head now – terrible shame, innit?' His father-in-law took the same view. Miksa sank his entire savings of £500 into renting a workshop and taking on more mechanics from the squadron. Five years later his company, Mellowhide Products of Rochdale, was the largest manufacturer of flexible PVC in the country, and he was a millionaire.

Most of the airmen did not aspire to such heights, and were content to make a decent living. Flight Lieutenant Bronisław Malinowksi started a mechanical workshop near Croydon and, having made enough money to set himself up, took a publican's course and settled down to pulling pints. This seems to have been a popular option. In the 1960s Bruno Kudrewicz, another fighter pilot, became the publican of the White Hart at Thatcham, a comrade of his was the host at the Antelope in

Warwick, and Witold 'Lanny' Lanowski, a Mustang pilot who moved to the RAF, ran a pub in Poplar on his retirement.

Many went back to the land and became farmers in parts of the country as varied as Devon, where the former bomber navigator Andrzej Matysiak bred the largest herd of pedigree Devon cattle, and Scotland, where former flight engineer Jan Rusin farmed turkeys. Stefan Knapp went to the Central School of Arts and Crafts, then the Slade, and became an artist.

But some could not ever quite get over the war. 'It demoralized you for the rest of your life, because you had to accept the fact that life was not that important and that, provided you survived, you could stuff the rest,' says Zbigniew Bobiński, a bomber pilot with 305. 'You had to force yourself to think of everything as here today, gone tomorrow; some kind of instinct of self-preservation dictated that you shouldn't take anything too seriously – and you had to hammer that into your head. So when, later, you came up against the ambition and competitiveness that are part of any career, you couldn't really be bothered; you did enough to be able to bring home enough money, and that was all. Some drank themselves to pieces.'

Bobiński and two colleagues found themselves jobs in India as pilots for Deccan Airways. They had a comfortable bungalow with plenty of servants in Hyderabad, and he had ample opportunity to go shooting game whenever he had a few days off. During a stopover in Bombay one night, he was visited in his hotel room by 'a lovely little blonde' who asked if it was true that he was a Polish airman. 'I always heard that Polish airmen were very chivalrous and ready to help a woman in trouble' she said, and begged him to hide her. It turned out that she was an Egyptian who had worked for British Intelligence during the war but was now reduced to smuggling gold. Her accomplice had been caught and the police were after her. Bobiński and his friends took her in but found that she did not fit into their way of life at Hyderabad, so they unloaded her on to a colleague working for another airline, Bogdan Krahelski, who was passing through.

After Independence and Partition, Bobiński changed to flying pilgrims from Karachi to Jedda, and in 1951 he and several others went to work for the CIA. The Americans had been using stateless and jobless Poles for murky operations since the end of the war (one Battle of Britain veteran was being trained in 1951 to parachute into Poland in order to steal a MiG and fly it out), and the Polish Air Force Association headquarters in Earl's Court were well known to the various government agencies. It is commonly believed that the hall porter worked for the CIA, the barman for British Intelligence, and one of the administrators for the KGB and the CIA at the same time. (Roman Rudkowski, a former commander of 301 and later of the Polish contingent in 138 Special Duties, also worked for the CIA, while posing as a KGB agent, with a Russian transmitter in his flat in Baron's Court.)

Bobiński and his colleagues, six pilots and six navigators in all, were taken to Germany and installed in a private house outside Frankfurt. They had very little idea of what they were to do. 'We didn't even talk amongst ourselves,' he relates. He was given a single-engined De Havilland Beaver plane that had belonged to a Canadian trapper and whose log-book showed no connection with any government agency. He was kitted out with Soviet civilian clothes, a Soviet watch and a cyanide pill. When he was sent on operations, he was given a series of navigational courses and minimal information. His flights took him over the Baltic states and Lake Ladoga. But the agent who had been dropped into the Soviet Union to co-ordinate activities had evidently defected, as the only time Bobiński was supposed to land in order to pick up someone, he noticed that what in the moonlight he had taken for hedges lining the improvised landing strip were in fact lorries full of soldiers. He gave full throttle before his wheels had touched the ground and just managed to get away, in a hail of bullets.

Bobiński, who made his last flight in 1953, survived, but others were less fortunate. Another group, operating over the Ukraine, was betrayed. A third, working out of Greece, was concentrating on Albania. Among these was Krahelski, who had taken the Egyptian blonde off Bobiński. His missions were hardly more successful, as Kim Philby was passing information to the Soviets and the planes were met with ferocious barrages of flak. 'It's worse than the Ruhr!' Krahelski complained; having finished his tour of duty he decided to take his girl off and settle down in Cairo on the money he had saved. Unfortunately, the blonde had been turned by the KGB, and somebody (it could have been the KGB or the CIA) put a bomb on board the Dakota in which the two flew off towards their well-earned retirement.

When the operations from Europe into Albania and the Soviet Union were shut down, some of the remaining pilots were transferred to Taiwan and, later, the Philippines. Here they baulked when ordered to strafe and bomb insurgent villages, and they were all retired. A handful of them surfaced in various post-colonial conflicts, notably in the Congo – where they came across an old comrade, 'Johnny' Zumbach.

Zumbach's post-war career was more colourful than most. In December 1944 he met a shady pre-war entrepreneur from Poland at the bar of the Wellington Club in London, and was soon moving uncut diamonds from London to Brussels in his Mustang. 'By the end of 1945 I had banked £3,000 in fees for helping him to keep the Antwerp dealers supplied until they regained their pre-war sources,' he writes. With a couple of British colleagues he started a charter company which specialized in transporting currency for laundering. 'Each trip was worth £10,000,' Zumbach explains. By 1948 their seven planes, piloted by five ex-fighter pilots, were smuggling Swiss watches to London, gold bars from Tangier to Paris, penicillin to Prague, Jews to Israel, and arms to various places. Then his partner ran off with their capital and they pursued him all the way to Rio de Janeiro, where the trail went cold. There followed an inglorious few years working in a towel factory, then in 1957 he opened a discothèque in the Champs-Elysées in Paris and took a pretty young wife. But it was not in his nature to stay in one place for long. In 1962 he was contacted by some old acquaintances and met Moise Tshombe in Geneva, who asked him to create an air force for Katanga, the province that had seceded from the Congo after the latter gained its independence from Belgium. He recruited another four Polish pilots and a team of ground staff in London, and they were soon bombing and strafing the Congolese forces, but he did not like Tshombe or his politics, and he took the earliest opportunity to return to his wife and his discothèque. In 1967 the siren call lured him to Biafra. He survived that war, too, but he remained heavily enmeshed in international intrigue, and when he died without apparent cause in 1986, many of his friends assumed that he had been liquidated by someone or other.

As careers go, few can be more intriguing than that of Henryk 'de' Kwiatkowski. Although he surrounds himself with the aura of a fighter pilot, he seems to have been a radio operator with one of the bomber squadrons (records list no fewer than five airmen by the name of Henryk Kwiatkowski). Be that as it may, he now lives at Lyford Cay in Nassau, in a luxurious house wedged between those of Stavros Niarchos and Julio Iglesias, keeps racehorses in England, Ireland, France and the United States, and in 1992 put down $17 million in cash to buy Calumet Farm, the most prestigious stud in Kentucky's blue-grass country. After the war, Kwiatkowski worked for Pratt & Whitney, the air-craft-engine manufacturer, in Montreal, but he also flew Pakistani pilgrims from Karachi to Jedda and the Shah back to Iran after the Mossadeq coup in 1953. He is also reported to have supplied AWACs to Saudi Arabia, and the plane that was used in the Entebbe raid of 1975 to Israel. He virtually created the used plane business, buying unwanted aircraft from large American or European carriers and selling them on to South American air-lines, then buying the planes these were replacing and selling *them* to third-world countries. He also pioneered aircraft-leasing on an ambitious scale, making a great deal of money in the process.

Most of the Polish airmen did not live so dangerously, or pursue such riches. There is a quiet dignity about the way they picked up the strands of what was left of their lives and worked hard at an enormous variety of jobs. Most of them showed courage, determination and initiative, those paramount traits of the force in which they had served. But even if they successfully put the war behind them, the past sometimes came back to haunt them.

Gabriel Rachuba, who left the Polish Air Force in 1948 and opened a small newsagent's in Edgbaston, only discovered in 1963 that the son he had believed to be dead was twenty-four years old and living in Wrocław. One airman married in Poland in 1938. In the following year he was deported by the Soviets and spent two years in the gulags, and it was not until 1942 that he got to England and joined the air force. Through the Red Cross he learnt that his wife had died in a camp in Siberia, so there was nothing to stop him marrying an English girl. But in the 1960s a relative living in Poland managed to trace his first wife, who was working on a collective farm near Minsk.

Although some never found it in them to forgive the betrayal of Yalta or to forget the shabby treatment they had met with from Britain after the war, most remained remarkably untouched by it. A certain wisdom made them realize that the grousing of civil-ians, the insults of trade union activists and the hatred of left-leaning intellectuals were of little consequence. It is extremely difficult to get a Polish airman settled in Britain to say anything other than that the British have been wonderful friends and allies. This does not stem from servility or from delusion, but from a remarkably cool appraisal of the realities of war and peace, and a warm appreciation of the deep and enduring friendship they did find here.

The anti-Polish feelings in Britain at the end of the war subsided with the passage of time, but they were replaced by political contempt on the part of the fashionably left-wing intellectual establishment. And no attempt was made to right even the purely social wrongs. Pensions were never granted, and the Polish Air Force Association and its small group of retired RAF friends continue to struggle to raise funds to look after their old and infirm.

The twenty-fifth anniversary of the Battle of Britain brought some acknowledgment of the role they had played, and a Pole was selected to be one of twenty to meet the Queen at the celebrations. Skalski and the other survivors in Poland were brought over for the banquet held in London for the première of the film *The Battle of Britain.* A monument to the Polish Air Force was unveiled in St Clement Danes, the RAF church in the City of London, and this was followed in 1990 by the unveiling of a plaque in the crypt of St Paul's Cathedral. The RAF lays on a band and a Spitfire to fly over the dwindling crowd of veterans who gather at the annual ceremony before the Northolt memorial. But arrogance and ignorance still occasionally combine to slight Polish feelings. In 1993 a grandiose Battle of Britain monument was erected on the cliffs of Dover commemorating every squadron that took part – every squadron except two, that is. Neither 302 nor 303, the highest scorer of the lot, is mentioned.

In 1988, as people began to prepare for the fiftieth anniversary of the outbreak of war, Skalski conceived the idea of tracing the two German airmen he had shot down on 1 September 1939. He had kept a note of their names, and wrote to a couple of West German newspapers. His enquiry elicited interest and was publicized widely; the two men were located, and a reunion was arranged with the help of German television, which wanted to film the meeting. On his arrival, Skalski was greeted by the Chief-of-Staff of the German Air Force, an admiral, and a gaggle of dignitaries. By the time he reached the Bavarian home of Friedrich Wimmer on 23 March 1990, the other airman had died, and only his widow could attend the meeting. The German air ace Adolf Galland was also present, at the request of German television, so that he could pay authoritative compliments to the valour and skill of the Polish airmen. He duly related that during the war the

Luftwaffe used to recognize the Polish squadrons by their for-
mation, and that he used to tell his young pilots to 'fight like the
Poles do'. Pole and Germans embraced in front of the cameras.
But they avoided talking about the war.

In Poland, too, people no longer want to talk about the war
very much – the page is finally being turned on that unfortunate
chapter of the nation's history – but the survivors have been honoured and there has been a certain amount of setting the record
straight and tying up loose ends.

On 3 September 1992, the standard of the Polish Air Force was
brought back to Poland aboard the Presidential plane, escorted
by 400 former pilots, including 16 commanders of Polish
squadrons based in Britain during the war. In a moving ceremony, it was handed over to the cadets of the Polish Air Force
training school at Dęblin, which had trained so many of the
airmen.

Yet real recognition has bypassed them. 'In looking back over
the war years,' wrote a senior RAF officer in 1946, 'I wonder if
mankind is yet aware of the credit that is their due.' It probably
never will be. It rarely falls to heroes to receive their reward.

Sources

PRECISE FIGURES ARE notoriously elusive when dealing with aerial combat. I have used the official RAF figures, revised downwards after the war, and other most recent assessments (as communicated to me by Mr Jerzy Cynk), except in the case of the Battle of Britain. The original wartime British figure of 2,692 enemy planes shot down was revised drastically after the war on the basis of German documentation – to 1,733. The Polish contribution of 203 within the figure of 2,692 was never revised separately. If one were to simply reduce it proportionally, one would be doing the pilots an injustice, as it is most unlikely that the Polish score would warrant reducing anything like as far as the overall score. The original global figure was inflated by the enthusiasm and inexperience that characterized the first stages of the Battle of Britain, and the whole process of awarding claims was tightened up considerably in August and September. On top of this, Polish figures were kept low by two other factors. One was that the British assumed the Poles would tend to inflate their claims, and therefore checked these more stringently. The other was that the Poles had anticipated this assumption, and kept their claims realistically modest. Their figure of 203 was arrived at after a review by the Air Ministry's Historical Commission in 1942. It is therefore probably fairly accurate - and almost certainly represents more than the 7.5 per cent of the total generally accepted.

Chapter 1: Knights Errant

Zumbach, *On Wings of War*; Skalski, interview; Dreja, *Czyż Mogli Dać Więcej*; 303 Diary, Sikorski, LOT A V 49/34/2; Urbanowicz, *Świt Zwycięstwa* and *Początek Jutra*.

Chapter 2: Growing Wings

Cynk, *History of the Polish Air Force*; Lisiewicz, *Destiny Can Wait*; Rayski, *Słowa Prawdy o Lotnictwie Polskim*; Kusiak, *Życie Codzienne Oficerów*; Cyprian, *Komisja Stwierdziła*; Meissner, *Wiatr w Podeszwach*; Szumowski, *Through Many Skies*; Drobiński, interview; Kołaczkowski, interview; Groszek, interview; Lęska, interview; Arct, *Rycerze Biało-Czerwonej Szachownicy*; Milewski, interview; Wandzilak, interview; Kaliniecki, interview; Kłaczkowski, 'Orzeł z Forest Hills'; Król, *W Dywizjonie Poznańskim*; *Lotnicy spod Znaku*; Zamoyski, interview; Andrews, *The Air Marshals*; Cieślak et al., *Samoloty Myśliwskie*

Września; Cynk, 'Air War Over Poland'; Stachiewicz, *Przygotowania Wojenne*; Rolski, *Uwaga Wszystkie Samoloty*; Urbanowicz, *Początek Jutra*; Schiele, *Blisko Nieba*.

Chapter 3: Black September

Skalski, *Czarne Krzyże nad Polska*; Krzemiński, *Wojna Powietrzna w Europie*; Cynk, 'Air War Over Poland'; Cieślak et al., *Samoloty Myśliwskie Września*; 303 Diary, Sikorski, LOT A V 49/34/1; Król, *W Dywizjonie Poznańskim* and *Lotnicy Spod Znaku*; Rolski, *Uwaga Wszystkie Samoloty*; Pawlak, *Polskie Eskadry w Wojnie Obronnej*; Czarnomski, *They Fight for Poland*; Szumowski, *Through Many Skies*; Arct, *Rycerze Biało-Czerwonej Szachownicy*; Szubański, *W Obronie Polskiego Neiba*; Zaczkiewicz, *Lotnictwo Polskie w Kampanii Wrześniowej*; Lisiewicz, *Destiny Can Wait*; Kosiński & Majsak, *My i Oni*; Laszkiewicz, *Opowieści Róży Wiatrów*; Arct, *Alarm w St Omer*; Urbanowicz, *Początek Jutra*; Zając, *Dwie Wojny*; Kwiatkowski, interview; Lutosławski, *Dno Nieba*; Meissner, *G For Genevieve*.

Chapter 4: Balkan Farce

Lisiewicz, *Destiny Can Wait*; Wasilewski, *Obyś Żył w Ciekawych Czasach*; Dreja, *Czyż Mogli Dać Więcej*; Sikorski, LOT A I 2/15; Skalski, *Czerwone Krzyże nad Polską*; Król, *W Dywizjonie Poznańskim*; PRO, AIR 2/4211; Milewski, interview; Szumowski, *Through Many Skies*; Garliński, *Poland in the Second World War*; Lutosławski, *Dno Nieba*; Tuskiewicz, *Polskie Sił y Powietrzne*; Cynk, 'Air War Over Poland'; Urbanowicz, *Początek Jutra*; Meissner, *Pióro ze Skrzydeł*; Karpiński, *Na Skrzydłach Huraganu*.

Chapter 5: French Fiasco

Arct, *Alarm w St Omer*; Król, *Walczyłem pod Niebem Francji*; Nycz, *W Powietrznym Zwiadzie*; PRO, AIR 2/4211; Urbanowicz, *Świt Zwycięstwa*; Kaliniecki, interview; Zając, *Dwie Wojny*; Jokiel, *Udział Polaków w Bitwie o Anglie*; Cynk, 'Air War Over Poland'; Schiele, *Blisko Nieba*; Rolski, *Uwaga Wszystkie Samoloty*; Kalinowski, *Lotnictwo Polskie*; Arct, *W Podniebnej Chwale*; Szumowski, *Through Many Skies*; Król, *Lotnicy spod Znaku*; 303 Diary, Sikorski, LOT A V 49/34/2; Meissner, *G for Genevieve*; Laszkiewicz, *Opowieści Róży Wiatrów*; Bobkowski, *Skice Piórkiem*; Pruszyński, *W Moskicie nad Trzecią Rzesza*; Lutosławski, *Dno Nieba*; Połoniecki, *Fly for Your Life*.

Chapter 6: Mist and Regulations

Arct, *Polish Wings in the West* and *W Podniebnej Chwale*; Rolski, *Uwaga Wszystkie Samoloty*; Slessor, *The Central Blue*; Milewski, interview; Zając, *Dwie Wojny*; Griffiths, *Winged Hours*; Smithies, *War in the Air*; PRO, AIR 2/4213 (Davidson's Report); *Nasze Wiadomości ze Świata*, Nos 2 & 3, 18–19 March 1940; No. 16, 2 April 1940; F/O G. Marsh in *Skrzydła*, 1–14 Sept. 42, 17/394; PRO, AIR 2/4213; PRO, AIR 2/7916; Urbanowicz, *Świt Zwycięstwa*; Jokiel, *Udział Polaków w Bitwie o Anglię*; *The Sunday Post*, 18 August 1940; Schiele, *Blisko Nieba*; Groszek, interview; Król, *W Dywizjonie Poznańskim*; 316 Diary, Sikorski, LOT A V 54/10; Węgrzecki, *Kosynierzy*; Schiele, *Spitfire*; 307 Diary, Sikorski, LOT A V 51/59; Lisiewicz, *Destiny Can Wait*; Kalinowski, *Lotnictwo Polskie*; PRO, AIR 19/162 (Report on pilot shortfall); Nahlik, interview; 303 Diary, Sikorski, LOT A V 49/34/3; Zumbach, *On Wings of War*; Andrews, *The Air Marshals*; Lucas, *Thanks for the Memory*; Meissner, *G for Genevieve*; Witorzeńc, interview; Tuskiewicz, *Polskie Siły Powietrzne*; Sikorski, LOT A I 2/15; 303 Diary, Sikorski, LOT A V 49/34/2; Jaworzyn, *No Place to Land*; Sword et al., *The Formation of the Polish Community*; *Skrzydła*, No. 10/387, 15–31 May 1942; Kwiatkowski, *Bomby Poszły*; Dreja, *Czyż Mogli Dać Więcej*;

Arct, *Alarm w St Omer* and *Polacy w Bitwie o Anglie*; Lutosławski, *Dno Nieba*; Wasilewski, *Obyś Żył w Ciekawych Czasach*; Spaight, *Battle of Britain*; Falkowski, *With the Wind in My Face*; Thompson, 'I Met the Men Who Saved Britain'; Joubert in *Skrzydła*, 15 March 1946, 5/478; Kellett in *Daily Telegraph*, 5 July 1946; Anon. British pilot in *Skrzydła*, 1–14 May 42, 9/386; Drobiński, interview; Bishop, *The Battle of Britain*; Skalski, interview; Król, *Polskie Dywizjony Lotnicze w Bitwie o Anglie*; Karpiński, *Na Skrzydłach Huraganu*; Banaszczyk, *W Bitwie o Anglie*; Crook, *Spitfire Pilot*; Gleave in *Skrzydła*, No. 9/482, 15 May 1946; Martel, interview; PRO, AIR 2/5196 (Dowding); Wandzilak, interview; 304 Diary, Sikorski, LOT A V 36/8; Thomson, interview.

Chapter 7: The Legend of 303

303 Diary, Sikorski, LOT A V 49/34/2; Kellett, interview; Smithies, *War in the Air*; Vincent, *Flying Fever*; Kent, *One of the Few*; Miksa, interview; Young, interview; Lisiewicz, *Destiny Can Wait* and *It speaks for itself*; Kalinowski, *Lotnictwo Polskie*; Tuskiewicz, *Polskie Siły Powietrzne*; Banaszczyk, *W Bitwie o Anglie*; Baley, *Two Septembers*; Dreja, *Czyż Mogli Dać Więcej*; Cobb in *Skrzydła*, No. 9/386; Król, *W Dywizjonie Poznańskim*; Wyndham, interview; Kołaczkowski, interview; Fiedler, *Dywizjon 303*; Austin, *Fighter Command*; Spaight, *The Battle of Britain*; Urbanowicz, *One Man's War*; Miller, *One-Man Polish Air Force*; Crook *Spitfire Pilot*; Forrester, *Fly for Your Life*; *Skrzydła*, No. 1/402, 1–5 January 1943; *The Daily Telegraph*, 25 October 1940; *The Evening News*, ditto; Kornicki, *Polish Air Force*; Thomson, interview; *Skrzydła*, 1/402, 1–5 January 1943; 315 Diary, Sikorski, LOT A V 53/3a; Nahlik, interview; Bildziuk, interview; Król, *Mój Spitfire*; Kent & Thurso, Sikorski, LOT A V 98/13; Polish Airmen's Appeal Review 1987

Chapter 8: Fighting on

Kalinowski, *Lotnictwo Polskie*; 307 Diary, Sikorski, LOT A V 51/59; 304 Diary, Sikorski, LOT A V 36/8; 316 Diary, Sikorski, LOT A V 54/10; *Skrzydła*, No. 19/396, 1–14 Oct. 42; Intelligence report, Sikorski, LOT A V 100/4a, Hucknall; Wandzilak, interview; Rosier, interview; Harvington, interview; Schiele, *Spitfire*; Rolski, *Uwaga Wszystkie Samoloty*; Lisiewicz, *Destiny Can Wait*; 315 Diary, Sikorski, LOT A V 53/3 & 3a; 309 Diary, Sikorski, LOT A V 61/35; Maclaren, *Poland at Arms*; 302 Diary, Sikorski, LOT A V 49/33/1; Austin, *Fighter Command*; Pruszyński, *Poland Fights Back*; Król, *W Dywizjonie Poznańskim*; Sheilah Graham in *News* (USA), 18 August 1941; Nycz, *W Powietrznym Zwiadzie*; Król, *Mój Spitfire*; Gabreski, *Gabby*; Arct, *Niebo w Ogniu*; Urbanowicz, *Świt Zwycięstwa*; Schiele, *Blisko Nieba*; Smithies, *War in the Air*; Andersz, interview; Arct, *Polacy w Bitwie o Anglie*; *The Fortnightly*, June 1941; *The Evening Citizen*, 9 January 1941; Kmiecik, interview; Northolt in *Skrzydła*, 21/491; Dreja, *Czyż Mogli Dać Więcej*; 302 Diary, Sikorski, LOT A V 49/33/1; Zumbach, *On Wings of War*; Drobiński, interview; Kołaczkowski in *Jednodniówka*.

Chapter 9: Bombing

Baley, *Two Septembers*; Kalinowski, *Lotnictwo Polskie*; Lisiewicz, *Destiny Can Wait*; Dreja, *Czyż Mogli Dać Więcej*; Ingham, *Polish Air Force in Lincolnshire*; Anderson, *Pathfinders*; Węgrzecki, *Kosynierzy*; *Skrzydła*, 15/392, 1–14 Aug. 1942; Sęp-Szarzyński, *W Służbie Latającego Smoka*; Bobiński, interview; Król, *Lotnicy Spod Znaku*; Smithies, *War in the Air*; Król, *Mój Spitfire*; 315 Diary, Sikorski, LOT A V 53/3a; Arct, *W Podniebnej Chwale*; Wasilewski, *Obyś Żył w Ciekawych Czasach*; Karpiński, *Na Skrzydłach Huraganu*; Maclaren, *Poland at Arms*; Meissner, *Pióro ze Skrzydeł*; Czarnomski, *They Fight for Poland*; Garliński, *Poland in World War II*; Tuskiewicz, *Polskie Siły Powietrzne*.

Chapter 10: A Growing Family

Sholto Douglas in *Skrzydła*, 15–30 October 1945, 22–3/472–3; Lisiewicz, *Destiny Can Wait*; 304 Diary, Sikorski, LOT A V 36/8; Kalinowski, *Lotnictwo Polskie*; Griffiths, *Winged Hours*; Miller, *One-Man Polish Air Force*; Arct, *Alarm w St Omer* and *W Pogoni za Luftwaffe*; Dreja, *Czyż Mogli Dać Więcej*; Lutosławski, *Dno Nieba*; Pruszyński, *W Moskicie nad Trecią Rzeszą*; Rolski, *Uwaga, Wszystkie Samoloty*; Lęska, interview; Kaliniecki, interview; Arct, *Niebo w Ogniu*; Maćkowski, *Rys Historyczny PLSK*; Alicja Kaliniecka, interview; Anna Bielec-Wisniewska, interview; Karpiński, *Na Skrzydłach Huraganu*; Trylski, *Błękitni Chłopcy*; Intelligence reports, Sikorski, LOT A V 100/4a; Mass Observation Archive, 622 & 734, March and June 1941; Knapp, *Square Sun*; Pruszyński, interview; Intelligence reports, Sikorski, LOT A V 100/4b, November 1944; Schiele, *Blisko Nieba*; Szumowski, *Through Many Skies*; Kwiatkowski, *Bomby Poszły*; Groszek, interview.

Chapter 11: The Home Front

Sheilah Graham in *News* (USA) 18 August 1941; Dreja, *Czyż Mogli Dać Więcej*; Zamoyski, interview; Węgrzecki, *Kosynierzy*; Połoniecki, *Fly for Your Life*; Bobiński, interview; Rosita Forbes, 'What They Think of Us', in unidentified paper, spring 1942, Sikorski, cuttings album; *Skrzydła*, 15–31 August 1942, 16/393; Kmiecik, interview; Griffiths, *Winged Hours*; Nycz, *W Powietrznym Zwiadzie*; 304 Diary, Sikorski, LOT A V 36/8; Mass Observation Archive, 569; *Glasgow Herald*, 25 March 1941; Gardiner, *Over Here*; Połoniecki, interview; 303 Diary, Sikorski, LOT A V 49/34/3; Cobb in *Skrzydła*, 130/372, 1–14 October 1941; Thomson, interview; Wandzilak, interview; Sikorski, LOT A V 50/3; Kwiatkowski, interview; 316 Diary, Sikorski, LOT A V 54/10; Król, *W Dywizjonie Poznańskim*; Lęska, interview; *Skrzydła*, 1–14 November 1941, 132/374; Mass Observation Archive, 541, 1669Q; Arct, *Polish Wings in the West*; Milewski, interview; Groszek, interview; Zumbach, *On Wings of War*; Harwood, Imperial War Museum; Bildziuk, interview; Meissner, *Pióro ze Skrzydeł*; *West Lancashire Evening Gazette*, 17 August 1942; *The Sunday Post*, 18 March 1941; Intelligence report, Sikorski, LOT A V 100/4a, October 1941; 300 Diary, Sikorski, LOT A V 34/13; *The Fortnightly*, June 1941; Milewski, interview; Corfield-Kobylińska, interview; Wyndham, *Love is Blue*; Schiele, *Spitfire*; Gnyś, *First Kill*; Pruszyński, *W Moskicie nad Trzecią Rzeszą*; Cobb in *Skrzydła*, 1–13 December 1942, 23–4/400–1; *The Blackpool Gazette*, 19 September 1942; 316 Diary, Sikorski, LOT A V 54/10; *Glasgow Daily Record & Mail*, 30 June 1942; *Skrzydła*, 15 May 1944, 9/435; and 1 September 1944, 17/443.

Chapter 12: No Victory

Lisiewicz, *Destiny Can Wait*; *Skrzydła*, 22/423; Kalinowski, *Lotnictwo Polskie*; Meissner, *Pióro ze Skrzydeł*; Arct, *W Pościgu za Luftwaffe*; Sławinski, *Pierwszy Myśliwski*; Krzemiński, *Wojna Powietrzna*; Intelligence report, Sikorski, LOT A V 100/33, March 1943; Ditto, Sikorski, LOT A V 100/4b; *Blackpool Evening Gazette*, 15 March 1945; Intelligence report, Sikorski, LOT A V 100/32; Orliński, letter to Urbanowicz, 20 v 81; Król, *Mój Spitfire*; Intelligence reports, Sikorski, LOT A V 100/4b, February and April 1944; *Skrzydła*, April 1944, 2/452; Schiele, *Blisko Nieba*; Arct, *Rycerze, Polacy w Bitwie o Anglię* and *W Pidniebnej Chwale*; Intelligence report, Sikorski, LOT A V 100/4b, September 1944; Połoniecki, *Fly for Your Life*; Pruszyński, *W Narwiku, Tobruku Moskicie*; Franks, *Battle of the Airfields*; Intelligence reports, Sikorski, LOT A V 100/4b, December 1944, January 1945; 300 Diary, Sikorski, LOT A V 34/14; Intelligence report, Sikorski, LOT A V 100/4b, March 1945; Tuskiewicz, *Polskie Siły Powietrzne*; 305 Diary, Sikorski, LOT A V 37/9; Knapp, *Square Sun*; *It Speaks for Itself*; Szumowski, *Through Many Skies*; Pruszyński, *W Moskicie nad Trzecią Rzeszą*.

Chapter 13: Redundancy

Lisiewicz, *Destiny Can Wait*; Tuskiewicz, *Polskie Siły Powietrzne*; Kalinowski, *Lotnictwo Polskie*; Sword, *Formation of the Polish Community*; Schiele, *Blisko Nieba*; Joubert in *Skrzydła*, 15 March 1946, 5/478; PRO, AIR 2/5782; 300 Diary, Sikorski, LOT A V 34/14; Intelligence report, Sikorski, LOT A V 100/4b, September 1945; Ditto, LOT A V 100/4c, February, April, June 1946; Knapp, *Square Sun*; *Skrzydła*, 15 September 1947; *Dziennik Polski*, 21 June 1947; Orwell in *Tribune*, 24 January 1947; Ingham, *Polish Air Force in Lincs*; Trylski, *Błękitni Chłopcy*; Solak, Imperial War Museum; Milewski, interview; Miksa, interview; Sikorski, LOT A V 98/14; *Skrzydła*, 1957–69; Bobiński, interview; Zumbach, *On Wings of War*; Colacello, *The Saviour of Calumet*; Skalski, interview; Gleave in *Skrzydła*, 15 May 1946, 9/482.

Bibliography

Oral Sources

Sqdn. Ldr. Tadeusz Andersz; Count Jan Badeni; Aniela Bielec-Wiśniewska; Roman Bildziuk; Sqdn. Ldr. Zbigniew Bobiński; Mrs B.K. Clements; Professor Richard Cobb; Sqdn. Ldr. Bolesław Drobiński; Wing-Cdr. Zbigniew Groszek; Lord Harvington; Flt. Lt. Andrzej Jeziorski; Capt. Alicja Kaliniecka; Sqdn. Ldr. Jerzy Kaliniecki; Wing-Cdr. Ronald Kellett; Flt. Lt. Jerzy Kmiecik; Patricia Corfield-Kobylińska; Wing-Cdr. Wojciech Kołaczkowski; Mrs Wacław Król; Sqdn. Ldr. Tadeusz Kwiatkowski; Capt. Anna Lęska; Air Vice-Marshal Aleksander Maisner; Flt. Lt. Ludwik Martel; Sqdn. Ldr. Włodzimierz Pilkington-Miksa; Capt. Tadeusz Milewski; Wing-Cdr. Andrzej Nahlik; Sqdn. Ldr. Bernard Połoniecki; Flt. Lt. Mieczysław Pruszyński; Count Edward Raczyński; Anna Radomska; Air Chief Marshal Sir Frederick Rosier; General Stanisław Skalski; Sqdn. Ldr. Henryk Szczęsny; Wing-Cdr. J.A. Thomson; Grp. Capt. Witold Urbanowicz; Grp. Capt. Stanisław Wandzilak; Flt. Lt. Jan Wieliczko; Sir Peter Wilkinson; Grp. Capt. Stefan Witorzeńc; Laura Wyndham; Wing-Cdr. J.R.C. Young; Count Jan Zamoyski

Archival Sources

Imperial War Museum, London
86/68/1 (Lady Isabelle Napier); 88/53/1 (Mrs J. Harwood); 90/11/1 (B.J. Solak); 92/2/1 (General L. Rayski)

Muzeum Wojska Polskiego, Warsaw
Poprawski, B., *Moje Wspomnienia Wojenne*

Polish Institute and Sikorski Museum, London
LOT A I: 2/15, 2/16
LOT A IV: 1/12, 1/13
LOT A V: 1/1, 1/4, 1/15, 1/36, 1/40–1, 1/44–5; 34/13, 34/14; 44/1; 48/8; 49/31–4, 49/69; 50/3–5; 51/59; 52/23–25; 53/3; 54/10–11; 55/3–4; 61/34–35; 98; 100/5–8, 100/15–16, 100/32–38, 100/41
Kol: 72 (Konarski); 139 (Suchoś); 164 (Kubała); 188 (Zając); 200 (Lisiewicz); 241 (Janus)

Public Record Office, London
AIR 2; 4211, 4212, 4213, 4626, 5196, 5782, 6154, 7196
AIR 19; 162

Sussex University
The Tom Harrisson Mass Observation Archive

Typescripts

Dzierżyński, O.E., *Memoirs*
Połoniecki, B., *Fly for Your Life*
Tuskiewicz, O., *Polskie Siły Powietrzne na Obczyźnie*, 1947

Printed Sources

Anderson, W., *Pathfinders*, London, 1946
Andersz, T., Interview, in *Skrzydła*, No. 138/264
Andrews, A., *The Air Marshals*, London, 1970
Arct, B., *W Pogoni za Luftwaffe*, Edinburgh, 1946
——*Zwichnięte Skrzydła*, Warsaw, 1948
——*W Podniebnej Chwale*, Warsaw, 1958
——*Rycerze Biało-Czerwonej Szachownicy*, Warsaw, 1960
——*Polacy w Bitwie o Anglię*, Warsaw, 1967
——*Alarm w St Omer*, Warsaw, 1969
——*Niebo w Ogniu*, Warsaw, 1970
——*Polish Wings in the West*, Warsaw, 1971
——*Policy w Walce z Bronią V*, Warsaw, 1972
Austin, A.B., *Fighter Command*, London, 1941
Baley, S., *Two Septembers*, London, 1941
Banaszczyk, E., *W Bitwie o Anglię*, Warsaw, 1973
Bartel, R.,Chojnacki, J., Królikiewicz, T., & Kurowski, A., *Z Historii Polskiego Lotnictwa Wojskowego 1918–1939*, Warsaw, 1978
Baykowski, J., *Polskie Siły Powietrzne w Wielkiej Brytanii*, London, 1947
Bethell, N., *The Great Betrayal*, London, 1984
Bishop, E., *The Battle of Britain*, London, 1960
Bobkowski, A., *Szkice Piórkiem*, Paris, 1957
Chromy, E., *Szachownice nad Berlinem*, Warsaw, 1967
Cieślak, K., Gawrych, W., Glass, A., *Samoloty Myśliwskie Września 1939*, Warsaw, 1987
Clostermann, P., *Feux du Ciel*, Paris, 1951
——*Le Grand Cirque*, Paris, 1950
Colacello, B., 'The Saviour of Calumet', *Vanity Fair*, October 1992
Crook, D.M., *Spitfire Pilot*, London, 1942
Cynk, J.B., 'Air War over Poland, September 1939', in *Air Pictorial*, Vol. 51, No. 9, September 1989
——*Polish Aircraft 1893–1939*, London, 1971
——*History of the Polish Air Force 1918–1968*, London, 1972
Cyprian, T., *Komisja Stwierdziła*, Warsaw, 1960
Czarnomski, F.B., *They Fight for Poland*, London, 1941
Damsz, J., *Lwowskie Puchacze*, Kraków, 1990
Deere, A., *Nine Lives*, London, 1991
Dreja, A., *Czyż Mogli Dać Więcej*, London, 1989
Falkowski, J., *Z Wiatrem w Twarz*, Warsaw, 1969
Fiedler, A., *Dywizjon 303*, London, 1942
——*Squadron 303*, London, 1942

——*Thank You, Captain, Thank You!*, London, 1945
Forrester, L., *Fly For Your Life*, London, 1956
Franks, N.L., *The Battle of the Airfields*, London, 1982
Gabreski, F., with Molesworth, C., *Gabby, A Fighter-Pilot's Life*, New York, 1991
Gardiner, J., *Over Here*, London, 1992
Garliński, J., *Poland in the Second World War*, London, 1985
Gnyś, W., *First Kill*, London, 1981
Griffiths, F., *Winged Hours*, London, 1981
Halpenny, B., *Action Stations, Lincolnshire & East Midlands*, Cambridge, 1984
——*Action Stations, Greater London*, London, 1991
Harlender, Z., *Na Podniebnych Szlakach*, Warsaw, 1935
Harris, A., *Bomber Offensive*, London, 1947
Hasiński, M., *Historia Szkoły Podoficerów Lotnictwa dla Małoletnich*, London, 1981
Ingham, M.J., *The Polish Air Force in Lincolnshire*, Lincoln, 1988
It Speaks for Itself: What British War Leaders said about the Polish Armed Forces 1939–45, London, 1947
James, J., *The Paladins*, London, 1990
Janczak, A., *Puchacze Czuwają w Mroku*, Warsaw, 1976
Jaworzyn, J., *No Place to Land*, London, 1984
Jednodniówka XIV Światowego Zlotu Stowarzyszenia Lotników Polskich, New York, 1982
Johnson, J., *Wing leader*, London, 1958
Jokiel, J., *Udział Polaków w Bitwie o Anglię*, Warsaw, 1968
Jordan, P., *Aviation in Poland*, London, 1946
Kalinowski, F., *35 Lat Lotnictwa Wojskowego i Myśli Lotniczej*, London, 1946
——*Lotnictwo Polskie w Wielkiej Brytanii*, Paris, 1969
Karolevitz, R.F. and Fenn, R.S., *Flight of Eagles*, Sioux Falls, 1974
Karpiński, S., *Na Skrzydłach Huraganu*, London, 1976 (4 Vols)
Kelly, T., *Hurricane and Spitfire Pilots at War*, London, 1986
Kent, J., *One of the Few*, London, 1971
Kmiecik, J., *A Boy in the Gulag*, London, 1983
Knapp, S., *The Square Sun*, London, 1956
Kołaczkowski, W., 'Orzeł z Foręst Hills', in *Przegląd Polski, Nowy Dziennik*, New York, 29 March 1990
Koliński, I., *Regularne Jednostki Wojska polskiego (Lotnictwo)*, Warsaw, 1978
Kosiński, L. & Majsak, D. (eds), *My i Oni; Wrzesień 1939*, Lublin, 1994
Kornicki, F., *Polish Air Force, Chronicle of Major Events*, London, 1993
Król, W., *W Dywizjonie Poznańskim*, Warsaw, 1966
——*Lotnicy Spod Znaku Poznańskiego Kruka*, Warsaw, 1971
——*Mój Spitfire WX–L*, Warsaw, 1975
——*Polskie Dywizjony Lotnicze w Wielkiej Brytanii*, Warsaw, 1976
——*Walczyłem pod niebem Francji*, Warsaw, 1978
——*Za Sterami Odrzutowca*, Warsaw, 1978
——*Zarys Działań Polskiego Lotnictwa w Wielkiej Brytanii 1940–1945*, Warsaw, 1990
Krzemiński, C., *Wojna Powietrzna w Europie 1939–1945*, Warsaw, 1983
Księga Lotników Polskich, Warsaw, 1989
Kurowski, A., *Lotnictwo Polskie w 1939*, Warsaw, 1962
——*Kraksy i Wzloty*, Warsaw, 1965
Kusiak, F., *Życie Codzienne oficerów Drugiej Rzeczypospolitej*, Warsaw, 1992
Kwiatkowski, H., *Poszły Bomby*, Warsaw, 1985
Laszkiewicz, S., *Sępy*, Warsaw, 1937
——*Chmurne Loty*, Warsaw, 1939
——*Opowieści Róży Wiatrów*, Letchworth, 1946
Lisiewicz, M. (ed.), *Destiny Can Wait*, London, 1949
Lucas, L., *Thanks for the Memory*, London, 1989

Lutosławski, R., *Dno Nieba*, Warsaw, 1958
Maćkowska, M., *Rys Historyczny P.L.S.K.*, London, n.d.
Maclaren, A., *Poland at Arms*, London, 1942
MacMillan, N., *The Royal Air Force in the World War*, London, 1944
Marsh, L.G., *Polish Wings over Britain*, London, 1943
Meissner, J., *G for Genevieve*, Edinburgh, 1944
———*L for Lucy*, Edinburgh, 1945
———*Żądło Genofewy*, Katowice, 1946
———*Pilot Gwiaździstego Znaku*, Warsaw, 1962
———*Jak Dziś Pamiętam*, Warsaw, 1967
———*Wiatr w Podeszwach*, Warsaw, 1971
———*Pióro ze Skrzydeł*, Warsaw, 1973
Miller, M., *One-Man Polish Air Force*, in *Air Classics*, Vol. 16, No. 9, 1980
Newman, B., *They saved London*, London 1952
Nycz, W., *W Powietrznym Zwiadzie*, Warsaw, 1982
Orlinski, B., *Do Krainy Wschodzącego Słońca*, Toronto, 1978
Orpen, N., *Airlift to Warsaw*, London, 1984
Orwell, G., *Collected Essays, Journalism & Letters*, Vol. IV, London, 1978
Paszkowski, K., *RAF kontra Luftwaffe*, Łódź, 1946
Pawlak, J., *Brygada Pościgowa Alarm*, Warsaw, 1977
———*Polskie Eskadry w Wojnie Obronnej 1939*, Warsaw, 1982
———*Brygada Bombowa – Kurs Bojowy!*, Warsaw, 1983
Peszke, M.A., 'The Operational Doctrine of the Polish Air Force in World War Two', in *Journal of the American Aviation Historical Society*, No. 18, 1973
———'The Prewar Polish Air Force', in *Aerospace Historian*, No. 27, 1981
Petrusewicz, S.A., ed., *Młodociani Lotnicy*, London, 1992
Pruszyński, K., *Poland Fights Back*, New York, 1944
Pruszyński, M., *W Tobruku, Narwiku i Moskicie*, Warsaw, 1948
———*W Moskicie nad III Rzeszą*, Warsaw, 1984
Rattigan, T., *The Flare Path*, London, 1942
Rayski, L., *Słowa Prawdy o Lotnoctwie Polskim 1919–1939*, London, 1948
Rolski, T., *Uwaga, Wszystkie Samoloty*, Warsaw, 1974
———*85 Dni pod Francuskim Niebem*, Warsaw, 1975
Romeyko, M. (ed.), *Polska Lotnicza*, Warsaw, 1937
———*Rayskie Czasy Lotnictwa Polskiego*, London, 1949
Rozwadowski, J., *Morski Dywizjon Lotniczy*, Albany, NY, 1973
———*Gwiaździsta Eskadra*, Albany, NY, 1976
Rzepniewski, A., *Wojna Powietrzna w Polsce – 1939*, Warsaw, 1970
Schiele, T., *Spitfire*, Katowice, 1957
———*Blisko Nieba*, Katowice, 1966
Sęp-Szarżyński, S., *W Słuzbie Latającego smoka*, London, 1957
Skalski, S., *Czarne Krzyże nad Polską*, Warsaw, 1971
Sławiński, K., *Lotnicy Września*, Warsaw, 1972
———*Pierwszy Myśliwski*, Warsaw, 1980
———*Lotnictwo Armii 'Pomorze'*, Pruszków, 1992
Slessor, J., *The Central Blue*, London, 1956
Smithies, E., *War in the Air*, London, 1990
Spaight, J.M., *The Battle of Britain*, London, 1941
Stachiewicz, W., *Przygotowania Wojenne w Polsce 1935–1939*, Paris, 1977
Stafford, D., *Britain and European Resistance*, London, 1980
Sword, K., with Davies, N. & Ciechanowski, J., *The Formation of the Polish Community in Great Britain*, London, 1989
Szołdrska, H., *Lotnictwo Podziemia*, Warsaw 1986
Szubański, R., *W. Obronie Polskiego Nieba*, Warsaw, 1978

Szumowski, T., *Through Many Skies*, Beverley, 1993
Thompson, D., 'I Met the Men Who Saved Britain', *Sunday Chronicle*, 3 August 1941
Trylski, J., Rusiecki, S., & Wiczkowski, T., *Błękitni Chłopcy*, London, 1988
Urbanowicz, W., *Ogień nad Chinami*, Warsaw, 1963
——*Początek Jutra*, Kraków, 1966
——*Myśliwcy*, Kraków, 1969
——*Świt Zwycięstwa*, Kraków, 1971
——'One Man's War', in *American Fighter Aces Bulletin*, Mesa, Arizona, Vol. 2, No. 4, 1985
Vincent, S.F., *Flying Fever*, London, 1972
Wasilewski, Z., *Obyś Żył w Ciekawych Czasach*, Warsaw, 1958
Wegrzecki, K., *Kosynierzy Warszawscy*, London, 1968
——*Lotnicy Polscy w Nottingham*, London, 1986
Wierzbicki, K., *Rosły nam Skrzydła*, Warsaw, 1977
Witkowski, A., *Tajemnica Lotu nad Prosnę*, Warsaw, 1991
Wyndham, L., *Love is Blue*, London, 1986
Wytrwał, J., *Behold! The Polish Americans*, Detroit, 1977
Zaczkiewicz, W., *Lotnictwo Polskie w Kampanii Wrześniowej 1939r*, Warsaw, 1947
Zając, J., *Dwie Wojny*, London, 1964
Zamoyska, P., *Jan, Portrait of a Polish Airman*, London, 1944
Zbierański, C., *O Narodzinach Lotnictwa Polskiego*, New York, 1958
Zieliński, J., *Asy Polskiego Lotnictwa*, Warsaw, 1944
Zumbach, J., *On Wings of War*, London, 1975.

Index